MOLIERE-
(Jean-Bap

The Bourgeois Gentleman
(Le Bourgeois Gentilhomme)

The Doctor In Spite of Himself
(Le Médecin malgré lui)

The Affected Damsels
(Les Précieuses Ridicules)

The Miser (L'Avare)
(Regular Edition)

The Miser (L'Avare)
(Short Edition)

***

Translated by
CARL MILO PERGOLIZZI

Prologue by
Claire Nicholas White

International Pocket Library
Division of Branden Publishing Co.
Boston

HOUSTON PUBLIC LIBRARY

. R01290 45056

© Copyright 1999
by Carl Milo Pergolizzi

Library of Congress Cataloging-in-Publication Data

Molière, 1622-1673.
    [Selections. English. 1999]
    Molière, four plays / translated by Carl Milo Pergolizzi :
       prologue by Claire Nicholas White.
         p. cm.
    Contents: The bourgeois gentleman -- The doctor in spite
of himself -- The affected damsels -- The miser (regular
edition) -- The miser (short edition).
      ISBN 0-8283-2038-1 (alk. paper)
    1. Molière, 1622-1673--Translations into English.
    I. Pergolizzi, Carlo Milo.
    II. Title.
    III. Title: Four plays.
    IV. Title: 4 plays.
      PQ1825.E5P47   1999
      842'.4--DC21   99-18379
                            CIP

INTERNATIONAL POCKET LIBRARY
Division of Branden Publishing Company
17 Station Street
Box 843 Brookline Village
Boston MA 02447

Contents

PROLOGUE

My name is Jean Baptise Poquelin.
My dad, upholsterer of class, has
made chairs on which the King
of France put down his royal ass.
Acting is my dubious profession,
a blemish on dad's reputation
So, not to cause him any shame,
I'm called Moliere. It's a good name.
I lived three hundred years ago,
but nothing's changed I'll have you know.
The foibles I made fun of then
are popular today again.
Take my *Tartuffe*, the holy man;
his hair was long, his virtue sham.
You who are fond of eastern sages
that meditate, and pay them wages,
Why are these saints such sudden rages?
As for *Alceste*, my *Misanthrope*,
who with corruption could not cope,
look at your young idealists
who fought the system
but missed the boat
and fell in the lists.
Then look at my two precious girls
who so loved literary pearls
they scorned their suitors.
Now I see girls storm the university,
and claim they want their liberty!
As for my doctors' strange proceedings,
their enemas and copious bleedings,
You have your share of quackery,
your drugs and your psychology,
your snake oil fads of the counter culture!
Not a sou would I a doctor pay,
And since we all must die some day,

better let nature have her way.
Let's use, dear friends,
our common sense.
Let laughter be our self-defense
against extreme, deluded men.
I, too, alas, was one of them.
Married a girl twenty years younger,
a shrew who claimed that I had wronged her.
That girl has led me such a life,
I wish I'd never taken wife!
Today our play is just a farce.
I'm told my humor is too coarse
and yet it won favor in court.
The King, you see, was not above such sport.
I wrote the play; I act the fool.
You, fellow man, my only school.
I died on stage playing
The Imaginary Invalid.
Ironic? Not if you consider
the play the thing and life the fibber,
For since I'm here with you tonight,
It's that Moliere has never died!

Claire Nicholas White
for Carl Milo Pergolizzi
as Jean Baptiste Poquelin
(aka Moliere)

INTRODUCTION

If you are fortunate enough to have written a play deemed the best of the year by French critics, you would be awarded a *Moliere*. This fact, in itself, attests to the extraordinarily high esteem in which Moliere is held by the French. Indeed, the French language itself is often referred to by the French as the language of Moliere. What was unfortunate for Moliere, however, was that his highly merited acclaim was painfully long in coming.

When he established his *Illustre Theatre* in 1643, the prevailing theatrical vogue was essentially neo-classical. Works by the early Greek and Roman tragedians and by Corneille, the French playwright who was the rage at that time, were almost the exclusive fare at the two major and long since established theaters of the day--the Hotel de Bourgogne and the Marais.

Competition with these two groups proved very difficult for Moliere. He despised their haughtiness and railed against their format that catered exclusively to the elite. He was a man of the people who loved to laugh and was ill-equipped to confront the predominantly tragical theatrical fare of that decade. His finances went from bad to worse and there were times when he couldn't pay for the candles needed to illuminate the stage. Therefore, his decision to leave the Parisian scene and to seek fortune for his theater in the provinces of France is readily understandable.

"Qui m'aime, me suive!" (Let those who love me follow me!) he exclaimed to his troupe; and follow him they did.

It turned out to be a fortuitous decision for it was during his sojourn in the provinces that he encountered the *Commedia dell'Arte*, a type of improvisational theatre specializing in irreverent farce. It originated in Italy and had been touring the provinces of France, Spain, and England since the middle of the 16th century. In contrast with the Parisian concept of theater, the *Commedia dell'Arte* catered to all strata of society and dealt with real-life character types that were usually satirical of the upper classes. Some of the major characters were *Scapino*, a master-duping servant (the precursor of *Figaro*); *Columbina*, a commonsensical maidservant; *Dottore*, a comical would-be scholar or doctor; *Pantalone*, a bumbling, easily deceived husband or father; and *Capitano*, a bragging soldier.

The influence of the *Commedia dell'Arte* on Moliere must have been indeed profound for, upon his return to Paris in 1658, he totally discarded the neo-classical vogue and set about writing farces satirical of the upper classes using many of the *Commedia dell'Arte* stock character types. His plays caused a sensation in Paris and Louis XIV himself afforded him the privilege of allowing his troupe to perform in the prestigious theatre of the Palais-Royal much to the jealousy and consterna-tion of the Hotel de Bourgogne and the Marais.

In the four plays in this volume, several of the *Comme-dia*'s stock character types are to be noted. For example, in *The Doctor in Spite of Himself*, there is *Sganarelle*, the comical, would-be doctor and scholar; *Jacqueline*, the commonsensical maidservant, and *Geronte*, the deceived father. In *The Affected Damsels* there is *Jodelet*, the boastful soldier, and finally in *The Miser*, you have *Valere*, a sophisticated version of the master-duping servant.

Care must be exercised, however, not to over-emphasize the *Commedia dell'Arte*'s influence on Moliere. Although he lifted some its character, there are many others in his writings that were of his origination and that had far more depth and sophistication such as the miser, the misanthrope, the religious bigot and the hypochondriac. What the *Commedia dell'Arte* did, essentially, was to cause him to set a new course for his literature that was eminently more consistent with his particular genius and social orientation--one that dealt with the common man and poked fun at the pretentiousness of the elite.

Although Moliere wrote of life in 17th century France, his instinct for comedy, his insight into the vagaries of human nature and his incisiveness of style serve to explain the durability of his popularity, particularly in the French-speaking world. However, it has been difficult for me to understand why more actors and theater-lovers from all over the world do not embrace him as true, universal champion of the theater for, aside from his genius as a playwright, he was a man who abided by the highest principles of the acting profession and this at a time when actors were subject to much of persecution and social banishment.

But it was his death, perhaps, that best illustrates his devotion to the theater. A performance of one of his major works, *The Imaginary Invalid*, was scheduled in which Moliere was to play the lead. Despite being desperately ill, he went on in true, show biz fashion only to collapse on stage during the final act. A few hours later, he was dead. On his death bed, he chose to be buried in unhallowed rather than renounce the theatrical profession to his confessor. *Quel beau geste!*

About ten years ago, the theater troupe to which I belonged called upon me to direct *The Doctor in Spite of Himself*, and I immediately set about reading translations. However, in my opinion, none that I read succeeded in conveying the full ironic and comic impact of Moliere's lines and so, being a teacher of French, I decided to do my own.

I had hardly completed the first page when I began to develop an appreciation of the difficulty of my task. The major problem stemmed from the basic structural differences between English and French.

The closing lines of ACT II provides a good case in point. Sganarelle, the *doctor*, has just agreed to cure a gentleman's sweetheart so that he (the gentleman) might marry her. Sganarelle closes the act with the following reassurance:

"...j'y perdrai toute ma médecine, ou la malade crèvera ou bien elle sera à vous."

If you don't know French, be assured that the delivery of this line convulses a French audience. If, however, we were to transliterate, we would have: "I shall use all my medicine for this; either the patient will die or she will be yours."

(End your acts like that and you had better serve very strong coffee during intermission!)

Sparing you a discourse on comparative linguistics, let me state simply that in French the punch word or phrase usually falls somewhere near the middle of the sentence, whereas in English, we prefer to place it at the end where it seems to have more impact, and where it provides greater allowance for audience reaction; so that if we take that same listless sentence and move the punch phrase to the end, we wind up with a much more appropriate English curtain line: "Benefiting from my entire knowledge of medicine, our patient will most assuredly be yours...unless, of course, she dies first."

It was on a late Saturday afternoon when I finally arrived at the last page of *Doctor*. I found myself actually reluctant to terminate my association with those madcap characters. I recall getting up from my typewriter and sitting by my kitchen window with a cup of coffee and a cigarette. I was gazing emptily upon the barren, wintry landscape when suddenly, from out of nowhere, a pigeon made a very abrupt landing on the window sill not two feet away from me. This startled me for you hardly see any pigeons in my area, least of all on your window sill. I set my coffee cup down ever so gently lest a precipitous motion put an end to this bizarre visitation. The bird remained absolutely motionless for a minute or so and then turned inward and suddenly it was I who was being observed.

The eerie, unblinking concentration of his stare and the sustained total immobility of his body became increasingly fascinating and some very peculiar thoughts started popping into my head. Messages were arriving via some subliminal route urging me back to my typewriter and to finish the play. But in spite of this, I continued to stare back. Then, another message: "Ridiculous!" I retorted, why the devil would you come back as a pigeon?"

But I returned to the typewriter and began work on that last page, peering occasionally over my shoulder to ascertain his continued presence. When at last the job was done, I scurried back to the window, but the perch was empty. I quickly scanned the horizon for a last glimpse of whoever or whatever it was, but he was gone, and a twinge of melancholy came over me with the bitter-sweet realization that his mission was accomplished and that I would see him nevermore.

Carl Milo Pergolizzi

The Bourgeois Gentleman

(LE BOURGEOIS GENTILHOMME)

TRANSLATOR'S NOTE: Using Lully's original musical score and with the help of a professional musician I have translated Lully's lyrics and synchronized them to his music. I know of no other translation that does this which may account for the fact that THE BOURGEOIS GENTLEMAN is among the least performed of Moliere's works on the American stage. The irony is that it is the most revered and most performed in France.

CHARACTERS:

MR JOURDAIN, a Bourgeois
MRS JOURDAIN, his Wife
DORANTE, a Nobleman
DORIMENE, a Noblewoman
LUCILLE, Mr. Jourdain's daughter
CLEONTE, his Valet and Suitor to Nicole
NICOLE, his Servant
MUSIC MASTER, DANCING MASTER
FENCING MASTER, PHILOSOPHY MASTER
MASTER TAILOR and HIS APPRENTICE
TWO LACKEYS
A STUDENT
SINGERS and MUSICIANS
COOKS

In the Turkish Ceremony: MUFTI, DERVISHES, TURKS, SINGERS and DANCERS

ACT I

Scene 1: **Music Master, Dancing Mstr, 3 Singers, 2 Violinists, 4 Dancers**

The overture is performed by a musical ensemble. At a table at Center Stage a student of the MUSIC MASTER composes a serenade requested by the master of the household.

MUSIC MASTER	**(To his Musicians)** Into this room, please. You may sit here until he comes.
DANCIN' MSTR	**(To his Dancers)** And you as well. This way, please.
MUSIC MASTER	Is it done?
STUDENT	Yes.
MUSIC MASTER	Let's see. That's' fine.
DANCIN' MSTR	Is this something new?
MUSIC MASTER	Yes, it's a melody for a serenade that I had him compose while waiting for our man to be awakened.
DANCIN' MSTR	May I look at it?
MUSIC MASTER	You will hear both melody and lyrics when he comes, which will be soon.
DANCIN' MSTR	Business is good for both of us these days, isn't it?
MUSIC MASTER	Indeed it is, thanks to the man we found here. What a sweet source of revenue he is, our Mr. Jourdain, with his notions of nobility and gallantry, and how wonderful it would be for your dancing and my music were everyone like him.
DANCIN' MSTR	I wouldn't go that far. If only he weren't such a poor student.

MUSIC MASTER He may learn poorly but he pays well and that is what our professions need more than anything else.

DANCIN' MSTR Yes, but I must confess that for me it's the glory, the recognition that counts. How distasteful it is in any of the fine arts to produce for fools, to have one's compositions sullied by the barbarism of a simpleton. True pleasure is only to be derived by working for people with a refined appreciation of the arts, who know how to respond to the beauty of a given work and how to gratify its creator with appropriate praise. Yes, the sweetest reward for the artist is the honor bestowed upon him by the adulation and celebrity of his work. Enlightened praise is the most exquisite form of satisfaction for the artist and, in my opinion, he can ask for no greater recompense than that for his efforts.

MUSIC MASTER I agree and I relish it as much as you do. There is certainly nothing more flattering than the applause of which you speak. But one does not live by praise alone, however enlightened it might be. It must be blended with something a bit more substantial. For me, the best way to praise is with an open purse. It's true that we are dealing here with a man of meager wit, who utters nothing but nonsense and whose applause is always ill-times and inappropriate; but his money more than compensates for the inadequacies of his judgment. There is discernment in his purse and gold in his praise. Thus our ignorant bourgeois is of

	more value to us than the highly cultured lord who introduced us here.
DANCIN' MSTR	There is an element of truth in what you say, but I feel that you overemphasize the importance of money, and that a true gentleman should never concern himself with anything as base as that.
MUSIC MASTER	You are, nevertheless, very quick to accept the money that our man gives you.
DANCIN' MSTR	Of course, but it takes more than that to make me happy. I only wish that along with his wealth, he possessed greater refinement of taste.
MUSIC MASTER	That would please me as well. After all, this is the very thing the two of us are striving to develop in him. But we must keep in mind, however, that it is through him that we are establishing our reputations, and that his purse paves the way for the praise of others.
DANCIN' MSTR	Here he comes.

Scene 2:   Mr Jourdain, Music Master, Dancing Mstr, Violinists, Singers, Dancers, Two Lackeys, Student.

MR JOURDAIN	Well, gentlemen, what have we here? May I look at your little ditty?
DANCIN' MSTR	How's that? What little ditty?
MR JOURDAIN	Eh? Over there… What do you call that? Your prologue or your dialogue of songs and dance?
DANCIN' MSTR	Aha!
MUSIC MASTER	Yes, sir. We're ready for you.
MR JOURDAIN	I'm sorry you had to wait for me, but the fact is that I am dressing myself today as

	do the people of quality, and I had a devil of a time trying to put on a pair of silk stockings that my tailor sent me.
MUSIC MASTER	We are here solely to await your pleasure, sir.
MR JOURDAIN	I would like both of you to stay until my new outfit arrives, so that you might see me in it.
DANCIN' MSTR	Whatever pleases you, sir.
MR JOURDAIN	You shall see me properly decked out from head to toe.
MUSIC MASTER	We do not doubt it, sir.
MR JOURDAIN	This oriental robe was especially made for me.
DANCIN' MSTR	It is truly beautiful, sir.
MR JOURDAIN	My tailor told me that people of quality dress like this in the morning.
MUSIC MASTER	That suits you perfectly, sir.
MR JOURDAIN	Lackeys! Hey there! My two lackeys!

The Two LACKEYS Enter.

1ST LACKEY	What is it, sir?
MR JOURDAIN	Nothing. I just wanted to know if you could hear me.

The LACKEYS bow and Exit.

MR JOURDAIN	**(To the MASTERS)** What do you think of my liveries?
DANCIN' MSTR	They are magnificent, sir.
MR JOURDAIN	**(Half-opening his robe to reveal a straight pair of breeches of red velvet and a green velvet spencer)** And this is

something casual for my morning exercises.

MUSIC MASTER   It is truly elegant, sir.

MR JOURDAIN   Lackeys!

The LACKEYS re-enter.

1ST LACKEY   Yes, sir?

MR JOURDAIN   The other lackey.

2ND LACKEY   Sir?

MR JOURDAIN   (Removes robe) Hold my robe. (To the MASTERS) How do I look?

DANCIN' MSTR   Very good. One couldn't possibly look any better.

MR JOURDAIN   Let's have a look at your little chore.

MUSIC MASTER   First I would like you to listen to a melody that he has just composed for the serenade that you commissioned. He is a student of mine with a true gift for this type of thing.

MR JOURDAIN   Yes, but this isn't something for a student to do; were you too good to do this yourself?

MUSIC MASTER   Sir, you must not be misled by the word "student," for the knowledge of this kind of student can match that of the greatest masters. Just listen and you will find the melody to be of incomparable beauty.

SINGER   (**Singing**) I languish here night and day,
And I've known naught but deep despair
Since I became the slave of your eyes oh so fair.
If you so poorly treat, Iris, one who loves thee,
Alas, what would you do were I your enemy?

Mr JOURDAIN	I find this song a little too dreary; it puts me to sleep. Couldn't you liven it up a bit here and there?
MUSIC MASTER	The music must coincide with the words, sir.
MR JOURDAIN	Someone taught me a really nice one a while ago. Hold on... How does it go?
MUSIC MASTER	In faith, sir, I have no idea.
MR JOURDAIN	There's lamb in it.
MUSIC MASTER	Lamb, sir?
MR JOURDAIN	Yes... Ah! **(Begins to sing)**

> Oh, how sweet and pretty
> Did my Jeannie appear.
> Oh, how fair and saintly,
> No lamb could be as dear.
> Alas, alas, so very cruel,
> My sweet faced Jeannie,
> The tiger would never be.

Mr Jourdain looks around him expectantly.

MR JOURDAIN	Now wasn't that nice?
MUSIC MASTER	As nice as could be.
DANCIN' MSTR	And you sing it so well.
MR JOURDAIN	That's without ever having learned music.
MUSIC MASTER	You ought to learn music as well as dancing, sir. These two arts are very closely related.
DANCIN' MSTR	And they open the mind to beautiful things.
MR JOURDAIN	Do the people of quality also learn music?
MUSIC MASTER	Yes, sir.
MR JOURDAIN	So then shall I. But I don't know where I'll find the time to fit it in for, in addition to the fencing master who is teaching me,

I have also engaged a philosophy master who is to start this morning.

MUSIC MASTER Philosophy is not without some importance, but music, sir. Music.

DANCIN' MSTR Music and dancing music and dancing, that's all that's really necessary.

MUSIC MASTER There is nothing more useful in a state than music.

DANCIN' MSTR There is nothing more necessary for mankind than dancing.

MUSIC MASTER Without music a state could not subsist.

DANCIN' MSTR Without dancing man can do nothing.

MUSIC MASTER All the disorder, all the wars that we see in the world stem from not learning music.

DANCIN' MSTR All of man's misfortunes, all the afflictions that fill the pages of history, all the blunders of politicians and the failures of great commanders, all of this was brought about by want of dancing skill.

MR JOURDAIN How is that?

MUSIC MASTER Is not war the outcome of a lack of union among men?

MR JOURDAIN That is true.

MUSIC MASTER And if all men were to learn music, would that not be a means of promoting harmony among them and of achieving universal peace?

MR JOURDAIN You are right.

DANCIN' MSTR When a man commits some breach of conduct, be it in the affairs of the family, government or army, don't we always say that he took the wrong step in the matter in question?

MR JOURDAIN Yes, we say that.

DANCIN' MSTR	And the act of taking a wrong step, could that be due to anything else but the lack of dancing skill?
MR JOURDAIN	That is true. Both of you are right.
DANCIN' MSTR	We point that out so that you might appreciate the excellence and usefulness of dancing and music.
MUSIC MASTER	Would you like us to show you our compositions?
MR JOURDAIN	Yes.
MUSIC MASTER	As I have already told you, this is a minor work that I composed a while back which demonstrates the various emotions that music can express.
MR JOURDAIN	Very good.
MUSIC MASTER	**(To the Singers)** Come forward. **(To Mr Jourdain)** You must picture dressed as shepherds.
MR JOURDAIN	Why always as shepherds? That's all you see everywhere.
DANCIN' MSTR	When you have people speaking to music, for the sake of believability they must do so as shepherds. For a prince or a townsman to his express his arduous feelings in a musical dialogue would be highly unnatural, and this is why the singing roles have always been assigned to shepherds.
MR JOURDAIN	All right, then. Let's see.

DIALOGUE TO MUSIC between a Two Male Singers and One Female Singer.*

> My heart in love's domain hath strayed,
> The tender prey to its snares must it be.
> For sighs and languishing do comprise

cruel love's serenade.

Surmount this barricade,
Foolish heart, naught's more sweet
Than is our liberty.

Ah! What a joy it is
When two hearts beat together.

MR JOURDAIN   Is that it?

MUSIC MASTER   Yes.

MR JOURDAIN   That's what I call a very nice piece of work, and there are some very wise sayings in it.

DANCIN' MSTR   And now, for my part, I present a little work comprised of some of the most beautiful movements and attitudes with which a dance might be varied.

MR JOURDAIN   Will they be shepherds again?

DANCIN' MSTR   They'll be whatever you like.

BALLET SEQUENCE with Four Dancers executing all the different movements and steps at the command of the Dancing Mstr.

DANCIN' MSTR   **(To the Dancers)** Ready, dancers, with solemnity... Begin. Let's go dancers, up tempo. Solemnly, now, for the saraband. And now, the bourree. Cheerfully, now, for the gaillarde. And now to conclude with the glorious Canarian air.

* This song becomes excessively tedious if sung in its entirety. For this reason, the Comedie Francaise sings an abbreviated version. My translation limits itself to the

excerpts sung by the Comedie Francaise and can be sung to the music. Attention to meter and rhyme necessitated some slight liberties with meaning.

ACT II

Scene 1: **Mr Jourdain, Music Master, Dancing Mstr, Lackeys**

MR JOURDAIN That was no stupid thing they just did. Those fellows really know how to flap about.

DANCIN' MSTR The dance will be all the more impressive once its blended with the music and, in the little ballet that we have prepared for you, you will see something truly elegant.

MR JOURDAIN That's for a little later, and the person that I'm having all this done for is to do me the honor of coming here for dinner.

DANCIN' MSTR All is in readiness.

MUSIC MASTER May I add, sir, that this is inadequate. A person with your sumptuous tastes and refined inclinations should hold concerts at his residence every Wednesday and Thursday.

MR JOURDAIN Do the people of quality hold them?

MUSIC MASTER Yes, sir.

MR JOURDAIN So then shall I. Will they be beautiful?

MUSIC MASTER Without a doubt. You will need three voices: a treble, a counter tenor, and a bass, which will be accompanied by a bass viol, a theorbolute, and a harpsichord for the sustained bass, and finally two violins for the ritournelles.

MR JOURDAIN You must also add a trumpet marine. Now there's an instrument that really pleases me, and that is very harmonious.

MUSIC MASTER Leave those matters to us, sir.

MR JOURDAIN	Well, anyway, don't forget to send me the musicians who are to sing at the table.
MUSIC MASTER	You will have everything you need.
MR JOURDAIN	But above all, make sure the ballet is beautiful.
DANCIN' MSTR	Everything will be as you like it including among other things, certain minuets that you shall see.
MR JOURDAIN	Ah! The minuet is my dance! I want you to see me dance it. Let's do it, master.
DANCIN' MSTR	A hat, sir, if you please.

Mr Jourdain takes the hat off his Lackey's head and wears it over his nightcap. The Dancing Mstr takes Mr Jourdain's hand and sings the melody to a Minuet to which he makes his student dance.

DANCIN' MSTR	La-la-la... Watch the cadence, if you please. La-la-la... Lift the right leg La-la--la...Try not to move your shoulder so much... La-la-la... Don't hold your arms so rigidly... La-la-la... Lift up your head... Kindly turn out your toes; don't turn them in... La-la-la... Hold your body straight...
MR JOURDAIN	Aha?
MUSIC MASTER	A matchless performance!
MR JOURDAIN	That reminds me; teach me how I should bow when greeting a marchioness, for I shall soon have need to know.
DANCIN' MSTR	How to bow when greeting a marchioness?
MR JOURDAIN	Yes, a marchioness by the name of Dori-mene.
DANCIN' MSTR	Give me your hand.

MR JOURDAIN   No, you just have to do it. I'll remember it.

DANCIN' MSTR   Well, if you wish to greet her with great respect, you must bow once and fall back; then, advancing towards her, you make three more bows bending down to her knees on the last one.

MR JOURDAIN   Let's see you do it.

The Dancing Mstr takes the three bows.

MR JOURDAIN   Good!

1ST LACKEY   (Entering) Sir, your fencing master is here.

MR JOURDAIN   Have him come in and give me my lesson. **(To the Music Master and Dancing Mstr)** I'd like you to watch me at this.

Scene 3: Mr Jourdain, Dancing Mstr, Music Master, Fencing Mstr, 1st Lackey.

FENCIN' MSTR   **(Taking two foils from the Lackey and handing one to Mr. Jourdain)** Let's begin, sir, with the salute. Your body erect, leaning slightly upon the left thigh. Your legs not so far apart. Your wrist opposite your hip. The tip of your sword at shoulder level. Your arm not quite so extended. Your left hand at eye level. Angle your shoulder more. Your head up. Assume a look of confidence. Advance. Your body steady. Hit me in quart and follow through. One, two. Recover. Once again, steadily. One, two. Jump backwards. When you thrust, sir, you must disengage your sword first and then have your body lean into that attack. One, two. Let's go. Hit me in tierce and follow through. Advance. Thrust from there. One, two. Recover. Once more. One, two. Jump backwards. (He scores two or three touches as he calls out.) On guard, sir. On guard!

MR JOURDAIN   Aha!

MUSIC MASTER   You're doing marvelously.

FENCIN' MSTR   As I have already told you, the whole secret of fencing consists of two things: to give and not to receive, and, as I showed you the other day by means of demonstrative reasoning, it is impossible to receive if you know how to deflect the sword of your adversary from the line of your body. This can be accomplished quite simply by a slight movement of the wrist either inward or outward.

MR JOURDAIN   In this way, therefore, a man of little courage can be sure to kill without being killed himself?

FENCIN' MSTR   Without a doubt. Did you not see the demonstration?

MR JOURDAIN   Yes.

FENCIN' MSTR   And from this you can see the basis for the esteem that the state must bestow upon the men of our profession, and why the science of arms is so vastly superior to all the useless sciences such as dancing, music and...

DANCIN' MSTR   Easy does it, my good fencing master. I'll have you speak more respectfully of dancing.

MUSIC MASTER   I'll thank you, sir, not to abuse the excellence of music.

FENCIN' MSTR   I find you both very laughable in your wish to compare your sciences to mine.

DANCIN' MSTR   Behold the man of importance.

MUSIC MASTER   Behold the funny animal with his plastron!

FENCIN' MSTR   My little dancing master, I'm going to teach you some very fancy steps; and you, my little musician, are going to have some very pretty tunes sliced out of you.

DANCIN' MSTR   I'll teach you your own trade, swashbuckler!

MR JOURDAIN   **(To Dancing Mstr)** Are you mad, quarreling with someone who understands tierce and quart, and who knows how to kill a man by demonstrative reasoning?

DANCIN' MSTR   I scoff at his demonstrative reasoning and at his tierce and his quart!

MR JOURDAIN   **(To the Dancing Mstr)** Gently, I say!

FENCIN' MSTR   **(To Dancing Mstr)** How's that? You impertinent dwarf!

MR JOURDAIN   Oh! My fencing master...!

DANCIN' MSTR   **(To Fencing Mstr)** How's that? You bulky drayhorse!

MR JOURDAIN   Oh! My dancing master...!

FENCIN' MSTR   If I go after you...

MR JOURDAIN   **(To Fencing Master)** Gently!

DANCIN' MSTR   If I lay my hands on you...

MR JOURDAIN   **(To Dancing Mstr)** Easy now!

FENCIN' MSTR   I'll slice you in such a way...

MR JOURDAIN   **(To Fencing Mstr)** Please...!

DANCIN' MSTR   I'll thrash you so that you...

MR JOURDAIN   **(To Dancing Mstr)** I beg you...

MUSIC MASTER **(To Dancing Mstr)** Let's teach him how to speak.

MR JOURDAIN **(To Music Master)** Good heavens! Stop this!

Scene 4: Mr Jourdain, Dancing Mstr, Music Master, Fencing Mstr, Philosophy Mstr, Two Lackeys

MR JOURDAIN **(As Philosophy Mstr enters)** Hello, my dear philosopher! You arrived in the nick of time with your philosophy. Come here and make these people stop fighting.

PHLSPHY MSTR What is it? What is the problem, gentlemen?

MR JOURDAIN Each of them is arguing about the superiority of his profession to the point where they're insulting each other and threatening to come to blows.

PHLSPHY MSTR Come now, gentlemen, Must you allow yourselves to be carried away by such passion? Haven't you read Seneca's learned treatise on anger? Is there anything more base and shameful than this passion which turns man into a ferocious beast? And must not our behavior be ever subject to the dictates of reason?

DANCIN' MSTR Indeed, sir, he has been offending both of us with his slurs on dancing which is my profession, and music, the specialty of my colleague here.

PHLSPHY MSTR A man of wisdom is above all the insults directed towards him, and the best answer to an offense is moderation and patience.

FENCIN' MSTR They both had the audacity to want to compare their professions with mine.

PHLSPHY MSTR Must you let that disturb you? Men should never fight over vainglory and rank, for the only true distinguishing attributes of mankind are wisdom and virtue.

DANCIN' MSTR I'll have him know that dancing is a science to which one could never pay sufficient homage.

MUSIC MASTER And for my part let him know that music is a science that has been revered throughout the centuries.

FENCIN' MSTR And I assert to both of them that the science of arms is the most beautiful and most necessary of all sciences.

PHLSPHY MSTR And just where does that leave philosophy? How dare the three of you address me with such arrogance, and give shamelessly the name of science to things that don't even merit the name of art, and that can only be classified under the shabby titles of gladiator, singer and mountebank?

FENCIN' MSTR Be gone, you mongrel of a philosopher!

MUSIC MASTER Be gone, you pedant good-for-nothing!

DANCIN' MSTR Be gone, you pompous pedagogue!

PHLSPHY MSTR How's that? Scoundrels that you are...!

The Philosophy Master lunges at them as the Dancing, Music and Fencing Masters beat him.

MR JOURDAIN My learned philosopher!

FENCIN' MSTR A plague on the animal!

MR JOURDAIN Gentlemen!

PHLSPHY MSTR Impudent dogs!

MR JOURDAIN My learned philosopher!

DANCIN' MSTR To blazes with the pompous ass!

MR JOURDAIN Gentlemen!

PHLSPHY MSTR   Villains!
MR JOURDAIN   My learned philosopher!
MUSIC MASTER   The devil take the impertinent runt!
MR JOURDAIN   Gentlemen!
PHLSPHY MSTR   Knaves! Tramps! Traitors! Impostors!
MR JOURDAIN   My learned philosopher! Gentlemen! My
                learned philosopher! Gentlemen!

All the Masters exit fighting.

MR JOURDAIN   Oh, fight on as you will; there's nothing I
                can do about it, and I'm not going to spoil
                my robe trying to keep you apart. I'd be
                crazy to butt into that and chance getting
                myself hurt.

Scene 5: Philosophy MSTR, Mr Jourdain, Two Lackeys

PHLSPHY MSTR   **(Straightening his collar and regaining
                his composure)** And, now to our lesson.
MR JOURDAIN   Ah, sir! I am sorely distressed by the
                beating they gave you.
PHLSPHY MSTR   That was nothing. A philosopher knows
                how to take things as they come and I'm
                going to compose a satire in the style of
                Juvenal that will cut them most splendidly
                to shreds. But enough of that. What is it
                that you wish to learn?
MR JOURDAIN   As much as I can for I have the most
                burning desire to be learned, and I am
                extremely angry with my parents for not
                making me study all the sciences when I
                was young.
PHLSPHY MSTR   A most reasonable sentiment. Nam sine
                doctrina vita est quasi mortis imago. You

	understand that... You know Latin, of course?
MR JOURDAIN	Yes, but let's make believe I don't. Tell me what it means.
PHLSPHY MSTR	That means that without science life is practically an image of death.
MR JOURDAIN	That Latin is right.
PHLSPHY MSTR	Are you familiar with any of the principles or fundamentals of the various sciences?
MR JOURDAIN	Oh yes. I know how to read and write.
PHLSPHY MSTR	Where would you like us to begin? Do you want me to teach you logic?
MR JOURDAIN	What's logic?
PHLSPHY MSTR	It is logic that teaches the three operations of the mind.
MR JOURDAIN	And what are they, these three operations of the mind?
PHLSPHY MSTR	The first, the second and the third. The first is to conceive properly by means of universals; the second is to judge properly by means of categories; and the third is to draw the correct conclusion by means of the figures Barbara, Celarent, Darii, Ferio, Baralipton, and so forth.
MR JOURDAIN	Those words are much too unlovely. I don't find that logic very nice. Let's learn something more pretty.
PHLSPHY MSTR	Would you care to learn ethics?
MR JOURDAIN	Ethics?
PHLSPHY MSTR	Yes.
MR JOURDAIN	What does it have to say, this ethics?
PHLSPHY MSTR	It deals with happiness, teaches men to moderate their passions and...
MR JOURDAIN	Oh, no! I'll have none of that! I'm as bilious as the devil, and no ethics is going

	to deny me my bellyful of passion when I feel like it.
PHLSPHY MSTR	Is it physics that you want to learn?
MR JOURDAIN	Physics? What's that about?
PHLSPHY MSTR	It is physics that explains the principles of natural things and the properties of the bodies, that discusses the nature of the elements metals, minerals, rocks, plants, and animals, and teaches us the causes of all the meteors, rainbows, will-o-the--wisps, comets, lightning flashes, thunder-claps, thunderbolts, rainfalls, snowfalls, hailstorms, winds, and whirlwinds.
MR JOURDAIN	There's too much hurly-burly in all that, too much confusion.
PHLSPHY MSTR	What is it then that you want me to teach you?
MR JOURDAIN	Teach me how to spell.
PHLSPHY MSTR	With pleasure.
MR JOURDAIN	Afterwards, you will teach me the almanac, so that I'll know when there's a moon and when there isn't.
PHLSPHY MSTR	So be it. However, to pursue your idea properly, and to treat this matter as a philosopher, I must proceed according to the order of things and begin by developing a precise understanding of the nature of the French letters and of the different way each is pronounced; and accordingly, I must tell you that the letters are divided into vowels...so-called because they express the voice, and into the consonants...so-called because they sound with the vowels and function only to mark the

	various articulations of the voice. There are five French vowels: A, E, I, O, U.
MR JOURDAIN	I understand all that.
PHLSPHY MSTR	The vowel A is pronounced by opening the mouth wide...A, A.
MR JOURDAIN	A, A. Yes.
PHLSPHY MSTR	The vowel E is pronounced by bringing the upper and lower jaws closer together...A, E.
MR JOURDAIN	A, E. A, E. Good heavens! Yes! Oh, how beautiful that is.
PHLSPHY MSTR	And the vowel I by bringing the jaws even closer tog -ether and drawing back the corners of the mouth towards the ear...A, E, I.
MR JOURDAIN	A, E, I, I, I, I, I. That's true! Long live science!
PHLSPHY MSTR	The vowel O is formed by re-opening the jaws and drawing the upper and lower lips close to each other at the corners: O
MR JOURDAIN	O, O. Nothing could be more true. A, E, I, O, I, O. That's really admirable! I, O. I, O.
PHLSPHY MSTR	The overture of the mouth forms an actual circle that represents an O.
MR JOURDAIN	O, O, O. You're right! Oh, what a beautiful thing it is to know something!
PHLSPHY MSTR	The vowel U is formed by bringing the teeth together without clenching them entirely, and extending the lips forward, drawing them close to each other but without having them meet: U
MR JOURDAIN	U, U. You're absolutely right! U!
PHLSPHY MSTR	Your lips should protrude as if you were pouting; therefore, when you wish to

	ridicule someone, all you have to do is say U.
MR JOURDAIN	U, U. That's true! Ah, why did I not study sooner so that I might know all this?
PHLSPHY MSTR	Tomorrow we shall discuss the other letters which are the consonants.
MR JOURDAIN	Are there as many curious things about them as there are in these?
PHLSPHY MSTR	To be sure. The consonant D, for example, is pronounced by placing the tip of your tongue above the upper teeth: Da.
MR JOURDAIN	Da, Da.. Yes! Ah, what beautiful things! What beautiful things!
PHLSPHY MSTR	The F by pressing the upper teeth against the lower lip: fa.
MR JOURDAIN	Fa, Fa. That's true! Ah, father and mother of mine, how mad I am at you!
PHLSPHY MSTR	And the R by curling the tip of the tongue back against the high point of the palate so that, being brushed by the air that escapes forcefully, the tongue yields and snaps back to its original position making a kind of trill: R-R-R-Ra.
MR JOURDAIN	R-R-R-Ra. R-R-R-Ra. That's true! Oh, what a clever man you are! And how much time I have wasted! R-R-R-Ra
PHLSPHY MSTR	I will explain all these curiosities to you in depth.
MR JOURDAIN	Pray, do. Moreover, I must tell you a secret. I am in love with a person of very high quality and I would like you to help me write something to her in a short letter that I would drop at her feet.
PHLSPHY MSTR	Very well.
MR JOURDAIN	That will be very gallant, right?

PHLSPHY MSTR   To be sure. Do you wish to write to her in verse?

MR JOURDAIN   No, no. No verse.

PHLSPHY MSTR   Then you only want prose?

MR JOURDAIN   No, I want neither prose nor verse.

PHLSPHY MSTR   But it's got to be one or the other, sir.

MR JOURDAIN   Why?

PHLSPHY MSTR   For the simple reason, sir, that one can only express one's self in prose or in verse.

MR JOURDAIN   Is there nothing then but prose or verse?

PHLSPHY MSTR   No, sir. All that is not prose is verse, and all that is not verse is prose.

MR JOURDAIN   And when one speaks, what's that?

PHLSPHY MSTR   Prose.

MR JOURDAIN   How's that? When I say: "Nicole, bring me my slippers and give me my nightcap," that's prose?

PHLSPHY MSTR   Yes, sir.

MR JOURDAIN   By Jupiter! I've been speaking prose for forty years without even knowing it, and I am greatly obliged to you for having taught me that. I would like you to put in the letter: "Beautiful marchioness, your beautiful eyes make me die of love;" but I would like that to be said in a gallant fashion, and that it have a more genteel turn.

PHLSPHY MSTR   Say that the fire of her eyes reduces your heart to ashes; that you suffer day and night from the throes of a...

MR JOURDAIN   No, no, no. I don't want all that. I only want what I said to you: "Beautiful marchioness, your beautiful eyes make me die of love."

PHLSPHY MSTR   But you must expand on that a bit.

MR JOURDAIN   No, I tell you, those are the only words I want in the letter but phrased in style and with a proper arrangement. I beseech you to show me the various ways they can be put.

PHLSPHY MSTR   Well, first of all, they can be arranged as you said: "Beautiful marchioness, your beautiful eyes make me die of love." Or: "Of love they make me die, beautiful marchioness, your beautiful eyes." Or: "Your beautiful eyes of love they make me, beautiful marchioness, die." Or: "Die your beautiful eyes, beautiful marchioness, of love they make me." Or: "They make me your beautiful eyes die, beautiful marchioness, of love." Or:...

MR JOURDAIN   But of all those ways, which is the best?

PHLSPHY MSTR   They way you said it: "Beautiful marchioness, your beautiful eyes make me die of love."

MR JOURDAIN   I have never studied and I got that with the first try. I thank you from the bottom of my heart, and I beseech you to come early tomorrow.

PHLSPHY MSTR   I shall not fail to do so. Remember now: Fa Fa Fa. (He exits)

MR JOURDAIN   **(To 1st Lackey)** How's that? My coat hasn't arrived yet?

1ST LACKEY   No, sir.

MR JOURDAIN   That blasted tailor makes me wait on a day when I have so many things to do. I'm boiling with rage! May the quartan fever strangle that wretched tailor! The devil take that tailor! The plague choke that tailor! If I had my hands on him now, that hateful tailor, that mongrel of a tailor, that treacherous tailor, I'd...

Scene 6: Mr Jourdain, Master Tailor, Apprentice Tailor (carrying coat), Lackey

MR JOURDAIN	Ah, there you are! I was about to get mad at you.
MSTR TAILOR	I was unable to come sooner, and I had twenty people working on your outfit.
MR JOURDAIN	The silk stockings that you sent me were so tight that I had a devil of a time trying to put them on, and there are already two runs in them.
MSTR TAILOR	They'll stretch easily.
MR JOURDAIN	Of course, they will if I keep getting runs; and these shoes you made me are hurting me ferociously.
MSTR TAILOR	Not at all, sir.
MR JOURDAIN	What do you mean, not at all?
MSTR TAILOR	No, they don't hurt you at all.
MR JOURDAIN	I tell you they are hurting me!
MSTR TAILOR	You're just imagining that.
MR JOURDAIN	I imagine it because I feel it. That's why!
MSTR TAILOR	Hold on, sir. Behold the most beautiful and best matched coat in all the court. To design a sedate outfit without using black is a true work of art, and I'd venture that your most gifted tailors in court wouldn't do as well had they six tries at it.
MR JOURDAIN	What the deuce is this? You've got the flowers upside down.
MSTR TAILOR	You never told me, did you, that you wanted them right side up?

MR JOURDAIN	Did I have to tell you that?
MSTR TAILOR	Yes, indeed. All the people of quality wear them thus.
MR JOURDAIN	People of quality wear them upside down?
MSTR TAILOR	Yes, sir.
MR JOURDAIN	Oh, well, in that case, I guess it's all right.
MSTR TAILOR	If you wish, I'll put them right side up.
MR JOURDAIN	No, no.
MSTR TAILOR	You just have to say the word.
MR JOURDAIN	No, I tell you, you did the right thing. Do you think the outfit will look well on me?
MSTR TAILOR	What a question! I'll defy any painter with his brush to do better. I have an apprentice at my place who is the greatest genius in the world when it comes to making breeches, and I have another whose talent for doublets makes him the hero of our time.
MR JOURDAIN	Are the wig and plumes as they should be?
MSTR TAILOR	Everything is just right.
MR JOURDAIN	**(Looking at the coat)** Aha, my dear tailor, this is something you made from the material of my last outfit. I recognize it.
MSTR TAILOR	Well, sir, the fact is that the material seemed so beautiful to me that I felt like using it to cut out a coat for myself. Would you like to try on your outfit?
MR JOURDAIN	Yes, give it to me.
MSTR TAILOR	Wait. That's not the way it's done. I have brought some people who will dress you to music. Clothes like these must be put on with ceremony. You there! Enter. Dress the gentleman as you do for people of quality.

Four Apprentices enter and two of them remove his exercise breeches while the other two remove his spencer. Then they put on his new outfit. Mr. Jourdain walks among them showing them his outfit to see if it's all right This is all done with orchestral accompaniment.

APPRENTICE	My Gentleman, may I request a gratuity for the apprentices?
MR JOURDAIN	What did you call me?
APPRENTICE	My Gentleman.
MR JOURDAIN	"My gentleman?" This is what it's like to dress a person of quality. Go about dressed as a bourgeois and you'd never anyone say to you: "My Gentleman."

He hands the Apprentice Tailor some money.

APPRENTICE	Your Lordship, we are deeply obliged.
MR JOURDAIN	"Your lordship!" Hoho! "Your lordship!" Hold on, my friend. "Your lordship" deserves something, and those are no little words, "Your lordship." Here you are, that's what your lordship gives you. He hands out more money.
APPRENTICE	Your lordship, we shall all drink to the health of your Grace.
MR JOURDAIN	"Your Grace!" Oh! Oh! Oh! Wait. Don't leave. "Your Grace" to me! **(Aside)** Good heavens, if he goes as far as Your Highness, he'll have my entire purse. **(Aloud as he hands out more money)** Here you are. That's for "My Grace."
APPRENTICE	We thank his Lordship most humbly for his generosity.

MR JOURDAIN   A good thing he stopped for I was about to
give him everything.

**The four Apprentice Tailors express their joy with a dance
upon their exit.**

ACT III

Scene 1: Mr Jourdain, Nicole, Two Lackeys

MR JOURDAIN	Follow me as I walk about town to show my new outfit; and take special care, both of you, to stay close behind me so that everyone will know that you are mine.
LACKEYS	Yes, sir.
MR JOURDAIN	Call Nicole for me. I have to give her some orders. Don't bother. There she is... Nicole!
NICOLE	What is it?
MR JOURDAIN	Listen.
NICOLE	Hahahahaha.
MR JOURDAIN	What are you laughing at?
NICOLE	Hahahahaha.
MR JOURDAIN	What's that hussy up to?
NICOLE	Hahaha... Oh, my, don't you look dandy! Hahaha.
MR JOURDAIN	What's that?
NICOLE	Hoho... Saints above! Hahahaha...
MR JOURDAIN	Little vixen that you are, are you making fun of me?
NICOLE	Oh, no sir. I'd just feel awful if I did... Hahahaha
MR JOURDAIN	I'll punch you in the nose if you laugh anymore.
NICOLE	Sir, I can't help it... Hahahaha
MR JOURDAIN	You won't stop?
NICOLE	Sir, please forgive me, but you look so funny that I can't keep from laughing... Hahahaha...
MR JOURDAIN	Did you ever see such insolence?

NICOLE	You couldn't look more funny if you tried... Hahaha
MR JOURDAIN	I'll...
NICOLE	Please excuse me, sir... Hahahahaha
MR JOURDAIN	See here, if I hear the slightest titter out of you, I'm going to give you the biggest slap that was ever given.
NICOLE	Very good, sir. It's... finished... I won't laugh anymore...heheh
MR JOURDAIN	See that you don't. Now in preparation for later on, you must clean...
NICOLE	Hahahaha...
MR JOURDAIN	You must clean thoroughly...
NICOLE	Hahahahaha...
MR JOURDAIN	I say that you must clean the parlor and...
NICOLE	Hahahahaha...
MR JOURDAIN	Again!
NICOLE	**(Crumbling with laughter)** Go to it, sir. I'd rather you hit me and let me laugh my bellyful. I'd be better for it. Hahahaha...
MR JOURDAIN	This is too much!
NICOLE	For mercy's sake, sir, please let me laugh... Hahaha...
MR JOURDAIN	If I lay my hands on you...
NICOLE	Sir, I shall split my sides if I don't laugh... hahaha
MR JOURDAIN	Did you ever see such a brazen female who laughs in my face instead of taking orders?
NICOLE	What do you want me to do, sir?
MR JOURDAIN	I want you to think about preparing the house for the company that will be arriving soon.
NICOLE	By the saints, sir, I don't feel like laughing anymore. All that company of yours makes

such a mess around here that all it takes to put me in a bad mood is to hear mention of it.

MR JOURDAIN   Perhaps for your sake I ought to shut the house up to everyone?

NICOLE   No, sir, not to everyone; just to certain people.

Scene 3:   Mr Jourdain, Nicole, Mrs. Jourdain, Two Lackeys

MRS JOURDAIN   Aha! Here's a new kettle of fish! What kind of a get-up is that? Do you care that little about what people will think to deck yourself out like that? Do you really want to be the laughing-stock wherever you go?

MR JOURDAIN   Only the fools will laugh at me, dear wife.

MRS JOURDAIN   Well, they've already started. In fact, your peculiar ways have been making people laugh for quite some time now.

MR JOURDAIN   And just who are these people, if you please?

MRS JOURDAIN   People who are right and who have more sense than you. For my part, I am scandalized by the life you are leading. I don't know what's become of our house. You'd think we were having daily carnivals here. And just so there'll be no let-up, we disturb the entire neighborhood with early morning screeching of fiddlers and singers.

NICOLE   Madame speaks the truth, sir. I'll never be able to keep a clean house with that bunch of people you have coming here. They have feet that look for mud in all sections of town just to bring it here; and poor

Francoise has just about worn himself out scrubbing the floors that your fancy masters dirty regularly every day.

MR JOURDAIN Hold on there, our servant Nicole, you've got a pretty sharp tongue for a peasant girl.

MRS JOURDAIN Nicole is right, and she's got more sense than you. I'd like to know what you expect to do with a dancing master at your age?

NICOLE And with a fencing master whose foot--stomping shakes the whole house and uproots the tiles of the parlor floor.

MR JOURDAIN Be quiet, my servant and my wife.

MRS JOURDAIN Do you want to learn how to dance for the time when your legs give out?

NICOLE Do you have a notion to kill someone?

MR JOURDAIN Be still, I tell you! You're ignorant creatures, the both of you, and you don't know the advantages of all that.

MRS JOURDAIN You ought to be thinking instead about marrying off your daughter who is of age now.

MR JOURDAIN I'll think about marrying off my daughter when the right party comes along; but I also want to think about learning the finer things.

NICOLE I also heard, madame, that he hired today, to top it all, a philosophy master.

MR JOURDAIN That's right. I want to be learned and to know how to reason about things with people of culture.

MRS JOURDAIN Soon you'll be going to the lycee for a whipping, at your age.

MR JOURDAIN	And why not? Would to heaven I be whipped right now in front of everyone and knew what they teach at the lycee.
MRS JOURDAIN	Oh, yes indeed, a lot of good that will do you.
MR JOURDAIN	To be sure.
MRS JOURDAIN	You really need all that to run your household.
MR JOURDAIN	Certainly. Both of you are talking like imbeciles, and your ignorance makes me ashamed. **(To Mrs Jourdain)** For example, do you happen to know what you're speaking right now?
MRS JOURDAIN	Yes, I know that what I'm saying is right and that you ought to be thinking about another way of life.
MR JOURDAIN	I'm not talking about that, I tell you. I'm asking you: what I am speaking with you and what I am saying to you now; what is it?
MRS JOURDAIN	Nonsense.
MR JOURDAIN	No, no. It's not that. What both of us are saying, the form of language we are using this instant.
MRS JOURDAIN	Well, what about it?
MR JOURDAIN	What is that called?
MRS JOURDAIN	That's called whatever one wants to call it.
MR JOURDAIN	That's prose, imbecile!
MRS JOURDAIN	Prose?
MR JOURDAIN	Yes, prose. All that prose is not verse, and all that verse is not prose. So there! That's what studying is all about. **(To Nicole)** And you, do you know what you have to do to say U?
NICOLE	What?

MR JOURDAIN	Go ahead. Say U and see.
NICOLE	All right, U.
MR JOURDAIN	Yes, but when you say U, what are you doing?
NICOLE	I'm doing what you tell me to do.
MR JOURDAIN	Oh, how strange it is to have to deal with simpletons! You extend the lips forward, and you bring the upper and lower jaws close together; U, do you see? I'm pouting: U.
NICOLE	Oh, yes, that's just dandy.
MRS JOURDAIN	Now isn't that admirable.
MR JOURDAIN	Other things are completely different. If only you had seen O, and DA, DA, and FA, FA.
MRS JOURDAIN	What's all that gibberish?
NICOLE	What's all that going to get you?
MR JOURDAIN	Seeing ignorant females drives me mad.
MRS JOURDAIN	Go on, you ought to send all those people packing with their stuff and nonsense.
NICOLE	And especially that lout of a fencing master who fills the house with dust.
MR JOURDAIN	Aha! That fencing master really gratesyou. I'm going to show you now just how impertinent you really are. **(He calls for the foils and gives one to Nicole.)** Now then, demonstrative reasoning, the line of the body. When you push in quart, you have only to do this; when you push in tierce, you just have to do that. In that way you'll never get killed. Isn't it nice to be so sure of things when you're fighting someone? Here, I'll show you. Make a few thrusts at me.

NICOLE	Very well, like this? **(Nicole makes several thrusts at him.)**
MR JOURDAIN	Gently now! Oh! Easy does it! A plague on the little vixen!
NICOLE	You told me to thrust.
MR JOURDAIN	Yes, but you're thrusting in tierce before thrusting quart, and you're not giving me the chance to parry.
MRS JOURDAIN	You are mad, my husband, with all your silly notions and you've been acting like this since you started mixing with the nobility.
MR JOURDAIN	When I mix with the nobility I show my sound judgment, and it's much better than mixing with your common folk.
MRS JOURDAIN	Oh, yes indeed. There's a great deal to be gained by keeping such fancy company; and you've been acting very smart with that fine count of yours whose got you so bamboozled.
MR JOURDAIN	Quiet! Think about what you're saying. Do you realize, my dear wife, who it is you're talking about when you speak of him. He's a person of much greater importance than you might think...a lord of great esteem at court, who speaks to the king just like I speak to you. Don't you consider it a great honor for me that a person of such quality be seen coming to my house so often, and that he call me his dear friend and treat me as if I was his equal? You could never imagine how kind he's been to me and how he has overwhelmed me by the compliments he has paid me in front of everyone.

MRS JOURDAIN	Oh yes, he's nice to you and pays you compliments as he borrows your money.
MR JOURDAIN	Indeed! Isn't it an honor for me to loan money to a man of such rank? And could I do any less for a lord who calls me his dear friend?
MRS JOURDAIN	And this lord, what does he do for you?
MR JOURDAIN	Things that would astonish you if you knew.
MRS JOURDAIN	How's that?
MR JOURDAIN	Enough. I can't explain that. All you have to know is that, if I loaned him money, he'll return it to me and soon.
MRS JOURDAIN	Yes, wait for that.
MR JOURDAIN	Certainly. Didn't he tell me so?
MRS JOURDAIN	Yes, yes, he won't fail to fail to do so.
MR JOURDAIN	He gave me his word as a gentleman.
MRS JOURDAIN	Fiddlesticks!
MR JOURDAIN	Ah! But you're a stubborn one, my dear wife. I tell you he'll keep his word; I'm sure of it.
MRS JOURDAIN	And I'm quite sure that he won't, and that all those compliments are to puff you up.
MR JOURDAIN	Hold your tongue. Here he comes.
MRS JOURDAIN	That's all we need now. He's here perhaps to borrow some more money from you. Just the sight of him turns my stomach.
MR JOURDAIN	Quiet, I say!

Scene 4: Mr Jourdain, Mrs Jourdain, Nicole, Dorante

DORANTE	My dear friend, Mr Jourdain, how are you?
MR JOURDAIN	Well enough, sir, to render you whatever service I may.

DORANTE	And, Mrs Jourdain there, how is she?
MR JOURDAIN	Mrs Jourdain is doing as well as she can.
DORANTE	My, my, Mr Jourdain! Your attire is absolutely matchless!
MR JOURDAIN	As you see.
DORANTE	You look thoroughly striking in that outfit, and there's not a gentleman at court that could top you.
MR JOURDAIN	Aha!
MRS JOURDAIN	**(Aside)** He scratches him where he itches.
DORANTE	Good heavens, Mr Jourdain, I could hardly wait to see you. I respect you more than any man in the world, and I was discussing you again this morning in the king's chambers.
MR JOURDAIN	You do me too much honor, sir. **(To Mrs Jourdain)** In the king's chambers!
DORANTE	Come now, put your hat on.
MR JOURDAIN	Sir, I know the respect that I owe you.
DORANTE	Good Lord, put it on. Let's not stand on ceremony, I beseech you.
MR JOURDAIN	Sir...
DORANTE	Put it on, I say, Mr. Jourdain; you are my friend.
MR JOURDAIN	Sir, I am your servant.
DORANTE	I'll not put my hat on unless you put on yours.
MR JOURDAIN	**(Putting on his hat)** I would rather be unmannerly than bothersome.
DORANTE	**(Aside)** I am your debtor, you know.
MRS JOURDAIN	Yes, we know only too well.
DORANTE	You have generously loaned me money on several occasions, and you have obliged me in what is certainly the most gracious of manners.

MR JOURDAIN	You jest, sir.
DORANTE	But I know how to acknowledge favors, and repay what is loaned.
MR JOURDAIN	I have no doubts about that, sir.
DORANTE	I'd like to settle our account, and I am here so that we might work it out together.
MR JOURDAIN	**(Aside, softly, to Mrs Jourdain)** There! Do you see your impertinence, wife?
DORANTE	I am a man who likes to discharge his debts as soon as possible.
MR JOURDAIN	**(Aside, softly, to Mrs Jourdain)** I told you!
DORANTE	Let's see how much I owe you.
MR JOURDAIN	**(Aside, softly, to Mrs Jourdain)** You and your ridiculous suspicions!
DORANTE	Do you remember the total amount of money you loaned me?
MR JOURDAIN	I believe so. I've kept a little memorandum. Here it is. On one occasion I gave you two hundred louis d'or.
DORANTE	That is true.
MR JOURDAIN	Another time. Six score.
DORANTE	Yes.
MR JOURDAIN	And once, one hundred and forty.
DORANTE	You're right.
MR JOURDAIN	These three items amount to four hundred and sixty louis which comes to five thousand and sixty francs.
DORANTE	Your figures are correct. Five thousand and sixty francs.
MR JOURDAIN	One thousand thirty-two francs to your plume merchant.
DORANTE	Exactly.
MR JOURDAIN	Two thousand eighty francs to your tailor.
DORANTE	That is true.

MR JOURDAIN   Four thousand three hundred and seventy-nine francs, twelve sous and eight deniers to your cloth merchant.

DORANTE   Very good. Twelve thousand and eight deniers. The account is accurate.

MR JOURDAIN   And one thousand seven hundred forty-eight francs, seven sous and four deniers to your saddler.

DORANTE   All true. What does that come to?

MR JOURDAIN   Sum total: Fifteen thousand and eight-hundred francs.

DORANTE   The sum total is exact. Fifteen thousand and eight hundred francs. Add to that the two hundred pistoles that you are going to give me, and that will make exactly sixteen thousand francs that I will pay the first chance I get.

MRS JOURDAIN   **(Aside to Mr Jourdain)** There. Didn't I tell you?

MR JOURDAIN   Hush!

DORANTE   Loaning me that sum won't put you out, I hope.

MR JOURDAIN   Oh, no!

MRS JOURDAIN   **(Aside to Mr Jourdain)** That man is milking you dry.

MR JOURDAIN   Hold your tongue!

DORANTE   If that would inconvenience you, I could go elsewhere.

MR JOURDAIN   No, sir.

MRS JOURDAIN   He won't be happy until he's put you in the poorhouse.

MR JOURDAIN   Quiet, I say.

DORANTE   You have only to say that this would cause the slightest difficulty.

MR JOURDAIN   Not at all, sir.

MRS JOURDAIN	(Aside) What a cajoler!
MR JOURDAIN	Keep quiet!
MRS JOURDAIN	(Aside) He'll drain the last sou out of you.
MR JOURDAIN	(Aside) Will you be still?
DORANTE	I have several people who would gladly oblige me, but since you are my best friend, I felt that asking anyone else would be an injustice to you.
MR JOURDAIN	You do me too much honor, sir. I shall go fetch what you need.
MRS JOURDAIN	(Aside) What? You're going to give him that too?
MR JOURDAIN	(Aside) What can I do? Do you expect me to refuse a man of such rank, a man who only this morning spoke of me in the king's chambers?
MRS JOURDAIN	(Aside) Off with you; you're a born dupe.

Scene 5: Dorante, Mrs Jourdain, Nicole

DORANTE	You are sad of countenance; what can be the matter, Mrs. Jourdain?
MRS JOURDAIN	My head may not be swelled up but it's still larger than my fist.
DORANTE	Where is your daughter? I don't see her.
MRS JOURDAIN	My daughter is doing quite nicely where she is.
DORANTE	How is she getting along?
MRS JOURDAIN	On her two legs.
DORANTE	Wouldn't you like to come with her one of these days to the ballet or comedy theater at court?
MRS JOURDAIN	Yes, indeed, we really feel like laughing. Don't we ever feel like laughing?

DORANTE	I imagine, Mrs Jourdain, that you had many suitors in your younger days, being as beautiful and sweetly humored as you were.
MRS JOURDAIN	Indeed, sir! Has Mrs Jourdain grown decrepit, and does she have the shakes already?
DORANTE	Ah! In faith, Mrs. Jourdain, I beg your pardon. It did not occur to me that you are young; I am absent of mind more than not, and I beseech you to forgive my impertinence.

Scene 6: Mr Jourdain, Mrs Jourdain, Dorante, Nicole

MR JOURDAIN	Here are two hundred louis d'or in exact count.
DORANTE	I assure you, Mr. Jourdain, that I am completely at your disposal, and that I am most eager to be of service to you at court.
MR JOURDAIN	I am much obliged, Sir.
DORANTE	If Mrs. Jourdain wishes to see the royal entertainment, I'll get her the best seats in the house.
MRS JOURDAIN	Mrs. Jourdain kisses your hand.
DORANTE	**(Aside to Mr Jourdain)** As I advised you in my letter, our beautiful marchioness will be here soon for the ballet and dinner; I finally got her to agree to attend the divertissement you're planning in her honor.
MR JOURDAIN	Let's move off a bit, for obvious reasons.

They move to one side of the stage.

DORANTE	It's been eight days since our last meeting, and I have not sent you news about the diamond you gave me which I was to present to her as a gift from you; but the fact is that I had a devil of a time overcoming her scruples, and it was only today that she agreed to accept it.
MR JOURDAIN	How did she like it?
DORANTE	She loved it! And, unless I'm sadly mistaken, the beauty of that diamond will have a very favorable effect on her feelings towards you.
MR JOURDAIN	Would to heaven that be so!
MRS JOURDAIN	**(Aside to Nicole)** Once he's with him, he can never part company.
DORANTE	I got her to appreciate the richness of the gift and the depth of your love.
MR JOURDAIN	Your kindness overwhelms me, and it confounds me to see a person of your quality stoop to do what you are doing for me.
DORANTE	You jest, sir. Do scruples of that sort carry any weight with friends? And would you not do the same for me were the occasion to arise?
MR JOURDAIN	Oh, certainly, and with the greatest of pleasure!
MRS JOURDAIN	**(To Nicole)** Oh how his presence weighs on me.
DORANTE	For my part, when it comes to serving a friend, nothing else matters; and when you told me in confidence about your arduous feelings for that delightful marchioness whom I know socially, you saw how quic-

	kly I offered to serve the cause of your love.
MR JOURDAIN	True. These favors are what confound me.
MRS JOURDAIN	**(To Nicole)** Will he ever leave?
NICOLE	They do get on well together.
DORANTE	You have taken the right steps to captivate her, for there is nothing that women love more than to have money spent on them. And your frequent serenades, your incessant bouquets, the superb fireworks on water, the diamond she received from you and the entertainment you are preparing for her, will all serve to express your love far more eloquently than any words that you yourself might utter.
MR JOURDAIN	If money could put me on the road to her heart, I would spend my last sou. A woman of quality has charms that dazzle me, and it is an honor that I would buy at any cost.
MRS JOURDAIN	**(To Nicole)** What are they talking about all this time? Sneak up on them and listen.
DORANTE	You will soon have the pleasure of seeing her and then you may feast your eyes to your heart's content.
MR JOURDAIN	To have a free rein, I have arranged to have my wife dine at my sister's where she will spend the entire afternoon.
DORANTE	You did the wise thing, for your wife's presence would complicate matters. I have given the necessary orders to the cook and have made all the arrangements for the ballet. It is I who planned the entire affair and, if my orders are carried out properly, I am sure that...

Mr Jourdain suddenly notices Nicole eavesdropping and slaps her.

MR JOURDAIN   Aha! That's for your impertinence! (To Dorante) Let us leave, if you please.

Dorante and Mr Jourdain exit

Scene 6: Mrs Jourdain, Nicole

NICOLE   By the saints, madame! I paid a high price for my curiosity, but I believe they're up to something. They're talking about some affair that they don't want you to attend.

MRS JOURDAIN   I've had suspicions about my husband for some time now, Nicole. Unless I'm sorely mistaken, there's some love affair in the works, and I've been trying to get to the bottom of it; but let's think about my daughter. You know how much Cleonte loves her. He's a fine lad and I want to help his courtship along and give him Lucille, if I can.

NICOLE   In truth, madame, I can't tell you how happy I am that you feel this way since your esteem for Cleonte is no greater than my love for his valet, and I would like our marriage to take place in the shadow of theirs.

MRS JOURDAIN   Go tell Cleonte that I want him here immediately so that I might be with him as he asks my husband for Lucille's hand in marriage.

NICOLE   I shall go at once, madame, and with great joy for this is the nicest errand I shall ever do.

Mrs Jourdain exits and Nicole is alone

NICOLE   Oh, how gladdened certain hearts will be when they hear what I have to say.

Scene 7: Nicole, Cleonte, Covielle

NICOLE   **(To Cleonte)** Ah! There you are. I've been looking for you. I am an ambassadress of joy and I come...

CLEONTE   Off with you, traitor! I'll have no more of your treacherous speeches.

NICOLE   Is this the way your receive me...?

CLEONTE   Be gone, I say. Go at once and tell your unfaithful mistress that she will no longer dupe the overly simple Cleonte.

NICOLE   What madness is this that grips him? My poor Covielle, tell me what this is all about.

COVIELLE   Your poor Covielle? You little minx! Quickly now! Out of my sight and leave me in peace.

NICOLE   What? You, too?

COVIELLE   Out of my sight, I say, and never speak to me again.

NICOLE   **(Aside)** Saints above! I wonder what's bitten the two of them. I must tell my mistress about this.

Scene 8: Cleonte, Covielle

CLEONTE   Can you imagine anyone treating a sweetheart like that...a sweetheart second to none in faithfulness and passion?

COVIELLE   It's a dreadful thing they did to us.

CLEONTE   I display towards a person all the ardor and tenderness conceivable. She is all that I love in this world, and she occupies my every thought. All my concern, all my desires, all my joy centers upon her. Everything I say, think or dream concerns her. She is the reason for the very breath I take and for every beat of my heart. And this is the worthy recompense for such affection! It's been two days now since I've seen her...two days that have seemed like two frightful centuries. I meet her by chance; my heart is transported by the sight of her. My face bursts with joy; I fly to her in ecstasy...only to have that unfaithful creature look the other way as she brushes past me as if never in her life had she seen me.

COVIELLE   My sentiments exactly.

CLEONTE   Could anything ever match, Covielle, the perfidy of that ungrateful Lucille?

COVIELLE   And that of that hussy, Nicole?

CLEONTE   After all the ardent sacrifices, sighs and vows that her charms drew out of me.

COVIELLE   After all those assiduous compliments, courtesies and favors that I have showered upon her in the kitchen.

CLEONTE   All the tears that I shed at her feet!

COVIELLE   All the buckets of water that I drew for her!

CLEONTE	All the ardor I've shown cherishing her more than myself.
COVIELLE	All the heat I've endured turning the spit for her.
CLEONTE	She avoids me disdainfully!
COVIELLE	She snubs me impudently!
CLEONTE	Such perfidy deserves the greatest punishment.
COVIELLE	Such treachery merits a thousand slaps in the face.
CLEONTE	Never speak to me of her again, I beseech you.
COVIELLE	I, sir? God forbid!
CLEONTE	You are never to proffer excuses for the actions of that unfaithful creature.
COVIELLE	Have no fear.
CLEONTE	No, all your speeches in her defense will be to no avail.
COVIELLE	I wouldn't dream of it!
CLEONTE	I am determined to retain my ill feelings and to break all communication with her.
COVIELLE	I agree with that.
CLEONTE	She is perhaps attracted by the looks of that fancy count that visits her, and the dazzling effect that gentility has upon her is quite obvious to me; but honor dictates that I not allow her fickleness to prevail. I shall match her step for step in her headlong rush to change things, so that it won't be she alone who will reap the satisfaction of this separation.
COVIELLE	Beautifully said. Those are my sentiments exactly.
CLEONTE	Help me retain my resentment towards her and to resist whatever remaining tender-

	ness I might feel towards her that might cause me to speak in her favor. Describe her to me in such a way as to have her appear contemptible in my eyes. Emphasize all the defects that you see in her that should arouse my displeasure.
COVIELLE	In her, sir? She's a childish snob, a pretentious coquette whose physical attributes are hardly enrapturing. I see nothing in her that is not mediocre, and you could find a hundred others more worthy of you. First of all, she has small eyes.
CLEONTE	That's true; her eyes are small, but they are full of fire. They sparkle, they pierce, they excite like nothing else on earth.
COVIELLE	She has a wide mouth.
CLEONTE	Yes, but it has charm that is not seen on other mouths. The desire that wells up in me when I gaze upon it renders it the most attractive and lovable mouth in the world.
COVIELLE	She is rather small of build.
CLEONTE	Yes, but she is graceful and well-proportioned.
COVIELLE	She affects a non-chalance of speech and action.
CLEONTE	That is true; but she does so with such gracefulness, and her ways are so engaging, so indescribably charming that they capture my heart.
COVIELLE	As for her wit...
CLEONTE	Ah! That she has, Covielle, the most refined, the most delicate.
COVIELLE	Her conversation...
CLEONTE	Her conversation is charming.
COVIELLE	She is always serious.

CLEONTE	Would you prefer a perpetual display of joviality? Is there anything more insufferable than a woman who laughs at anything?
COVIELLE	Lastly, she is as capricious as anyone I know in this world.
CLEONTE	Yes, she is capricious, I agree. But when a woman is beautiful, everything about her is becoming, and there is nothing we cannot endure from her.
COVIELLE	Well, since that's the way it is, it's obvious that you wish to love her always.
CLEONTE	I? I would rather die, and I shall hate her as much as I have loved her.
COVIELLE	How will you do that since you find her so perfect?
CLEONTE	My vengeance will be all the more striking because of this. As beautiful, attractive and lovable as I find her, I shall nevertheless hate her and leave her, and this will amply demonstrate my strength of will. Here she comes.

Scene 10: Cleonte, Covielle, Lucille, Nicole

NICOLE	**(To Lucille)** For my part, I was thoroughly shocked by it.
LUCILLE	It can be nothing else, Nicole, but what I said. But there he is.
CLEANTE	**(To Covielle)** I don't even want to speak to her.
COVIELLE	I shall do likewise.
LUCILLE	What is this all about, Cleonte? What's troubling you?
NICOLE	What ails you, Covielle?

CLEONTE	What is it that grieves you thus?
NICOLE	What is it that puts you in such a bad humor?
LUCILLE	Have you lost your tongue, Cleonte?
NICOLE	Are you dumb, Covielle?
CLEONTE	Oh, what a brazen creature!
COVIELLE	Oh, what a Judas!
LUCILLE	I can see that our recent meeting has upset you.
CLEONTE	**(To Covielle)** Aha! She realized what she has done.
NICOLE	The reception we gave you this morning got your dander up.
COVIELLE	**(To Cleonte)** She has guessed where the shoe pinches.
LUCILLE	Isn't it true, Cleonte, that this is the cause of your resentment?
CLEONTE	Yes, faithless one, that is it, since speak I must; and I say to you that you are wrong to believe that your unfaithfulness will prevail, for it shall be I who will be first to break our relationship, thereby depriving you of the satisfaction of rejecting me. It will be difficult, of course, for me to overcome my love for you. This will occasion much anguish. I shall suffer for a time but I shall get over it; and I would rather put a dagger through my heart than to be so weak as to return to you.
COVIELLE	**(To Nicole)** That goes for me, too.
LUCILLE	That's much ado about nothing. I'd like to explain to you, Cleonte, why I avoided you this morning.
CLEONTE	**(Drawing away from her)** No, I don't want to hear it.

NICOLE	**(To Covielle)** I'd like to tell you why we passed you by so quickly.
COVIELLE	**(Drawing away from her)** No, I don't want to listen.
LUCILLE	**(Following Cleonte)** I want you to know that this morning...
CLEONTE	**(Retreating further)** No, I tell you.
NICOLE	I want you to understand...
COVIELLE	**(Retreating further)** No traitoress.
LUCILLE	Listen!
CLEONTE	I'll have none of it.
NICOLE	Let me explain.
COVIELLE	I am deaf.
LUCILLE	Cleonte!
CLEONTE	No.
NICOLE	Covielle!
COVIELLE	Not at all!
NICOLE	Stop this!
CLEONTE	Nonsense.
NICOLE	Hear me!
COVIELLE	Folderol!
LUCILLE	Wait a moment!
CLEONTE	In no way.
NICOLE	A little patience.
COVIELLE	Fiddlesticks.
LUCILLE	Just two words.
CLEONTE	No, it's over.
NICOLE	One word.
COVIELLE	No, it's finished.
LUCILLE	**(Stopping the chase after Cleonte)** Very well then. Since you refuse to listen, you can keep your opinions and do whatever you please.

NICOLE	**(Also stopping)** Since that's the way you're going to act, you can take it anyway you like.
CLEONTE	**(Turning to Lucille)** All right, let's hear what you have to say.
LUCILLE	**(Avoiding Cleonte)** I no longer wish to discuss it.
COVIELLE	**(Turning to Nicole)** Very well, what was that all about?
NICOLE	**(A avoiding Coville)** I no longer wish to explain it to you.
CLEONTE	**(To Lucille)** Tell me...
LUCILLE	**(Still drawing away)** No, I shall tell you nothing.
COVIELLE	**(Following Nicole)** Explain to me...
NICOLE	**(Drawing away)** No, I shall explain nothing.
CLEONTE	For pity's sake...
LUCILLE	No, I say.
COVIELLE	Have a heart...
NICOLE	I'll have none of it.
CLEONTE	I beseech you.
LUCILLE	Let me be.
COVIELLE	I beg you.
NICOLE	Go away.
CLEONTE	Lucille!
LUCILLE	No.
COVIELLE	Nicole!
NICOLE	In no way.
CLEONTE	For heaven's sake!
LUCILLE	I don't want to.
COVIELLE	Speak to me!
NICOLE	Not at all.
CLEONTE	Remove my doubts.
LUCILLE	No, I shall do nothing.

COVIELLE	Ease my mind.
NICOLE	No, I don't feel like it.
CLEONTE	Very well, ingrate, since you care so little about my suffering, and since you refuse to explain your abuse of my love for you, I shall make this our last meeting and go off to some distant place and die of a broken heart. **(He starts to leave)**
COVIELLE	**(Following Cleonte)** Me, too.
LUCILLE	Cleonte!
NICOLE	Covielle!
CLEONTE	**(Stops)** Yes?
COVIELLE	**(Stops)** What is it?
LUCILLE	Where are you going?
CLEONTE	Where I told you.
COVIELLE	We are going off to die.
LUCILLE	You're going to die, Cleonte?
CLEONTE	Yes, cruel one, since this is your wish.
LUCILLE	I? I want you to die?
CLEONTE	Yes.
LUCILLE	Who told you this?
CLEONTE	**(Nearing her)** What else am I to make of your refusal to remove my suspicions?
LUCILLE	Am I to blame? Had you only been willing to listen to me, would I not have told you that the incident that has so sorely grieved you was due to the presence this morning of an old aunt who is convinced that a girl is dishonored by the mere approach of a man, who lectures us constantly on this subject and who depicts all men as devils to be shunned?
CLEONTE	This is the truth you're telling me, isn't it, Lucille?
COVIELLE	You're not lying to us?

LUCILLE	Nothing could be more true.
NICOLE	That's exactly the way it was.
COVIELLE	**(To Cleonte)** Well, do we accept this?
CLEONTE	Ah, Lucille, just one word from your mouth and the anguish in my heart is appeased. Who can resist the persuasion of one's beloved?
COVIELLE	With what ease do these infernal creatures cajole us!

Scene 11: Mrs. Jourdain, Cleonte, Lucille, Covielle, Nicole

MRS JOURDAIN	I am pleased to see you, Cleonte, and you arrive just in time. Here comes my husband. This is the moment for you to ask for Lucille's hand in marriage.
CLEONTE	Ah, madame, what sweetness do your words contain, and how they respond to the yearnings of my heart! Could ever there be a more delightful order, a more precious favor?

Scene 12: Cleonte, Mr. Jourdain, Mrs Jourdain, Lucille, Nicole, Covielle

CLEONTE	Sir, for some time now I have wanted to make a certain request of you. The matter is of such moment to me that I have decided to do so personally rather than engage anyone else to act in my behalf, and, without further ado, I shall request of you the glorious honor of becoming your son-- in-law.
MR JOURDAIN	Before giving you my answer, may I ask you, sir, if you are a gentleman?

CLEONTE	Sir, most people can answer that question with little hesitation or difficulty. They have no qualms about assuming that title, and seem to do so nowadays with the blessings of society. As for myself, I must confess that my convictions in this regard are somewhat stronger. I feel that all forms of imposture are unworthy of a man of honor, and that it is shameful to disguise what heaven has made us by parading about with a stolen title and presenting a false image of one's self For my part, I was born of parents who held positions that were undoubtedly honorable. I acquired the honor that comes from six years of service in the military and my resources are sufficient for me to maintain a passably high rank in the world. But despite all of this, I don't have the slightest intention of bestowing upon myself a title to which others in my place would feel justified in laying claim, and I shall state to you frankly that I am not a gentleman.
MR JOURDAIN	Let's shake on that, sir. My daughter is not for you.
CLEONTE	How's that?
MR JOURDAIN	You are not a gentleman; you shall not have my daughter.
MRS JOURDAIN	What's all this gentleman stuff? Does our family descend from Saint Louis?
MR JOURDAIN	Hold your tongue, wife. I know what you're leading up to.
MRS JOURDAIN	Don't both of us descend from plain working people?

MR JOURDAIN	There goes that slanderous tongue of yours again!
MRS JOURDAIN	And wasn't your father a tradesman just like mine?
MR JOURDAIN	The plague take that woman! It's always the same story with her. If your father was a tradesman, that was his bad fortune; but it is only the ignorant who would say that of my father. For my part, all I have to tell you is that I want a gentleman for a son-in-law.
MRS JOURDAIN	What your daughter needs is a husband who suits her. She'd be better off with an upright young man who is rich and handsome than with a penniless and homely gentleman.
NICOLE	That's true. We have the son of a gentleman in our village who is the clumsiest and biggest nincompoop I ever saw.
MR JOURDAIN	Hold that impertinent tongue of yours! You are forever sticking your nose into the conversation. I have enough money for my daughter; all that I need is honor, thus it is my wish that she be a marchioness.
MRS JOURDAIN	A marchioness?
MR JOURDAIN	Yes, a marchioness.
MRS JOURDAIN	God forbid!
MR JOURDAIN	My mind is made up.
MRS JOURDAIN	And my mind will never consent to it. There can be painful disadvantages to marrying above one's station. I don't want a son in-law who'll reproach my daughter for her parents; nor do I want her children to be ashamed to call me Grandma. If she had to visit me dressed as a grand lady,

and if by accident she failed to greet some-one in the neighborhood, they would be quick to say all kinds of nasty things about her. Things like: "Look at the fancy marchioness with her haughty airs. She's the daughter of Mr. Jourdain. When she was little, she was only too happy to play the fine lady with us. She wasn't always as uppish as that. Her two grandfathers sold cloth at St. Innocent's Gate, and they made lots of money for their children for which they're probably paying now in the other world, for you don't get rich by being honest." I'll have none of that tittle-tattle. In a word, I want a man who'll be beholden to me for my daughter, and to whom I can say: "Sit there, son-in-law, and join me for dinner."

MR JOURDAIN   There's that small mind of yours at work again, always clinging to the bottom rung of the ladder. No more discussion! My daughter will be a marchioness in spite of everyone and, if you keep pestering me, I'll make her a duchess! **(He exits)**

MRS JOURDAIN Cleonte, you mustn't let this discourage you. **(To Lucille)** Follow me, child, and tell your father firmly that you either marry Cleonte or you marry no one.

Scene 13: Covielle, Cleonte

COVIELLE   You really handled that nicely with your fancy notions.

CLEONTE   What would you have me do? For me, it was a matter of principle.

COVIELLE	Principles with a man like that? Can't you see that he's mad, and would it have cost you anything to go along with his fancies?
CLEONTE	You're right; but I didn't think I would have to give proof of nobility to be the son-in-law of Mr. Jourdain.
COVIELLE	Ha! Haha!
CLEONTE	What are you laughing at?
COVIELLE	At a way I just thought to trick our man into giving you what you want.
CLEONTE	How?
COVIELLE	The idea is really very funny.
CLEONTE	What is it?
COVIELLE	There was a certain masquerade performed just recently that fits in perfectly here, and I plan to make it a part of a little joke I shall play on our foolish friend. The whole thing is a bit farcical, but with him we could venture anything. There's no need for elaborate subterfuge for he'll play his role marvelously and will believe whatever nonsense we deem to tell him. I have the actors and the costumes. Leave everything to me.
CLEONTE	But tell me...
COVIELLE	I'll explain it all to you, but let's withdraw from here for here he comes.

Scene 14: Mr. Jourdain, Lackey

MR JOURDAIN	What the devil was that all about? All that they can criticize me for is my respect for nobility. For my part, there is nothing more beautiful than to hobnob with great lords. With them, there is nothing but

honor and civility, and I would give two fingers of my hand to have been born a count or a marquis.

1ST LACKEY Sir, the count is here and he's got a lady with him.

MR JOURDAIN Good heavens! I've got some orders to give. Tell him I'll be with them in a moment.

Scene 15: Dorimene, Dorante, Lackey

1ST LACKEY The master said to tell you he'll be with you in a moment.

DORANTE Very good.

The Lackey exits

DORIMENE I don't know, Dorante. Allowing you to bring me to a house where I know no one is another strange thing for me to do.

DORANTE Where else would you have me entertain you then, madame, since our fear of gossip has ruled out your house or mine?

DORIMENE But you fail to mention that little by little I am compromising myself by accepting each day your lavish testimonials of love. My defenses are futile; there is a genteel persistence about you that overcomes my resistance and causes me to comply with all your wishes. It began with your frequent visits which were followed in turn by declarations of love, serenades, entertainments and gifts. I opposed all these things, but you are not one to lose heart, and my resolve grows weaker with each day. I find myself no longer capable of contesting anything, and I believe that this will ultimately lead to marriage...something I had not even remotely considered.

DORANTE   In faith, madame, you should be married already. You are a widow and depend on no one but yourself. I am my own master and love you more than life itself. What is there to keep you from making the rest of my days those of untold bliss?

DORIMENE   Good heavens, Dorante! There are many qualities that both parties must have in order to live happily together, and the two most reasonable people in the world can often have difficulty in establishing a satisfying union.

DORANTE   You are wrong, madame, to anticipate so many difficulties, and the experience that you have had provides no conclusions for others to draw.

DORIMENE   Well, my conclusion is always the same. The expenses that you undergo in my behalf trouble me for two reasons: one is that they commit me more that I care to be. and the other...please, don't take offense...the other is that I am sure that they are more than you can afford, and I don't want that.

DORANTE   Ah! Madame, I beg you not to esteem so highly something that is unworthy of my love for you, and to allow... **(Mr. Jourdain interrupts him with his entrance)** Here is the master of the household.

Scene 16: Mr Jourdain, Dorante, Dorimene, Lackey

MR JOURDAIN	**(After making his second bow to Dorimene and finding himself too close to complete with the third bow)** Er... Step back a little, madame.
DORIMENE	How's that?
MR JOURDAIN	Just one step, please.
DORIMENE	What?
MR JOURDAIN	Back up a little for the third.
DORANTE	Madame, Mr. Jourdain is very strong on etiquette.
MR JOURDAIN	Madame, it is a great glory for me to see myself being so fortunate to be so happy to have the good fortune of your having had the kindness to grant me your presence; and, if I merited enough to...um...merit a merit like yours, and if heaven...envious of my good fortune...had granted me...the advantage of seeing myself worthy...of the...um...
DORANTE	That will do, Mr. Jourdain. Madame does not care for great compliments and she recognizes your nimble wit. **(Aside to Dorimene)** As you can tell by his manners, you're dealing with a rather ridiculous bourgeois.
DORIMENE	**(Aside to Dorante)** That's rather obvious.
DORANTE	Madame, here is my best friend.
MR JOURDAIN	You do me too much honor.
DORANTE	A gentleman to the core.
DORIMENE	I hold him in very high esteem.
MR JOURDAIN	I have done nothing as yet, madame, to deserve such consideration.

DORANTE	**(Aside to Mr Jourdain)** Take care not to mention the diamond you gave her.
MR JOURDAIN	Can't I even ask how she likes it?
DORANTE	How's that? You must do nothing of the sort. That would be most ungentlemanly of you and, to act as a man of refinement, you must pretend that it was not you who gave her this gift. **(Aloud)** Mr. Jourdain says, madame, that he is delighted to have you as his guest.
DORIMENE	He does me great honor.
MR JOURDAIN	**(Aside to Dorante)** How obliged I am to you, sir, for speaking to her thus in my behalf
DORANTE	**(Aside to Mr. Jourdain)** I can't tell you how difficult it was for me to get her to come here.
MR JOURDAIN	**(Aside to Dorante)** I don't know how I can ever repay you for it.
DORANTE	He says, madame, that he considers you the most beautiful person in the world.
DORIMENE	How very gracious of him.
MR JOURDAIN	Madame, it is you who are gracious, and...
DORANTE	Let us proceed with the dinner.
1ST LACKEY	**(Entering and addressing Mr Jourdain)** Everything is ready, sir.
DORANTE	Let's sit at the table and bring in the musicians.

Six cooks perform a dance which constitutes the third interlude, concluded by bringing in a table laden with various dishes for the feast, Mr Jourdain, Dorimene and Dorante take their seats.

ACT IV

Scene 1: Mr. Jourdain, Dorante, Dorimene, Lackeys, Cooks, Singers

DORIMENE

Really, Dorante, what's a thoroughly sumptuous meal!

MR JOURDAIN

You jest, madame. I only wish that it was more worthy of you.

DORANTE

Mr. Jourdain is right, madame, to speak thus, and he obliges me by the excellent manner in which he does you the honors of his household. I agree with him that the dinner is not worthy of you. Since it is I who ordered it, and since I am not as enlightened in these matters as are some of my friends, its preparation is not particularly ingenious. You will find in it certain culinary incongruities and some barbarous examples of taste. If Damis had a hand in it, all would have been done according to rule. It would have abounded in elegance and erudition, and he would have expanded upon each course, thereby convincing you of his exceptional competence in the science of good eating. He would have spoken to you of bread "de rive," slanted and golden at each end and with a crust that crumbles tenderly in the mouth; of a fragrant, velvety wine with a heartiness that does not overpower; of a breast of lamb garnished with parsley; of a loin of veal "de riviere" this long, white, delicate, pate of almonds in the mouth; a partridge imbued with a surprising aroma; and, for his chef d'oeuvre, he would have intoned upon a pearled bouillon soup backed up by a young plump turkey bordered by squabs and crowned with white onions stuffed with chicory. However, for my part, I can only confess my ignorance, and join Mr. Jourdain in his most proper wish that the dinner were more worthy of being offered to you.

DORIMENE   My only response to that compliment lies in the way I am eating.

MR JOURDAIN   Ah! Such beautiful hands!

DORIMENE   My hands are very ordinary, Mr. Jourdain, but you're probably referring to the diamond which is indeed beautiful.

MR JOURDAIN   Me, madame? Heaven keep me from ever wishing to discuss it; that would not be very gentlemanly on my part, and the diamond is a mere trifle.

DORIMENE   You are very gallant.

MR JOURDAIN   You are much too kind.

DORANTE   **(After signaling to Mr Jourdain)** Come now, some wine for Mr Jourdain, and for these gentlemen who will be so kind as to sing a drinking song for us.

DORIMENE   To blend good food with music is to provide the perfect seasoning. How admirably you do entertain me!

MR JOURDAIN   Madame, it is not...

DORANTE   Mr Jourdain, let us listen to these gentlemen; their singing will surpass anything we might say.

The Singers take glasses and sing two drinking songs accompanied by the orchestra.

DRINKING SONG:
Be always faithful, forever be true
To your beloved; Then you will know
All the joy that love can bestow.

Often in anger and passion,
We're spiteful and unyielding,
But love's sole demand
Is to love constantly.

A sip or two, Louise,
As we begin the round,
Ah, how a glass that you hold becomes a thing of
beauty!
You and the wine combine to overpower me,
And my heart for them both is by love doubly
bound.

Glass in hand, you and I,
Let's vow, let's vow, my beauty,
To love for all eternity.

Bring on the wine,
Let good cheer flow for everyone!
Pour it, my lad, pour it;
Pour it; pour it freely,
Until they say "Enough!"

DORIMENE   No one could possibly sing any better.
                That was absolutely beautiful.
MR JOURDAIN   I see here, madame, something even more
                beautiful.

DORIMENE	Dear me! Mr. Jourdain is more gallant than I thought.
DORANTE	How's that? Madame, for whom do you take Mr. Jourdain?
MR JOURDAIN	I would have her take me for what I would say.
DORIMENE	Again!
DORANTE	You don't know him.
MR JOURDAIN	She shall know me whenever she pleases.
DORIMENE	Oh, you're too much for me.
DORANTE	He is a man with a ready wit; but you have not observed, madame, that Mr. Jourdain waits until you have served yourself and then eats what you leave.
DORIMENE	Mr Jourdain is a man who charms me...
MR JOURDAIN	If I could charm your heart, I would be...

Scene 2: Enter Mrs Jourdain

MRS JOURDAIN	Aha! Look at the fine company we have here, and I can see that I was not at all expected. Thus it was for this beautiful affair, my dear husband, that you were so anxious to pack me off to your sister's for dinner. Downstairs looks like a playhouse and up here I'm interrupting what could pass for a wedding banquet. So this is how you squander your money! You send me away and then lavish fine ladies with music and entertainment.
DORANTE	What do you mean, Mrs. Jourdain? Where did you get the bizarre notion that your husband is squandering his money, and that it is he who is regaling this lady? Please know that this is my affair and that

	your husband's role was merely to avail me of his home. I would thank you to observe things more carefully before you speak.
MR JOURDAIN	Yes, you impertinent creature! It is the count who is giving all this to the lady here who is a person of quality. He has done me the honor of accepting my house and of desiring my company .
MRS JOURDAIN	Folderol! I know what I know.
DORANTE	May I suggest a better pair of spectacles for you, Mrs. Jourdain.
MRS JOURDAIN	I have no need of spectacles, sir, for I see things very clearly. I have you know that I am not a fool, and that I have sensed for some time now that something was going on. May I say, sir, that it is highly unworthy of a great lord like yourself to prey on the foolishness of my husband? And you, madame, please know that it ill befits a great lady like yourself to spread dissension in a household and to allow my husband to be in love with you.
DORIMENE	What is the meaning of all of this? Really, Dorante! You abuse me by subjecting me to the delusions of this intemperate person.

Dorimene exits.

| DORANTE | (**Following Dorimene**) Madame! Hold on! Where are you running? |
| MR JOURDAIN | Madame! My dear count! Offer her my apologies and try to bring her back. |

Mr Jourdain turns to Mrs Jourdain

MR JOURDAIN   Ah! Brazen creature that you are! Here's more of your fine doings. Insulting me like that in front of everyone and chasing people of quality from my house.

MRS JOURDAIN   To hell with their quality!

MR JOURDAIN   You wretch! I don't know what keeps me from cracking your skull with the pieces of the dinner that you came here to disturb. **(The table is removed).**

MRS JOURDAIN   Who cares about that? I am defending my rights, and all womankind will back me!

MR JOURDAIN   You would do well to stay clear of my temper!

Scene 3: Mrs Jourdain exits as Covielle enters in disguise

MR JOURDAIN   What an unfortunate time to arrive. I felt like saying such pretty things, and never was my wit so sharp. (Seeing Covielle but not recognizing him) But what is this I see?

COVIELLE   Sir, I don't know if I have the honor of being known by you.

MR JOURDAIN   No.

COVIELLE   **(Lowering his hand to a foot from the ground)** I knew you when you were no taller than that.

MR JOURDAIN   Me?

COVIELLE   Yes, you were the most beautiful child in the world, and all the ladies would hold you in their arms and kiss you.

MR JOURDAIN   They kissed me?

COVIELLE   Yes. I was a very close friend of your late father.

MR JOURDAIN   Of my late father?

COVIELLE	Yes. He was a most respectable gentleman.
MR JOURDAIN	What did you say?
COVIELLE	I said he was a most respectable gentleman.
MR JOURDAIN	My father?
COVIELLE	Yes.
MR JOURDAIN	You knew him well?
COVIELLE	Certainly.
MR JOURDAIN	And did you know hin to be a gentleman?
COVIELLE	Most assuredly.
MR JOURDAIN	Who can understand this world?
COVIELLE	How's that?
MR JOURDAIN	There are foolish people who tell me he was a shopkeeper.
COVIELLE	He, a shopkeeper? That's utter slander. He never was that. He was always considerate, always eager to be of service, and, since he was an expert in fabrics, he would go everywhere for his selections and have them brought to his place so that he might give them to his friends...for money.
MR JOURDAIN	Sir, I am delighted to make the acquaintance of someone who can attest to the fact that my father was a gentleman.
COVIELLE	Sir, I shall proclaim that to the entire world.
MR JOURDAIN	I shall be much obliged. May I ask the purpose of your visit
COVIELLE	Since my last meeting with your late father, the distinguished gentleman, I have traveled all over the world.
MR JOURDAIN	All over the world!
COVIELLE	Yes.

MR JOURDAIN	I'd say that's quite a ways from here.
COVIELLE	To be sure. I returned from these long voyages just four days ago and because of my concern for anything that might affect you, I come here to bring you the best news in the world.
MR JOURDAIN	Pray what might that be?
COVIELLE	Did you know that the son of the Great Turk is here?
MR JOURDAIN	Me? No.
COVIELLE	How's that? He has an absolutely magnificent cortege. Everyone goes to see him, and he has been received in this country as a lord of great importance.
MR JOURDAIN	In faith, I did not know that.
COVIELLE	What is to your advantage is the fact that he is in love with your daughter.
MR JOURDAIN	The son of the Great Turk?
COVIELLE	Yes, and he wants to be your son-in-law.
MR JOURDAIN	My son-in-law, the son of the Great Turk?
COVIELLE	The son of the Great Turk, your son-in-law. And since I have been to see him, and since I understand his language perfectly, we had a long conversation during which he said: "Acciam croc soler ouch alla moustaph gidelum amanahem marahini oussere carbulath?" That is to say: "Have you not seen the beautiful young person who is the daughter of Mr. Jourdain, the Parisian gentleman?"
MR JOURDAIN	The son of the Great Turk said that about me?
COVIELLE	Yes. When I replied that I was a special friend of yours, and that I had seen your

daughter, he said: "Marababashem!" ...
That is to say: "Ah! How I love her!"

MR JOURDAIN   Marababashem means "Ah! How I love her!"

COVIELLE   Yes.

MR JOURDAIN   In faith, you did well to tell me that because I myself would have never believed that this Marababashem could have meant "Ah! How I love her!" It's an admirable language, this Turkish.

COVIELLE   More admirable than you might believe. Do you know what Cacaracamouchen means?

MR JOURDAIN   Cacaracamouchen? No.

COVIELLE   That means "My dear soul."

MR JOURDAIN   Cacaracamouchen means "My dear soul."

COVIELLE   Yes.

MR JOURDAIN   That's marvelous! Cacaracamouchen, my dear soul. Who would have thought that? I find that amazing!

COVIELLE   Finally, sir, to conclude my message, I must tell you that he is coming to ask for your daughter's hand in marriage and, in order that his father-in-law be worthy of him, he wishes to make you a Mamamouuchi, which is a great dignitary in his country.

MR JOURDAIN   A Mamamouchi?

COVIELLE   Yes, a Mamamouchi which means in our language a paladin. Paladin! It's one of those ancient titles that...er..., you know...paladin! There is nothing more noble than that in the world, and you will rank among the greatest lords on earth.

MR JOURDAIN   The son of the Great Turk does me great honor, and I beseech you to conduct me to his home so that I might thank him.

COVIELLE   How's that? Why, he's at this moment on his way here.

MR JOURDAIN   He's coming here?

COVIELLE   Yes, and he's bringing with him all the ceremonial trappings for your investiture.

MR JOURDAIN   I must say he's very prompt.

COVIELLE   His love cannot tolerate any delay.

MR JOURDAIN   The only problem is that my daughter is as stubborn as can be and has this fellow Cleonte on her mind and swears that she won't marry anyone but him.

COVIELLE   She'll change her mind once she sees the son of the Great Turk, and then a wonderfully romantic episode will take place here. The fact is that the son of the Great Turk resembles Cleonte...well almost anyway. I have just seen him...they showed him to me, and the love that she has for one could easily be passed on to the other and...

Cleonte, disguised as the son of the Great Turk, enters with three PAGES carrying his train.

COVIELLE   I hear him coming... There he is!

Scene 4: Mr. Jourdain, Covielle (in disguise), Cleonte (in disguise), 3 Pages

CLEONTE   Amboushabim oqui boraf, Jordina, salama-lequi.

COVIELLE   **(To Mr. Jourdain)** That is to say: "Mr. Jourdain, may your heart be all year like a rose bush in bloom." This illustrates the obliging manner of speech in those countries.

MR JOURDAIN I am the most humble servant of His Turkish Highness.

COVIELLE **(To Cleonte)** Carigar camboto oustin moraf.

CLEONTE Oustin yoc catamalequi basurn base all moran.

COVIELLE He says that heaven should give you the strength of lions and the prudence of serpents.

MR JOURDAIN His Turkish Highness does me too much honor, and I wish him all kinds of prosperity.

COVIELLE Ossa binamen sadoc babally oracaf ouram.

CLEONTE Bel-men.

COVIELLE He says that you are to go with him quickly to prepare yourself for the ceremony so that afterwards you might see your daughter and conclude the marriage.

MR JOURDAIN All that in two words?

COVIELLE Yes, the Turkish language is like that; it says a lot in few words. Now go with him quickly where he wishes.

Mr Jourdain exits with Cleonte and the pages, leaving Covielle alone on stage.

COVIELLE Hahaha! My God, that was funny! What a dupe! Had he learned his role by heart, he couldn't have possibly played it better. Hahaha!

Scene 5: Dorante, Covielle

Dorante enters.

COVIELLE	Would you be so kind, sir, as to help us in a certain bit of business that is in progress?
DORANTE	Ah! Ah! Covielle! Who would have recognized you? What an outfit!
COVIELLE	You see! Hahaha!
DORANTE	What are you laughing at?
COVIELLE	At something that really calls for it, sir.
DORANTE	How's that?
COVIELLE	Sir, I could give you several tries at guessing the stratagem we are using on Mr. Jourdain to persuade him to give his daughter to my master.
DORANTE	What the stratagem is I cannot guess, but I can guess that it will succeed since it is you who is behind it.
COVIELLE	I see that you know me well, sir.
DORANTE	Tell me what it is.
COVIELLE	Let us withdraw to make room for what I see coming. You will be able to witness a part of the affair as I tell you the rest.

Dorante and Covielle withdraw as the Turkish Ceremony begins.

THE TURKISH CEREMONY

Mufti, Turks, Dervishes, Mr. Jourdain, Singers and Dancers.

Six Turks enter gravely, two by two to the sound of instruments. Each pair carries a carpet with which they dance several steps. They then raise their carpets high and the Turkish singers and musicians pass underneath. The Mufti and his company of Dervishes complete the procession. The Turks then spread the carpets on the ground and kneel on them while the Mufti and his Dervishes remain standing in the middle. As the Mufti invokes Mohammed in pantomime with contorted gestures and grimaces, the Turks prostrate themselves, singing "Alli, " and then return to a kneeling position with arms raised singing "Allah. " This switching continues until the invocation is over at which point they all rise and sing "Allah eckber" **(God is Great)**, and two Dervishes escort Mr. Jourdain **(now in Turkish garb, but sans turban and sabre)**.

TEXT	TRANSLATION
MUFTI **(To Jourdain)**	
Se ti sabir, ti respondir	If you know, you answer;
Se non sabir,	If you don't know
Tazir, tazir.	Quiet, quiet.
Mi star mufti.	I be mufti.
Ti qui star, ti?	Who be you?
Non intendir?	You don't understand?
Tazir, tazir.	Quiet, quiet.

Two Dervishes lead Mr. Jourdain offstage.

The Language being spoken is lingua franca, a hybrid language comprised of Italian, French, Spanish, Greek and Arabic; it was used in Mediterranean ports. The translation is provided merely for edification and is not meant to be sung.

TEXT		TRANSLATION
MUFTI	Dice, Turque,	Tell me, Turk,
	qui star quista?	who be that one?
	Anabista?	An Anabaptist?
	Anabista?	An Anabaptist?
TURKS	Ioc.	No.

MUFTI Zuinglista?	A Zuinglian?
TURKS Ioc.	No.
MUFTI Coffita?	A coffite?
TURKS Ioc.	No.
MUFTI Hussita? Morista? Fronista?	A Hussite? A Moor? ???
TURKS Ioc ioc, ioc.	No, no, no!
MUFTI Ioc, ioc, ioc! Star Pagana?	No, no, no. Is he a pagan?
TURKS Ioc.	No.
MUFTI Luterana?	A Lutheran?
TURKS Ioc.	No.
MUFTI Puritana?	A Puritan?
TURKS Ioc.	No.
MUFTI Bramina?	A Brahman?
TURKS Ioc, ioc, ioc.	No, no, no.
MUFTI Ioc, ioc., ioc. Mahametana?	No, no, no A Mohamedan?
TURKS Hi Valla. Hi Valla.	Yes, that's it. Yes, that's it.
MUFTI Como chamara?	What's his name?
TURKS Jordina.	Jourdain.
MUFTI (Leaping at him) Jordina?	Jourdain?
TURKS Jordina.	Jourdain.
MUFTI Mahameta, per Jordina. Mi pregar sera e matina Voler far un paladina De Giordina, de Giordina Dar Turbanta e dar scarcina	To Mohamed for Jourdain. I pray day and night That he make a paladin of Jourdain, of Jourdain Give him a turban and a sword

Con galera	With a galley
e brigantina	and brigantine
Per defender Palestina	To defend Palestine
Mahameta,	To Mohamed,
per Giordina	for Jourdain
Mi pregar sera e matina	I pray day and night.
(To the Turks)	
Star bon Turca, Giordina	Is Jourdain a good Turk?
TURKS Hi Valla; Hi valla!	Yes, that's it. Yes, that's it.

MUFTI **(Dancing and singing)**
Ha la ba la chou ba la ba la ba la...

Mufti exits.

TURKS Ha la ba la chou ba la ba la ba la...

Mufti re-enters wearing an oversized ceremonial turban decorated with four or five rows of lighted candles. Two Dervishes accompany him bearing the Koran and wearing pointed hats which are also set with lighted candles. The other two dervishes bring in Mr. Jourdain who is terrified by the ceremony and they make him kneel with his hands on the ground so that the Mufti might use his back as a sort of stand for the Koran. The Mufti makes a second burlesque invocation closing and opening his mouth without tittering a word; he then speaks vehemently, alternating between soft and thunderous tones, slaps his sides as if to force out the words, pounds on the Koran front time to time and turns its pages precipitously. Finally, he raises his hands and shouts...

MUFTI   Hou!

During the second invocation, the Turks bow and straighten up three times singing "Hou!" each time.

MR JOURDAIN	(After they remove the Koran from his back) Ah!
MUFTI	(To Mr. Jourdain) Ti non star furba? *You are not a knave?*
TURKS	No, no, no!
MUFTI	Non star forfanta? *You are not an impostor?*
TURKS	No, no, no!
MUFTI	Donar Turbanta. *Give the turban.*
TURKS	Ti non star furba? No, no, no. Non star fortanta? No, no, no. Donar turbanta.

The Turks put the turban on Mr. Jourdain's head singing and dancing to the music.

MUFTI	(Giving the sword to Mr. Jourdain) Ti star nobile, non star fabbola. *You're a noble and that's no fable.* Pigliar sciabbola. *Take the sword.*

The Turks draw their swords, dancing about, beating Mr. Jourdain with their swords, and repeat these words:

MUFTI	Dara, dara, bastonnara. *Hit him, hit him with a with a stick.*

The Turks repeat the words, dancing about Mr. Jourdain and beating him with sticks.

MUFTI   Non tener honta *Don't be ashamed* Questa star l'ultima affronta. *This is the last affront.*

The Mufti begins his third invocation, leaning on the dervishes who support him reverently; the Turks then exit with the Mufti and, as they do, they sing, dance, and leap about him bringing along Mr. Jourdain in their wake.

ACT V

Scene 1: Mr. Jourdain, Mrs. Jourdain

MRS JOURDAIN Oh my God! Have mercy on me! What is this I see before me? What a figure! Are you about to play the mummer? Is it masquerade time? Speak, why don't you? What is this? Who decked you out like that?

MR JOURDAIN Listen to that brazen creature speaking like that to a mamamouchi!

MRS JOURDAIN What's that?

MR JOURDAIN Yes, you must treat me with more respect now that they made me a mamamouchi.

MRS JOURDAIN What kind of beast is that?

MR JOURDAIN Mamamouchi in our language means paladin.

MRS JOURDAIN Balleting? At your age your dancing the ballet?

MR JOURDAIN What an ignoramus! I said paladin. It's a very high dignitary, and they just now performed the ceremony making me one.

MRS JOURDAIN What ceremony?

MR JOURDAIN Mahameta per Jordina.

MRS JOURDAIN What does that mean?

MR JOURDAIN Jordina, that is to say, Jourdain.

MRS JOURDAIN What about Jourdain?

MR JOURDAIN Voler far un paladina de Jordina.

MRS JOURDAIN What?

MR JOURDAIN Dar turbanto con galera.

MRS JOURDAIN What the deuce does that mean?

MR JOURDAIN	Dara, dara, bastonnara!
MRS JOURDAIN	What kind of gibberish is that?
MR JOURDAIN	Non tener honta, questa star l'ultima affronta.
MRS JOURDAIN	What is the meaning of all this?
MR JOURDAIN	**(Dancing and singing)** Hou la ba, ba la chou, ba la ba, ba la da. **(He falls to the ground)**
MRS JOURDAIN	Heaven help us! My husband has gone mad!
MR JOURDAIN	**(Rising)** Be still, insolent one! You must show respect to your mamamouchi.

Mr Jourdain exits.

MRS JOURDAIN	Where did this madness come upon him? Quickly now, I must prevent him from going out. **(Notices Dorante and Dorimene)** Aha! That's all I need to know! I've got trouble closing in on me from all sides!

Mrs Jourdain exits.

Scene 2: Dorante and Dorimene

DORANTE	Yes, madame, you're about to witness the most amusing episode conceivable. Were you to search the world over, you would not possibly find a man more mad than he; and then, madame, we must serve the cause of Cleonte's love by assisting in his little masquerade. He is a very decent lad and worthy of our concern.

DORIMENE	I think very highly of him, and he is deserving of good fortune.
DORANTE	Aside from that, madame, a ballet shall be performed here which we should not miss for it will be much to our liking, and I also must see if an idea of mine will succeed.
DORIMENE	I have seen the magnificent preparations, and these are things, Dorante, that I can no longer endure. Yes, it is my wish finally that you put an end to these lavish expenditures on my behalf, and to see that you do, I have decided to marry you with no further delay. The true secret to all these things is that they lead ultimately to marriage.
DORANTE	Ah! Madame, is it possible that you favor me with such sweet decision?
DORIMENE	This is only to avoid your total impoverishment since it is obvious that at this rate you will soon be without a sou.
DORANTE	How obliged am I to you, madame, for your concern over my estate!
DORIMENE	I shall make good use of both; but here comes your man. What a vision of splendor!

Scene 3: Mr. Jourdain, Dorante, Dorimene

DORANTE	Sir, madame and I have come to render homage to your newly bestowed dignity, and to rejoice with you over the forthcoming marriage of your daughter to the son of the Great Turk.

MR JOURDAIN	**(After making three bows Turkish-style)** Sir, I wish you the strength of snakes and the wisdom of lions.
DORIMENE	Sir, I am extremely pleased to be among the first to congratulate you over the high degree of glory to which you have been elevated.
MR JOURDAIN	Madame, I wish that your rosebush will be in bloom all year, and I am infinitely obliged to you for taking part in the honors that are happening to me, and I am very glad to see you here again so that I might apologize most humbly for the nastiness of my wife.
DORIMENE	That was nothing. Such comportment is excusable on the part of a woman to whom your heart is so precious, and it is not at all strange that the possession of a man like you should inspire fits of alarm.
MR JOURDAIN	The possession of my heart is a thing that you have completely acquired.
DORANTE	As you see, madame, our Mr. Jourdain is not among those who allow themselves to be blinded by their own prosperity; despite his rise to glory, he still deigns to recognize his friends.
DORIMENE	That is the mark of a truly generous person.
DORANTE	Where is his Turkish Highness? We would like to pay him our respects as friends of yours.
MR JOURDAIN	Here he comes now. I've sent for my daughter to give him her hand.

Scene 4: Cleonte (in disguise), Covielle (in disguise), Jourdain, Dorante, Dorimene

DORANTE   **(To Cleonte)** Sir, we bow before your highness as friends of your father-in-law and extend our most respectful assurance of our very humble services.

MR JOURDAIN   Where is that interpreter to tell him who you are and to have him understand what you say. You will see that he'll answer you, and that he speaks Turkish marvelously. Hey there! Where the devil did he go? **(To Cleonte)** Straf, strif, strof, straf. This gentleman is a grande segnore, grande segnore, grande segnore, and the lady is a dama, granda dama.

Cleonte pretends not to understand, and Mr. Jourdain begins pointing and making elaborate gestures.

MR JOURDAIN   Oh, my... Him, sir, him French mamamouchi, and her, her French mamamouchi lady... I can't speak more clearly than that... Ah, good. Here comes the interpreter.

Scene 5: Mr. Jourdain, Cleonte, Dorante, Dorimene, Covielle

Covielle enters in disguise

MR JOURDAIN   Where have you been? We can't say anything without you. **(Pointing to Cleonte)** Tell him that the gentleman and lady are people of high quality and that they come

	to pay their respects as my friends, and to assure him of their services. **(To Dorante and Dorimene)** Watch how he answers.
COVIELLE	Alabala crociam acci boram alabamen.
CLEONTE	Catalequi tubal ourin soter amalouchan.
MR JOURDAIN	What did I tell you!
COVIELLE	He said that the garden of your family should forever be sprinkled by the rain of prosperity.
MR JOURDAIN	I told you he speaks Turkish!
DORANTE	How remarkable.

Scene 6: Lucille, Mr. Jourdain, Dorante, Dorimene, Cleonte, Covielle

MR JOURDAIN	Come join us, my daughter, and give your hand to this gentleman who is doing you the honor of asking to marry you.
LUCILLE	What is this, father? What type of garb is that? Are you playing in some comedy?
MR JOURDAIN	No, no, this is no comedy; it is a very serious matter. You are to be honored more greatly than anyone could possibly wish. **(Pointing to Cleonte)** Behold, the husband that I give you.
LUCILLE	To me, father?
MR JOURDAIN	Yes, to you. Come now, join hands with him and be thankful to Heaven for your good fortune.
LUCILLE	I do not want to get married.
MR JOURDAIN	Well, I want it, and I am your father.
LUCILLE	I'll do nothing of the sort.
MR JOURDAIN	Enough of that! Come now, your hand.
LUCILLE	No father, as I told you, there is no power on earth that can force me to have any

other but Cleonte as a husband, and I will resort to the most drastic measures rather to allow myself to... **(Suddenly recognizing Cleonte beneath his disguise.)** It is true that as my father you are entitled to my complete obedience, and you may, therefore, dispose of me however you wish.

MR JOURDAIN   Ah! I am delighted to see you regain your sense of duty so promptly. How pleasing it is to have an obedient daughter.

Scene 7: Lucille, Mr. Jourdain, Cleonte, Covielle, Dorante, Dorimene, Mrs. Jourdain

MRS JOURDAIN   Well now, what do we have here? They tell me you're going to marry your daughter off to a mummer.

MR JOURDAIN   Is there no holding that impertinent tongue of yours? You're always sticking that shrewish nose of yours into everything, and there's no way of teaching you to be sensible.

MRS JOURDAIN   You're the one without a modicum of sense, and you flit from one folly to another. What is it this time? What do you plan to do with these people?

MR JOURDAIN   I plan to marry our daughter to the son of the Great Turk.

MRS JOURDAIN   The son of the Great Turk?

MR JOURDAIN   **(Pointing to Covielle)** Yes. Pay him your compliments through the interpreter over there.

MRS JOURDAIN	I don't need any interpreter; I'll tell him myself to his face that he'll not have my daughter.
MR JOURDAIN	There you go again! Will you be still?
DORANTE	Come now, Mrs. Jourdain, are you really turning down such an honor? You are rejecting his Turkish Highness as a son-in--law?
MRS JOURDAIN	By the saints, sir, mind your own business.
DORIMENE	This is a great glory that should not be refused.
MRS JOURDAIN	Madame, I shall thank you also not to trouble yourself with matters that do not concern you.
DORANTE	Our concern for your welfare stems only from our feelings of friendship for both of you.
MRS JOURDAIN	I can do quite nicely without your friendship.
DORANTE	Your daughter, however, has agreed to comply with the wishes of her father.
MRS JOURDAIN	My daughter has agreed to marry a Turk?
DORANTE	Most assuredly.
MRS JOURDAIN	She can forget her Cleonte?
DORANTE	What is there that one would not do to become a great lady?
MRS JOURDAIN	If she ever did anything like that, I'd strangle her with my own hands.
MR JOURDAIN	Enough of your cackling. I'm telling you that the marriage will take place.
MRS JOURDAIN	And I'm telling you that it won't
MR JOURDAIN	Oh, this is too much!
LUCILLE	Mother!
MRS JOURDAIN	Be gone, traitoress!

MR JOURDAIN	What? Are you now criticizing her for obeying me?
MRS JOURDAIN	She's my daughter as well as yours!
COVIELLE	**(Still in disguise, To Mrs. Jourdain)** Madame!
MRS JOURDAIN	And what have you got to say?
COVIELLE	Just a word.
MRS JOURDAIN	I've got no use for your "word."
COVIELLE	**(To Mr. Jourdain)** Sir, if I could just have a word with her alone, I promise you that she'll comply with your wish.
MRS JOURDAIN	Never!
COVIELLE	Would you just listen to me?
MRS JOURDAIN	No.
MR JOURDAIN	Listen to him.
MRS JOURDAIN	No, I don't care to.
MR JOURDAIN	He'll tell you.
MRS JOURDAIN	I don't want him to tell me anything.
MR JOURDAIN	Did you ever see such a stubborn woman? Would it harm you to listen to him?
COVIELLE	All I ask is that you listen; you may then do as you please.
MRS JOURDAIN	All right then, what is it?
COVIELLE	**(Aside to Mrs. Jourdain)** We have been trying to catch your eye for an hour. Don't you see that all this is simply to have us conform to the foolish notions of your husband, that we are using this disguise to dupe him, and that the son of the Great Turk is none other than Cleonte himself.
MRS JOURDAIN	**(Aside to Covielle)** Aha!
COVIELLE	**(Aside to Mrs. Jourdain)** And that I, Covielle, am the interpreter?
MRS JOURDAIN	Ah! Well, in that case, I shall yield.
COVIELLE	Act as though you know nothing.

MRS JOURDAIN   **(Aloud)** Yes, that settles it! I consent to the marriage.

MR JOURDAIN   Ah! At last everyone is acting sensibly. **(Aside to Mrs. Jourdain)** You didn't want to listen to him, but I knew that once you did, you'd know just who it is we have here in the son of the Great Turk.

MRS JOURDAIN   Yes, I see things very clearly now and I like what I see. You may send for the notary.

DORANTE   Very well put. And now, Mrs. Jourdain, to complete your happiness and to remove whatever feelings of jealousy you may have had concerning your husband, I shall announce that my lady and I plan to avail ourselves of the services of the same notary.

MRS JOURDAIN   I consent to that also.

MR JOURDAIN   **(Aside to Dorante)** That was just to fool her, wasn't it?

DORANTE   **(Aside to Mr. Jourdain)** Of course. We must amuse her with this little pretense.

MR JOURDAIN   **(Aside)** Good, good! **(Aloud)** Quickly now, summon the notary.

DORANTE   As we await his arrival and his drawing up of the contracts, let us see our ballet which we present for the entertainment of his Turkish Highness.

MR JOURDAIN   An excellent idea. Let's take our places.

MRS JOURDAIN   And Nicole?

MR JOURDAIN   I give her to the interpreter, and my wife to whoever will take her.

COVIELLE   Sir, I thank you. **(Aside)** If a greater fool than this could ever exist, all the way to Rome would I travel to announce it.

The play ends with the ballet, **THE BALLET OF NATIONS.** The second of the French segment, sung and danced by 3 women and 3 men in costumes from Poitiers.

> Wander with me
> Off to yon meadow
> There to behold
> A tale of love unfold
>
> There neath the tree
> Two doves intoning
> Sweet sounds of love and fidelity
>
> So glad of heart
> We can also be,
> If you'd love me
> For all eternity.
>
> Oh! How sweet is the world!
> Oh! How bright are the days!
> When two hearts are as one,
> And the power,
> The rapture of love
> Unfolds its wondrous ways!   THE END

The Doctor
In Spite of Himself

CHARACTERS

SGANARELLE, A Woodcutter
MARTINE, His Wife
GERONTE, An Elderly Gentleman
LUCINDE, His Daughter
LEANDRE, A Suitor
VALERE, Geronte's Servant
LUCAS, Geronte's Servant
JACQUELINE, Lucas' Wife & Geronte's Wetnurse
THIBAULT, A poor Old Man
PERRIN, His Son
MR ROBERT, A Neighbor

The play takes place in the woods of France and at Geronte's home.

ACT I

The scene represents a wooded area not far from Sganarelle's home.

Scene 1: Sganarelle, Martine

SGANARELLE	No. I tell you I'll have none of that. I'm the master here and I'll say what I want.
MARTINE	And I'm telling you that I want my say too, and that I didn't marry you just to put up with your pranks.
SGANARELLE	Oh, what a pain it is to have a wife, and how right Aristotle was to say that a wife is worse than a demon!
MARTINE	Aren't you the clever one with your stupid Aristotle!
SGANARELLE	Clever indeed! I defy you to find another woodcutter who can reason as well as I, who was an apprentice to a celebrated physician for six years and who, as a mere slip of a lad, could recite his Latin primer by heart.
MARTINE	Pompous idiot!
SGANARELLE	Whining shrew!
MARTINE	Cursed be the hour and the day when I decided to say yes.
SGANARELLE	Cursed be that cuckold of a notary that made me sign my ruination.
MARTINE	Oh, yes, indeed, you're the one with reason to complain. Ingrate! Should you not spend your day thanking God for having me as your wife? And did you deserve to marry a person like me?

SGANARELLE	It is true that the honor you bestowed upon me was overwhelming, and that our wedding night was for me a deep source of pride...but don't force me to go into that for I shall say certain things that...
MARTINE	What things?
SGANARELLE	Enough. Let's drop the subject. Let it suffice that we know what we know, and that you very fortunate to have found me.
MARTINE	In what way do you consider me fortunate to have found you? A man who is bringing me to the poorhouse, a debaucher, a deceiver, who eats everything I have.
SGANARELLE	You lie. I drink some of it, too.
MARTINE	Who sells, piece by piece, everything in the house.
SGANARELLE	I'm thrifty.
MARTINE	Who even sold my bed!
SGANARELLE	Now you'll get up earlier.
MARTINE	So that there's not a piece of furniture left in the entire household.
SGANARELLE	All the more easy to move out.
MARTINE	And who does nothing but gamble and drink from morning till night.
SGANARELLE	Only to avoid boredom.
MARTINE	And while you play and drink, what am I to do with my family?
SGANARELLE	Whatever you like.
MARTINE	I've got four unfortunate children on my hands.
SGANARELLE	Put them down.
MARTINE	Who constantly ask to be fed.
SGANARELLE	Feed them the whip, then. Come now, when I've had enough to eat and drink, I

want everyone in my house to have his fill.

MARTINE	And do you believe, drunkard, that this can go on forever.
SGANARELLE	Easy does it, please, dear wife.
MARTINE	That I should be forever subject to your insolence and debauchery?
SGANARELLE	Let's not get carried away, dear wife.
MARTINE	That I am beyond finding a way to have you face up to your duty?
SGANARELLE	My dear wife, you know that my endurance is short, and that my arm is long.
MARTINE	To hell with your threats.
SGANARELLE	My little wife, my sweetheart, as usual you're itching for it.
MARTINE	I'll show you that I in not afraid of you at all.
SGANARELLE	My dear spouse, you feel like taking a little something from me don't you?
MARTINE	Do you think your words frighten me?
SGANARELLE	Sweet object of my desires. I shall box your ears.
MARTINE	Drunkard that you are!
SGANARELLE	I shall beat you.
MARTINE	Sot!
SGANARELLE	I shall thrash you.
MARTINE	Drunken beast!
SGANARELLE	I shall throttle you.
MARTINE	Traitor! Insulter! Deceiver! Coward! Rogue! Knave! Tramp! Cad! Scoundrel! Villain! Thief!

Sganarelle takes up a stick and beats her.

SGANARELLE	You really have a thirst for it, don't you?

MARTINE Oh! Oh! Oh! Oh!

SGANARELLE Well, this is the best way to quench it.

Scene 2: Sganarelle, Martine, Mr. Robert

MR ROBERT Stop! Hold on! Enough! For shame! What is this? How disgraceful! A plague on the rogue who beats his wife thus!

MARTINE **(Hands on her hips, she forces Mr. Robert back as she speaks and eventually slaps him)** I want him to beat me!

MR ROBERT Oh! Well, in that case, I...er...approve wholeheartedly.

SGANARELLE Who are you to interfere?

MR ROBERT I was wrong.

MARTINE Is it any of your business?

MR ROBERT You are right.

MARTINE The impertinence of this man who wants to prevent husbands from beating their wives!

MR ROBERT I take it all back.

MARTINE Is this any concern of yours?

MR ROBERT In no way.

MARTINE Then mind your own business.

MR ROBERT I shall not say another word.

MARTINE I like to get beaten.

MR ROBERT So be it.

MARTINE It's no skin off your nose.

MR ROBERT That is true.

MARTINE And you are a fool to butt into things that don't concern you! **(She slaps him)**

MR ROBERT **(Turning to Sganarelle, who also forces him backwards as he speaks and who eventually beats Mr. Robert with the stick and drives him away)** My good man, you have my most humble apologies.

Go to it. Beat her; thrash her. I'll even help you if you want.

SGANARELLE   I don't feel like it.

MR ROBERT   Well, that's different.

SGANARELLE   I want to beat her if I want to, and I don't want to beat her if I don't want to.

MR ROBERT   Very good.

SGANARELLE   She's my wife and not yours.

MR ROBERT   Without a doubt.

SGANARELLE   And it's not for you to give me orders.

MR ROBERT   Certainly not...

SGANARELLE   I do not need your help.

MR ROBERT   That's fine with me.

SGANARELLE   And you are impertinent to interfere with other people's business. To quote the immortal Cicero: "Family quarrels are for quarrelsome families.. And for no one else!"

Sganarelle begins to beat Mr. Robert and routs him from the stage, then turns to Martine and tries clasp her hand but she withdraws.

SGANARELLE   Oh, come now. Let's make peace. Shake hands.

MARTINE   Yes, after giving me such a beating.

SGANARELLE   That's nothing. Shake.

MARTINE   I don't want to.

SGANARELLE   Eh?

MARTINE   No!

SGANARELLE   My little wife.

MARTINE   Not at all!

SGANARELLE   Come now, I tell you.

MARTINE   I'll have none of it!

SGANARELLE   Come, come, come.

MARTINE   No, I want to be angry.

SGANARELLE	Nonsense! It was such a trivial affair. Let's go.
MARTINE	Let me be!
SGANARELLE	Shake hands, tell you!
MARTINE	You treated me too badly.
SGANARELLE	Oh, very well then, I apologize. Now let's shake hands.
MARTINE	I accept your apology. **(Aside)** But he shall pay for it.
SGANARELLE	You're so foolish to let that disturb you. These are little things that good fellowship requires from time to time. A gentle thrashing between friends only serves to stimulate affection. Look here, I'm going off to the woods now, and I promise you today more than a hundred pieces of firewood!

Scene 3: Martine (alone)

MARTINE	Go... I may smile outwardly but my resentment runs deep, and I shall not forget! The seething within me shall not stop until I find a way to get back at you. I know only too well that a wife always has the means for revenge against a husband. But this situation calls for more than the usual forms of wifely retaliation. No! For his shameful abuse of me, the rogue must pay, and pay dearly.

Scene 4: Martine, Lucas, Valere

LUCAS	The devil take us both if we don't have a tough job on our hands! And I got no idea who we're gonna get for this.

VALERE	What do you want to do? We have to obey our master, don't we? Besides, his daughter is our mistress and her health concerns us both. Her marriage, which her illness has delayed, would give us claim to a reward. Horace, as you know, is very generous and is quick to pay for services rendered; and although our mistress may have shown some affection for a certain Léandre, you know very well that her father has not seen fit to accept him a son-in-law.
MARTINE	(**Musing aside**) Why can't I think up a good scheme for revenge?
LUCAS	But where did our master get such a stupid notion? All them doctors we called couldn't do nothin'.
VALERE	Well, sometimes, if you keep on looking, you find things that you couldn't find before...and often in very unlikely places.
MARTINE	Yes, whatever the cost, I must get even. The beating he gave me still sticks in my throat!

As she muses over her revenge, she accidentally bumps into Valere and Lucas.

MARTINE	Oh! I beg your pardon, gentlemen. I didn't see you. I was trying to find an answer to a difficult problem.
VALERE	We all have our problems in this world, madame. We, too, are looking for something that would give us great pleasure to find.

MARTINE	Might I be of service to you in your search?
VALERE	It's possible. You see, we are looking for a very able man, a special type of doctor, capable of relieving the daughter of our master of a malady which has suddenly deprived her of her power of speech. Several doctors have already exhausted all their science to no avail, but sometimes you stumble upon people with amazing secrets, with unusual kinds of remedies, and these people often succeed where others fail. We are looking for just such a person.
MARTINE	**(Aside, with an idea)** Oh! What a scheme for vengeance flashes through me! **(Turning back to Lucas and Valere)** Gentlemen, you could not possibly have found anyone in a better position than I to help you. It so happens we have a man here who is the most marvelous man in the world for curing hopeless cases.
VALERE	And where, I beseech you, can we find him?
MARTINE	You'll find him in that little clearing over there passing the time of day cutting wood.
VALERE	A doctor who cuts wood?
LUCAS	Who is collectin' herbs for his medicine, you mean?
MARTINE	No, I mean he's cutting wood. I tell you he's truly an extraordinary gentleman...capricious, eccentric, temperamental, whom you will never take for what he is. His manner of dress is peculiar, and he sometimes assumes an air of ignorance that

belies the wealth of science within him; and there is nothing he shuns more than the occasion to use his marvelous medical talents which heaven itself has bestowed upon him.

VALERE   This touch of the bizarre in great men is truly fascinating. It is as though a trace of madness were mixed in with their science.

MARTINE   Yes, but I'm afraid the madness in this case is greater than one might expect, for it sometimes causes the poor fellow to prefer to be beaten rather than to acknowledge his profession; and I warn you that once the madness grips him, you will never get him to admit that he is a doctor unless each of you pick up a stick and beat the madness out of him. Only then will he confess. This is what we do here when we have need of him.

VALERE   What a strange form of madness!

MARTINE   That is true, but after that you will see that he will perform miracles.

VALERE   And by what name does he go?

MARTINE   By the name of Sganarelle; but he is easy to recognize. He has a large, black beard and wears a green and yellow suit with a ruff.

LUCAS   A green and yella suit? What's he, a Parrot doctor? Ha, ha, ha.

VALERE   But is he truly as good as you say he is?

MARTINE   What's that? I tell you he's a man who performs miracles. Six months ago, a woman was given up for dead by all the other doctors, and even as preparations for her burial were being made, it was decided

	to summon by force the man of whom we speak. Upon seeing her, he put into her mouth a drop of some mysterious liquid, and at that very instant, she got up from her bed and began to walk about her room as if nothing had happened.
LUCAS	Ah!
VALERE	It must have been a drop of liquid gold!
MARTINE	That may very well be. However, it was not quite three weeks later that a child of twelve fell from a steeple to the pavement below where he broke his head, arms and legs. Our man had no sooner been brought to the scene when he began to rub a certain ointment of his own concoction all over the boy's body. The child thereupon rose to his feet and ran off to play marbles.
LUCAS	By jingo! That's the man we need all right! Let's go get him quick!
VALERE	Our thanks, madame, for the service you-'ve rendered us.
MARTINE	Yes, but remember the warning I gave you.
LUCAS	You just leave that to us, ma'am; if it's a beating he be lookin' for, we be only too happy to oblige.
VALERE	**(As they leave Martine and go in search of Sganarelle)** How fortunate we were to have met that woman. She has given me the greatest hope for success.

Scene 5: Valere, Lucas, Sganarelle

SGANARELLE	**(Singing)** La, la, la…

VALERE	**(Aside to Lucas)** I hear someone singing and cutting wood.
SGANARELLE	**(Entering with a bottle in one hand and an axe in the other)** La, la, la... Whew! After all that hard work, I deserve a drink. **(He puts down the axe and takes a swig from the bottle).**
SGANARELLE	That wood is as salty as the devil. **(Continues singing)** Kisses and hugs, sweet pretty bottle, Kisses and hugs for your little glug-glugs. But how men would be jealous of me, if wine from you would always flow, Ah! Ah! Ah! My bottle of pleasure, Why do you empty so? Ah! Ah! Ah! Sweet little treasure, Promise you'll never go. **(Stops singing)** Come now! Why all this sadness? I'll have none of that!
VALERE	**(Softly to Lucas)** there he is! In the flesh!
LUCAS	**(Aloud, oafishly)** By jingo! You're right! We found him!
VALERE	Sssshhh! Let's get closer.
SGANARELLE	**(Kissing the jug)** Ah, my wicked little darling, how I love you! **(He starts to sing again, then lowers his voice and hesitates as he realizes he's being observed by Lucas and Valere)** But how men would be jealous of me If wine from you would always flow **(Stops singing abruptly, spying Lucas and Valere)** Ah! Oh! Who the devil are those two after?

VALERE	That's him. No doubt about it.
LUCAS	There he be! The spittin' image of the lady's description!
SGANARELLE	**(Aside)** They look at me as they confer. What are they up to?

Sganarelle places the bottle on the ground Valere bows in greeting. Sganarelle, thinking Valere is reaching for the bottle, quickly snatches it up again and puts it on the other side of him. Lucas bows and Sganarelle snatches the bottle away from Lucas' reach and holds it close to his chest (comical by-play may continue.)

VALERE	Sir? are you not the one who is called Sganarelle?
SGANARELLE	What's that?
VALERE	I am asking, sir, if it is you who goes by the name of Sganarelle?
SGANARELLE	Yes and no, depending on what you want.
VALERE	We only wish to pay him the highest respect within our power.
SGANARELLE	Well, in that case, my name is indeed Sganarelle.
VALERE	Sir, we are delighted to have found you, for we have been told that you can provide us with the help we desperately need, and we are here to implore you to do so.
SGANARELLE	Well, if it has anything to do with my little business, gentlemen, I shall be only too pleased to serve you.
VALERE	Sir, you are too kind. But may I ask, sir, that you put your hat on. The sun might do you harm.
LUCAS	Betta cover yer head, sir.

SGANARELLE	(**Aside**) My, my... These two really stand on ceremony, don't they?
VALERE	Sir, you must not consider it strange that we come to you. Competent people are always in demand, and we have been advised as to your ability.
SGANARELLE	Well, it is true that I'm the best woodcutter in the world...
VALERE	My good man...
SGANARELLE	When it comes to my work, I spare nothing. It is beyond reproach.
VALERE	That is not exactly what we had in mind, sir.
SGANARELLE	But, I sell at a hundred and ten sous per hundred
VALERE	Let's speak no more of that, I beseech you, sir.
SGANARELLE	I assure you that I could not possibly sell them for less.
VALERE	We know all about it, sir.
SGANARELLE	Well, if you know all about it, you must know my prices
VALERE	Sir, this mockery ill-becomes your
SGANARELLE	I am not mocking anything, nor will I lower my price.
VALERE	Let's change the subject, sir, I beg of you.
SGANARELLE	You might be able to buy wood more cheaply elsewhere; after all, there are all kinds of wood, but you shall never match the quality of...
VALERE	Come now, sir, let's speak no more of this.
SGANARELLE	I swear to you that you shall not match my work at double the price.
VALERE	Enough, I tell you!

SGANARELLE	No, I tell you sincerely, that I could not in conscience sell for less; nor could I over-charge.
VALERE	Must it be, sir, that a person of your station derive pleasure from such degrading pretense...that he lower himself by speaking thus? Why should a man so knowledgeable, a famous doctor like yourself, wish to conceal from the world the nature of his wondrous talent?
SGANARELLE	(**Aside**) He's mad.
VALERE	We beseech you, sir, give up this pretense.
SGANARELLE	What's that?
LUCAS	No use tryin' ta fool us, sir. We know what we know.
SGANARELLE	What on earth do you mean? Whom do you take me for?
VALERE	For what you are... a great doctor.
SGANARELLE	(**Laughing**) Doctor yourself. I never was a doctor and I never will be.
VALERE	(**Softly to Lucas**) His madness is taking hold. (**To Sganarelle**) Sir, we ask you most respectfully to discontinue these denials and to spare us the necessity of a more extreme form of persuasion.
SGANARELLE	Spare you what?
VALERE	The need to do something that would grieve us sorely.
SGANARELLE	Indeed! Well, you can do whatever you like; the fact remains that I am not a doctor and that I understand none of this.
VALERE	(**Softly to Lucas**) I'm afraid we'll have to administer the cure. (To Sganarelle) Sir, for the last time, I beg you to admit what you are.

LUCAS	Oh, come on now. Quit yer dilly-dallying and confess nice and simple that yer a doctor.
SGANARELLE	This is too much
VALERE	What is the use of denying what is already known?
LUCAS	Why do you do such stoopid things? Where does it get ya?
SGANARELLE	Gentlemen, if I've told you once, I've told you a thousand times: I am not a doctor!
VALERE	**(Meandering about, looking for a stick)** You are not a doctor?
SGANARELLE	No.
LUCAS	**(Following Valere's lead)** Yer not a docta?
SGANARELLE	No, I tell you. **Valere and Lucas each pick up sticks and beat him)**.
VALERE	Very well, then. Since you insist, you leave us no choice.
SGANARELLE	Oh! Oh! Oh! Gentlemen! All right! I'll be whatever you want!
VALERE	Why do you force us to use violence, sir?
LUCAS	Why do ya give us the trouble o' havin' to beat ya?
VALERE	I assure you, sir, that I regret it most deeply.
LUCAS	Me, too, sir. I'm terrible sorry.
SGANARELLE	What the devil is this all about, gentlemen? Is this some type of joke, or has some delusion taken hold of you causing you to imagine me a docta?
VALERE	What's that? You still don't give up? You still deny being a doctor?
SGANARELLE	The devil take me if I am!
LUCAS	It's not true that yer a docta?

SGANARELLE	No, by all the saints! **(They begin beating him again)** Oh! OOOH! All right! All right, gentlemen! Since you insist, yes, I am a doctor, an apothecary too if you like. I'll admit to anything rather than get beaten.
VALERE	Ah! Now that's more like it, sir. I am delighted to see you so reasonable.
LUCAS	Ya bring joy to my heart, when ya talk like that.
VALERE	I most humbly beg your forgiveness.
LUCAS	Please excuse the libaty we took.
SGANARELLE	**(Aside)** Good Lord! Could it be that I'm the one who is mistaken here, and that I have become a doctor without even knowing it?
VALERE	Sir, you shall not regret confessing to us what you are; I assure you that your truthfulness will be rewarded.
SGANARELLE	But, gentlemen, tell me, could it not be that you yourselves are mistaken? Is it absolutely certain that I am a doctor?
LUCAS	Yes, by Jingo!
SGANARELLE	Really and truly?
VALERE	No doubt about it.
SGANARELLE	The devil take me if I knew it.
VALERE	How's that? Why you're the most able doctor in the world.
SGANARELLE	Aha!
LUCAS	A doctor who cured I dunno how many sicknesses.
SGANARELLE	Indeed!
VALERE	For six hours a woman had been given up for dead and just as they were about bury her, you gave her a drop of some mysteri-

	ous liquid and in a flash, the woman rose and began to walk about the room.
SGANARELLE	Good heavens!
LUCAS	A twelve year old boy fell off a steeple and broke his head, legs and arms, and then you come along and rub some kinda ointment on him, and just like that he gets up and goes off to play marbles.
SGANARELLE	Bless my soul!
VALERE	Finally, sir, if you would agree to come with us, we can assure you great personal satisfaction as well as the opportunity to earn as much as your heart might desire.
SGANARELLE	I'll earn as much as I want?
VALERE	Yes.
SGANARELLE	Ah! Well, in that case,. I am most assuredly a doctor. I had forgotten it before, but now it all comes back to me. What is the problem? Where must we go?
VALERE	We shall take you there. The problem concerns a girl who has lost her speech.
SGANARELLE	Good heavens, I haven't found it. Ha ha!
VALERE	**(Softly to Lucas)** He likes his little joke, that one. **(Aloud)** Let's go, sir.
SGANARELLE	Without a doctor's robe?
VALERE	We shall get you one.
SGANARELLE	**(Handing his bottle to Valere)** You there, hold that. That's where I keep my herbs. (To Lucas, spitting on the ground) And, you. Walk on that. Doctor's orders.
LUCAS	**(Walking as told)** By jingo! That's what I call a docta! And I betcha he does the job 'cause he's a real clown!

Act II

Scene 1: At the home of Geronte, Valere, Lucas, Geronte, Jacqueline

VALERE	Yes, sir, I believe you will be satisfied, for we have brought you the greatest doctor in the world.
LUCAS	No, sir, you'll never find a betta doctor than him. All them others couldn't even polish his boots.
VALERE	He's a man who has brought about marvelous cures.
LUCAS	Who even cured dead people.
VALERE	However, as I told you, he is somewhat capricious, and there are moments when his mind seems to wander, and you would not take him for what he is...
LUCAS	Yes, I'm afraid he likes his little joke, sir, and ... now please don't get upset, sir, but sometimes he acts like he was a tiny bit cracked.
VALERE	But fundamentally he is all science, and very often he makes statements that are quite ingenious.
LUCAS	When he's got a mind for it, he talks like it was coming right out of a book.
VALERE	His reputation is already widespread and he is respected by everyone.
GERONTE	I am dying to meet this man. Bring him to me at once.
JACQUELINE	By the saints, sir, this one won't do no better than all them others. It's just gonna be more of the same old claptrap, and I

think that the best medicine you can give
your daughter is a fine, handsome husband
that she really has a liking for.

GERONTE   Now, now, my dear wetnurse, you're
            quite a meddler, aren't you?

JACQUELINE I tell you all them doctors won't do no
            good at all. There's only one medicine that
            works on a girl, and that's a husband. All
            that there rhubarb and senna they been
            givin' her won't amount ta nothin'.

GERONTE   What man would accept her with her
            present infirmity? And when I made plans
            for her marriage, did she not oppose me?

JACQUELINE It's no wonder. You wanted to strap her to
            a man she don't love. Why didn't you
            choose that handsome Léandre, a man she
            really fancies? I'm sure she woulda obeyed
            you then; and I'm sure that if you wanted
            to give her to him, he'd take her just as
            she is.

GERONTE   Léandre is not suitable; he's not rich like
            the other fellow.

JACQUELINE He's got a rich uncle who made him his
            heir.

GERONTE   How much money he's got coming means
            nothing to me. It's what he's got now that
            counts. There is a great risk of disappoint-
            ment when you rely on the money that
            someone else is holding for you. Death has
            a way of turning a deaf ear to the wishes
            and prayers of would-be inheritors, and
            gray hair very often precedes the windfall
            of a dead benefactor.

JACQUELINE Well, anyway, I've always heard that in
            marriage or in anything else, happiness is

more important than money. Parents have that damned habit of always askin': "What does he have?" or "What does she have?" or of sayin' things like: "Our good friend Peter married off his daughter to fat Thomas who had more vineyards to offer than young Robin." Meanwhile, it's Robin that she really fancies, and now the poor creature looks like a dried up fruit and hasn't spent a happy day since. Let that be an example for you, sir. Happiness is all we got in this here world, and a happy marriage for my daughter is more important to me than all the Gold in Bauce!

GERONTE   Good grief, wetnurse, how you rattle on! Be quiet, I beg of you! You're too concerned about this, and your curdling your milk.

LUCAS   **(Punctuating each sentence with a stroke of his fist on Geronte's shoulder)** By jingo, keep quiet! **(Pound)** You're a bold one, you are! **(Pound)** Our master don't need yer speeches and he knows **(Pound)** what he's got **(Pound)** to do. Stick to milkin' yer baby and stop playin' the philosopher! **(Pounds to the ground)**.

GERONTE   **(Laing face up)** Easy does it! Oh! Gently!

LUCAS   I wanna learn her to show you more respect, sir.

GERONTE   Yes, but those gestures are not necessary.

Scene 2: Valere, Lucas, Jacqueline, Geronte, Sganarelle

VALERE   Sir, prepare yourself, for here is our doctor.

GERONTE	Sir, I am delighted to receive you at my home, for we have great need of your services.
SGANARELLE	**(Wearing a doctor's robe and a sharply pointed hat)** Hippocrates says... that we should both be wearing our hats.
GERONTE	Hippocrates says that?
SGANARELLE	Yes.
GERONTE	Well, if Hippocrates says it, then it must be done.

Geronte waves to Lucas to retrieve his hat.

SGANARELLE	My good doctor, having learned the marvelous things.
GERONTE	Er... To whom are you speaking, sir?
SGANARELLE	Why, to you, sir.
GERONTE	I am not a doctor?
SGANARELLE	You are not a doctor?
GERONTE	No, in truth.
SGANARELLE	Do you mean it?
GERONTE	I certainly do.

Sganarelle begins beating Geronte with a stick he's hidden under his robe.

GERONTE	Oh! Oooh! Ow! Ooooh!
SGANARELLE	Well, you're a doctor now, for that's all the training I ever got.
GERONTE	**(Angrily, to Valere)** What the devil kind of man did you bring here?
VALERE	I told you, sir, that he's a rather frivolous doctor.
GERONTE	Yes, and I'll send him on his way with his frivolity.

LUCAS	Don't pay no attention to him, sir, it's only to make ya laugh.
GERONTE	Such buffoonery does not please me.
SGANARELLE	Sir, I most humbly beg your forgiveness for the liberty that I took.
GERONTE	Your servant, sir.
SGANARELLE	I deeply regret…
GERONTE	It was nothing.
SGANARELLE	…the beating…
GERONTE	No harm done.
SGANARELLE	…that I had the honor to give you.
GERONTE	Let's speak no more of it. Sir, I have a daughter with a strange affliction.
SGANARELLE	I am delighted, sir, that your daughter has need of me, and I wish from the bottom of my heart that you and your entire family were also sick so that I might show you how eager I am to serve you.
GERONTE	I am obliged to you for these sentiments.
SGANARELLE	I assure you that I speak to you from the most noble depths of my soul.
GERONTE	You do me too much honor, sir.
SGANARELLE	What is your daughter's name?
GERONTE	Lucinde.
SGANARELLE	Lucinde! **(French pronunciation is more suitable here; it's much more beautiful).** Ah, what a beautiful name to practice on! Lucinde!
GERONTE	I'll go see what she's doing.
SGANARELLE	Who is that robust woman?
GERONTE	She's my child's wetnurse.
SGANARELLE	**(Aside)** Mmm. Now, there's a tasty morse if I ever saw one. **(Aloud)** Ah, wet-nurse, charming wet-nurse, my medicine is the most humble slave to your productive

bosom. Oh, to be the fortunate child suckled by such beauty.

He places his hand on her breast, much to Lucas' displeasure.

SGANARELLE All my remedies, all my science, all my skill is at your service, and...

LUCAS By yer leave, doctor, I'll thank you to keep yer hands off my wife. **(He yanks Sganarelle away)**

SGANARELLE What's that? She's your wife?

LUCAS Yes.

SGANARELLE Ah! Truly, I did not know that and I rejoice in the love you have for each other.

He pretends a gesture of embrace toward Lucas, then slips back to the wetnurse.

LUCAS **(Yanking him away again, positioning himself between them)** Easy does it, if you please.

SGANARELLE I assure you that I am delighted that you are joined together; I congratulate her on having a husband like you; and I congratulate you on having a wife so beautiful, so wise, **(He yanks Lucas aside and dashes to wetnurse)** and with such formation!

LUCAS Hey there! Not so many compliments, I'm askin' ya. **(Yanks Sganarelle in turn)**

SGANARELLE Don't you want me to rejoice with you over such a beautiful assemblage?

LUCAS With me as much as you want but no more of that with my wife.

SGANARELLE   I am sharing equally in the good fortune of you both, and **(continuing the same maneuver)**...if I embrace you to show you my joy; **(He slips back into the wetnurse's arms)**... I embrace her as well for the same reason.

LUCAS   **(Yanking him off a third time)** By the saints, doctor, enough of this here horseplay!

Scene 3: Sganarelle, Lucas, Jacqueline, Geronte

GERONTE   Sir, my daughter will be brought to you shortly.

SGANARELLE   I await her, sir, with all the medicine.

GERONTE   Where is it?

SGANARELLE   **(Taps his forehead)** In here.

GERONTE   Oh! Very good.

SGANARELLE   **(Heading for Jacqueline once more)** But since I am interested in all of your family, I must test the milk of your wetnurse and examine her breasts.

Lucas pulls him away once more.

LUCAS   No, no, we don't need no more o' that!

SGANARELLE   But it is a doctor's function to examine the bosoms of wet nurses.

LUCAS   Not with my wife ya won't.

SGANARELLE   Are you so impertinent as to oppose the will of a doctor?

LUCAS   To hell with you!

SGANARELLE   **(Facing him squarely)** I shall give you the fever!

JACQUELINE	**(Spinning Lucas around by his arm)** Off with you now. Am I not big enough to defend myself should he do something he oughtn't? Away with you!
LUCAS	Well, I don't want no more of his feelin' ya like that.
SGANARELLE	Shame on the rogue who is jealous of his wife.
GERONTE	Here is my daughter.

Scene 4: Geronte, Sganarelle, Jacqueline, Lucas, Valere, Lucinde

SGANARELLE	Is this the patient?
GERONTE	Yes, she is my daughter, and it would break my heart if she were to die.
SGANARELLE	May she do no such thing! Especially without doctor's orders.
GERONTE	**(To Lucas)** Bring up a chair.
SGANARELLE	**(Sitting between Geronte and Lucinde)** Now there's a patient who is not at all displeasing and I maintain that a man of sound mind and body would find her highly desirable.

Lucinde giggles a bit, soundlessly.

GERONTE	You have made her laugh, Sir!
SGANARELLE	So much the better; when the doctor makes the patient laugh, it is the best sign in the world. **(To Lucinde)** Well, now, what is the problem?

Lucinde remains silent.

SGANARELLE	What is the matter with you?... What is the nature of your sickness?
LUCINDE	**(Bringing her hand to her mouth in a strange effort to communicate)** Ah! Ee! Oh!
SGANARELLE	What's that?
LUCINDE	Ah! Ee! Oh!Ah! Eel Oh!
SGANARELLE	What?
LUCINDE	Ah! Ee! Oh!
SGANARELLE	Ah, Ee, Oh? I don't understand you at all. What the devil kind of language is that?
GERONTE	Sir, that is her sickness. She has become dumb, and up to now we have not been able to determine the cause, and this accident has caused her marriage to be postponed.
SGANARELLE	Why is that?
GERONTE	The one whom she is to marry wishes to wait until she is cured before going through with it.
SGANARELLE	And who is this fool who does want his wife to be dumb? Would to God mine had that sickness. I would be the last person in the world to cure her.
GERONTE	In any event, sir, we beg you to employ all your skill to relieve her of this affliction.
SGANARELLE	Ah! You need not be concerned. Tell me, does this malady cause her much suffering?
GERONTE	Yes, sir.
SGANARELLE	So much the better.
GERONTE	Eh?
SGANARELLE	Does she experience great pain?
GERONTE	Oh, very great pain.

SGANARELLE	Excellent.
GERONTE	Eh?
SGANARELLE	Does she go...you know where?
GERONTE	...Yes.
SGANARELLE	Copiously?
GERONTE	Oh, I know nothing about that.
SGANARELLE	And is the substance praiseworthy?
GERONTE	I have no knowledge of these things.
SGANARELLE	**(To Lucinde)** Give me your arm. **(She does; he listens for a moment and turns to Geronte)** We have here a pulse that tells me that your daughter is dumb.
GERONTE	Ah, yes! Sir, that is indeed her sickness; you have discovered it right off.
SGANARELLE	Aha!
JACQUELINE	**(To Lucas)** Did you see how he guessed right off what ails her?
SGANARELLE	We great doctors know everything right from the outset. A know-nothing would have been confused, and would have said to you it is this, it is that, but as for me, I hit the mark with very first shot, and I inform you that your daughter is dumb.
GERONTE	Yes...but I would like you to tell me where that comes from.
SGANARELLE	Nothing could be more simple; that comes from the fact that she has lost her powers of speech.
GERONTE	Very good. But the cause, if you please, of her loss of speech.
SGANARELLE	All our best authors will tell you that it is due to an obstruction of the action of the tongue.
GERONTE	Yes, but what are your feelings about this obstruction of the action of the tongue?

SGANARELLE   Well, Aristotle on this subject says... some very beautiful things.

GERONTE   I believe it.

SGANARELLE   Ah! What a great man he was!

GERONTE   Without a doubt.

SGANARELLE   A truly great man. **(Raising his forearm)** A man who was greater than me I by... **(Lowering his forearm almost to the ground)**...that much. But to get back to our discussion, I maintain that this obstruction of the action of the tongue is caused by certain humors that among us scholars are referred to as peccant humors...peccant, that is to say...peccant humors; the extent to which the vapors formed by the exhalation of the influences which arise in the region of the maladies, coming...so to speak...to...um...do you understand Latin?

GERONTE   No.

SGANARELLE   You know no Latin at all?

GERONTE   Not a syllable.

SGANARELLE   **(With enthusiastic, comical gesturing)** Cabricias, arci thuram, catalamus, singulariter nominativo, haec Musa, "...the Muse..." bonus, bona, bonum, Deus sanctus, estne oratio latinas? Etiam... Yes... Quare... Why?... Quia substantivo et adjectivum, concordat in generi, numerum, et cassus!

GERONTE   Ah! What have I not studied!

JACQUELINE   What a smart man he is!

LUCAS   Yeah, that was so beautiful that I didn't understand a single word.

SGANARELLE   Now, when the vapors of which I speak pass from the left side where the liver is located to the right side where the heart is, it happens that the lung, which we call in Latin "armyan," having communication with the brain, which in Greek we refer to as "nasmus," by means of the vena cava, which in Hebrew we call "cubile," meets on its way the aforementioned vapors which fill the ventricles of the omoplate; and because the aforementioned vapors... Please follow this train of thought, I beg of you...and because the aforementioned vapors have a certain malignity... Listen carefully to this, I beseech you.

GERONTE   Yes.

SGANARELLE   ... Have a certain malignity which is caused... **(Exploding)** Be attentive, please!

GERONTE   **(Cowering)** I am.

SGANARELLE   ... Which is caused by the acridity of the humors engendered in the concavity of the diaphragm, it happens that these vapors... Ossabandus, nequeys, nequer, potarinurn quipsa milus! And there precisely is what causes your daughter to be dumb!

JACQUELINE   Ah! How nice he said that!

GERONTE   No doubt about it, no one could possibly reason better than that. There's only one thing that surprised me, however, and that is the location of the liver and the heart. It seems to me that you are placing them improperly. Is not the heart on the left and the liver on the right?

SGANARELLE   Ahem, yes. That's the way it used to be, but we great doctors have changed all that;

	we now use completely new methods in the practice of medicine.
GERONTE	This is something I did not know and I ask you to forgive my ignorance.
SGANARELLE	No harm done; besides, you are not required to be as knowledgeable as we are.
GERONTE	To be sure. But, sir, what do you believe must be done for this illness?
SGANARELLE	What I believe must be done?
GERONTE	Yes.
SGANARELLE	My advice is that she be put back to bed and be given as a remedy a quantity of bread dipped in wine.
GERONTE	Why that, sir?
SGANARELLE	Because there exists in the mixture of bread and wine a sympathetic virtue that produces speech. Have you not observed that this is the only food given to parrots and that it's by eating this that they learn to speak?
GERONTE	That is true! Ah! What a great man! (To Lucas) Quickly, some bread and wine.

Lucas exits.

SGANARELLE	I shall return this evening to check on her condition. (Jacqueline begins to leave but Sganarelle stops her).
SGANARELLE	Hold on woman. (To Geronte) Sir, I simply must administer some of my little cures to your wetnurse.
JACQUELINE	Who? Me? I'm as healthy as a horse.
SGANARELLE	So much the worse, wetnurse, so much the worse. Such great health is to be feared, and you would do well to submit to some

	friendly bloodletting, or, perhaps, to a soothing enema.
GERONTE	But, sir, I must avow that I do not comprehend your methods. Why should one be bled when there is no ailment?
SGANARELLE	That is of no importance. It is the method itself that is salutary, and, as one drinks to satisfy a future thirst, so must one be bled for future sicknesses.
JACQUELINE	By the saints, I'll have none of that, and I'll not turn my body into an apothecary shop. **(She exists)**
SGANARELLE	You are resistant to treatment, but we'll find a way to make you more reasonable. **(To Geronte)** Sir, I bid you good day.
GERONTE	Wait a moment, please.
SGANARELLE	What do you wish to do?
GERONTE	**(Opening his purse)** Give you some money.
SGANARELLE	**(Extending his hand behind him as he turns away)** I shall accept none of it, sir.
GERONTE	Sir...
SGANARELLE	None at all.
GERONTE	Just a moment.
SGANARELLE	In no way.
GERONTE	I beseech you...
SGANARELLE	You jest, sir.
GERONTE	**(Putting money in Sganarelle's open palm)** There you are.
SGANARELLE	I'll do nothing of the sort.
GERONTE	Eh?
SGANARELLE	It is not money that motivates me.
GERONTE	I believe it.
SGANARELLE	**(After taking the money and hefting it in his hand)** Is this good weight?

GERONTE   Yes, sir.

SGANARELLE   I am not one of those mercenary doctors, you know.

GERONTE   I believe it.

SGANARELLE   **(After having taken the money)** Is this good weight?

GERONTE   Yes, sir.

SGANARELLE   I am not one of those mercenary doctors, you know.

GERONTE   I know.

SGANARELLE   Profit means nothing to me.

GERONTE   I never thought that for a moment. **(Exits)**

SGANARELLE   **(Alone, looking at the money he has received)** Good heavens, that wasn't bad at all, and providing...

Scene 5: Sganarelle, Leandre

LEANDRE   Sir, I've been waiting for you for quite some time, and I've come to beg your assistance.

SGANARELLE   **(Taking Leandre's pulse)** Oh, that's a very bad pulse.

LEANDRE   I am not the least bit sick, sir, and I do not come to you for that.

SGANARELLE   Well, if you are not sick, why the devil didn't you say so?

LEANDRE   Well, sir, to put it briefly, my name is Leandre, and I am in love with Lucinde, the girl you have just treated. However, because of her father's ill feelings towards me, I have not even been able to approach her, and I venture to ask you to serve the cause of my love by helping me with a plan of mine by which I might relay to her

	a brief message that is absolutely vital to my happiness and to my life.
SGANARELLE	Whom do you take me for? How dare you come to me for help in your affair of love? How dare you abuse a doctor's dignity with tactics of that nature?
LEANDRE	Sir, please don't shout.
SGANARELLE	I'll shout as much as I like! You are an impertinent young man!
LEANDRE	Please, sir, more softly!
SGANARELLE	A blunderer!
LEANDRE	I beseech you!
SGANARELLE	I shall teach you that I am not the man for that, and that it is the height of insolence...

Leandre extracts a purse a purse full of money which suddenly catches Sganarelle's attention. Leandre holds the purse and jingles the coins inside.

LEANDRE	Sir? (He hands Sganarelle the purse)
SGANARELLE	... To wish...to...use me... **(He pockets the purse)** I am not, of course, referring to you, sir, for you are a gentleman, and I would be delighted to be of service to you; but there are certain impertinent people in this world who shamefully misjudge character, and this, I must confess, makes me very angry.
LEANDRE	I apologize, sir, for the liberty that...
SGANARELLE	You jest, sir. Now, what is this all about?
LEANDRE	You shall discover, sir, that the illness that you wish to cure is just a pretense. The doctors have come up with all sorts of diagnoses. Some have called it a disorder of the brain, while others blamed in turn

the bowels, spleen and liver. But it is certain that love is its true cause, and that Lucinde came up with this sickness simply to avoid a marriage that was being imposed upon her. However, rather than chance being seen together, let us withdraw from here and, as we walk, I shall tell you what I would like you to do...

SGANARELLE Lead on, sir, for your words have inspired in me the deepest feelings of tenderness for your love. Benefiting as she will from my entire knowledge of medicine, our patient will most assuredly be yours...unless, of course, she dies first.

ACT III

Scene 1: Sganarelle, Leandre (in disguise) in Geronte's garden

LEANDRE   It seems that I look very convincing dressed as an apothecary, and since the father has hardly seen me, it is not likely that he will recognize me with this change of clothes and wig.

SGANARELLE   I agree.

LEANDRE   All that I would like from you is to have you teach me five or six impressive medical terms so that when I speak, I might appear as a man of competence.

SGANARELLE   Come, come now; that's not at all necessary. The costume alone will suffice. Besides, I don't know any more about medicine than you do.

LEANDRE   What's that?

SGANARELLE   The devil take me if I know a thing about medicine! Look, you are a gentleman and I shall confide in you as you have in me.

LEANDRE   How's that? You are really not a...

SGANARELLE   No, I tell you. They made me a doctor in spite of myself. I've never had any experience with anything a learned as that. I only got as far as the sixth grade in school. I have no idea how they came by such a fanciful notion. But when I saw how strongly they insisted that I be a doctor, I decided to become one at the expense of whomever it might concern. However, you will never believe how widely the error has spread and how readily everyone has believed in my competence. People from all over seek me, and if this keeps up, I believe I shall devote the rest of my life to medicine. I consider it to be the best trade of all, for regardless of whether your work is good or bad, the pay is still the same; we work as we please and we never suffer the aftermath of a bad job. Now should a cobbler spoil a piece of leather as he makes a pair of shoes, he must pay for it. But a doctor can spoil a man without having to pay a sou. There are no blunders for us; it is always the fault of the one who dies. Finally, the beauty of this profession lies in the fact that there exists among the dead the highest level of gentility and discretion, for never has a dead man been known to complain about the doctor who killed him.

LEANDRE It is true that the dead are very considerate in that regard.

SGANARELLE **(Seeing two men approaching)** There are some people over there who look like they are coming to consult me. Go to the home of your lady and wait for me.

Scene 2: Sganarelle, Thibault, Perrin.

THIBAULT Sir, me an my son, Perrin, have been looking for you.

SGANARELLE What is it?

THIBAULT His poor mother, whose name is Perrette, has been sick in bed for six months now.

SGANARELLE   **(Extending his hand, expecting money)**
What do you want from me?

THIBAULT   We'd like you to give us a little something to cure her.

SGANARELLE   I must first learn the nature of her sickness.

THIBAULT   Ah, she's got hypocrisy, sir.

SGANARELLE   Hypocrisy?

THIBAULT   Yes , sir, I mean she's swollen all over, and they say she got a bunch of serosities inside her, and that her liver, her stomach and her spleen, as you like to call it, instead of making blood don't make nothing but water now; and every other day she has a daily fever with lots of tiredness and pains in her leg muscules. She got so much flam in her throat that she sounds like she's about to choke. Sometimes, she gets such syncopes and fits of conversion that we think she's a goner for sure. No disrespect to you, sir, but we got an apothecary in our village who gave her a whole batch of treatments and, again no disrespect sir, it done cost me more than a dozen gold pieces on enemas, serums, infections of jacinth and on stimulizers that they made her take; but the apothecary said that all wasn't strong enough. He wanted to give her a drug called ametic wine, but to tell you the truth, sir, I didn't let him do it because they say them big doctors are killing off I dunno how many folks with that there stuff.

SGANARELLE	**(His hand still extended and gesturing for payment)** Let's get to the facts, my friend; let's get to the facts.
THIBAULT	Well, the fact is, sir, that we come to ask you what we ought to do.
SGANARELLE	I don't understand you at all.
PERRIN	Sir, my mother is sick and here are two pieces of gold that we offer for one of your remedies.
SGANARELLE	Ah! You I understand! Now there's a lad who speaks clearly and expresses himself properly. You say that your mother is hydropic, that is to say sick with dropsy, that her entire body is swollen, that she is feverish with pains in her legs, and that she is occasionally subject to syncopes and convulsions, by that I mean fainting spells?
PERRIN	Ah! Yes, sir. That's it exactly!
SGANARELLE	I understood you immediately, but I'm afraid you have a father who doesn't know how to state his case. You are now asking me for a cure?
PERRIN	Yes, sir.
SGANARELLE	A cure that will cure her?
PERRIN	That's what we had in mind, sir.
SGANARELLE	Here, take this. It is a form of cheese that you must make her eat.
PERRIN	A piece of cheese, sir?
SGANARELLE	Yes, it is a special preparation of cheese that contains gold, coral, pearls and quantities of other precious substances.
PERRIN	Sir, we are very grateful to you and we shall give this to her right away.
SGANARELLE	Off with you now, and if she dies, be sure to give her a nice funeral.

Scene 3: Jacqueline, Sganarelle, Lucas

SGANARELLE	Ah! Here comes that beautiful wetnurse. Oh! Wetnurse of my heart, how delighted I am to see you again. The sight of you is the rhubarb, the cassis and the senna that purges all the melancholy from my soul.
JACQUELINE	By the saints, doctor, you talk much too fancy for me. All that there Latin is beyond me.
SGANARELLE	Get sick, wetnurse, I beg of you; get sick for my sake. Nothing would make me more happy than to be able to cure you.
JACQUELINE	Thanks, but I don't want no one curing me.
SGANARELLE	Of, how I pity you, beautiful wetnurse, on having such a jealous and disagreeable husband.
JACQUELINE	What can I do, sir? It is the penance for my wrongdoings, and where they tie the goat, that's where she's gotta graze.
SGANARELLE	Come now! An uncivilized bumpkin like that! A man who's always watching you and won't let anyone talk to you!
JACQUELINE	Alas! You ain't seen nothin' yet. What you seen was just a little sample of his bad humor.
SGANARELLE	Is it possible that a man could be so base of heart as to maltreat a person like you? Ah, how many men from around here do I know who would consider themselves fortunate just to kiss the tips of your cuddly little feet. Why must it be that a person so well formed should fall into such hands, and that animal, a brute, an imbecile, a

fool...pardon me, wetnurse, if I speak thus of your husband.

JACQUELINE   Ah, sir, you don't have to tell me how much he deserves them names.

SGANARELLE   Yes, my dear, he certainly does, and he also deserves to have you plant a little something on his head as punishment for his suspicious mind.

JACQUELINE   Well, if I wasn't lookin' out for him, he could, in truth, force me to do something naughty.

SGANARELLE   Indeed, you would not be wrong to get back at him with someone else, for I tell you he is a man who truly deserves it; and, beautiful wetnurse, if I were so fortunate to be chosen for...

At this point, Lucas has already entered and has listened to their dialogue. They both suddenly become aware of him. Each goes off in opposite directions, the doctor in great comical fashion.

Scene 4: Geronte, Lucas

GERONTE   (Entering) Hey there, Lucas! Did you not see the doctor hereabout?

LUCAS   Oh yes, devil take him. I seen him all right, and my wife, too.

GERONTE   Where on earth can he be?

LUCAS   I dunno but I hope the devil carried him off.

GERONTE   Go see what my daughter is doing.

Lucas exits and Sganarelle returns with Leandre (in disguise).

GERONTE	Ah sir! I was just inquiring as to your whereabouts.
SGANARELLE	I was in your courtyard pleasantly relieving myself of some excess drink. How is the patient?
GERONTE	A little worse since your remedy.
SGANARELLE	So much the better.
GERONTE	Eh?
SGANARELLE	That's a sign that it's working.
GERONTE	Yes, but by working I'm afraid that it might kill her.
SGANARELLE	Be not concerned, for I have cures that scoff at everything. In fact, I'm actually looking forward to her deaththroes.
GERONTE	**(Pointing to Leandre)** Who is this man with you?
SGANARELLE	**(Making pumping gestures, imitating an apothecary administering an enema)** He is...
GERONTE	What?
SGANARELLE	...the one...
GERONTE	Eh?
SGANARELLE	...who gives...

Suddenly it becomes clear to Geronte.

GERONTE	Oh! I understand you.
SGANARELLE	Your daughter will have need of him.

Scene 6:   Sganarelle, Geronte, Lucinde, Jacqueline, Leandre

JACQUELINE	**(Entering)** Here's your daughter, sir. She wants to talk a little.

SGANARELLE   That will do her good. **(To Leandre)** Off
with you, apothecary, and take her pulse
so that I might confer with you on her
sickness.

**At this point, Sganarelle pulls Geronte off to one side and
puts his arm around his shoulder, concealing Geronte's
sightline from his daughter and Leandre. Sganarelle
places his hand on Geronte's chin so that each time
Geronte tries to look beyond, Sganarelle jerks the poor
man's head back.**

SGANARELLE   Sir, whether or not it is true that women
are more easy to cure than men is one of
the great and subtle questions among doctors. I beg you to listen to this, if you
please. Some say no while others say yes;
as for me, I say yes and no; to the extent
that the incongruity of the opaque humors
which are found in the natural temperament of women causes the animal in them
to want to dominate always their more
genteel capacities, one observes that the
capriciousness of the opinions depends
upon the oblique movement of the moon's
circle; and, as the sun that casts its beams
on the concavity of the earth, finds...

LUCINDE   **(Suddenly to Leandre)** No! I can't possibly change the way I feel about this!

GERONTE   There! My daughter speaks! Oh, admirable
doctor! Oh, wonderful remedy! How in-
debted I am to you, sir, for this marvelous
cure, and what can I do for you after such
a service?

SGANARELLE	**(Pacing and wiping his brow)** Whew! Now there was a tough disease to cure!
LUCINDE	Yes, father, I have regained my speech but only to tell you that I will have no other husband but Leandre, and that it is useless for you to want to give me to Horace.
GERONTE	But...
LUCINDE	I have made up my mind and there is nothing that could make me change it.
GERONTE	What's that?
LUCINDE	No use giving me practical reasons.
GERONTE	If...
LUCINDE	All your speeches will do nothing.
GERONTE	I...
LUCINDE	On this matter I am determined.
GERONTE	But...
LUCINDE	No paternal authority can force me to marry against my will.
GERONTE	I have...
LUCINDE	All your efforts will be in vain.
GERONTE	The...
LUCINDE	And I would rather throw myself into a convent than marry a man whom I do not love.
GERONTE	But...
LUCINDE	**(In deafening tones)** No! By no means! No contracts! You're wasting your time! I'll do nothing like that! That's settled!
GERONTE	Ah! Such impetuosity of language! There's no way to oppose it. **(Pleadingly to Sganarelle)** Sir, I beg you to make her dumb again.
SGANARELLE	I'm afraid that's impossible, sir. The best I can do is to make you deaf.
GERONTE	**(Appreciatively)** Thank you.

SGANARELLE	**(Bowing)** Your servant, sir.
GERONTE	**(To Lucinde)** Do you think, therefore...
LUCINDE	No! All your reasons will not affect my heart.
GERONTE	You shall many Horace this very evening!
LUCINDE	I would marry Death!
SGANARELLE	Good heavens! Stop all this, I beseech you. Allow me to remedy this affair. A sickness has taken hold of her, and I know the cure that must be administered.
GERONTE	**(Amazed)** Is it possible, sir, that you can cure this sickness of mind as well?
SGANARELLE	Yes, leave it to me; I have cures for everything, but for this I shall call upon the services of our apothecary. **(To Leandre)** Ahem, I would like to have a word with you... You will observe the arduous feelings that she has for this Leandre are entirely contrary to the wishes of her father, that there is no time to lose, that the humors have turned very sour, and that it is necessary to find promptly a cure for this malady lest it worsen with delay. For my part, there is only one that comes to mind, and that is a pinch of purgative flight that you will mix properly with two drams of matrimonium in pill form. She may perhaps offer resistance to this cure, but since you are very competent in your field, I'm sure that you will do your best to see that she takes the medicine. Go now, and have her walk about the garden in order to prepare the humors, while I converse here with the father; but above all, don't waste any time. Get on with the

cure; quickly now, on with the specific remedy.

Scene 7: Sganarelle, Geronte

GERONTE	What drugs, sir, were those that you just prescribed? I don't believe I ever heard mention of them.
SGANARELLE	They are drugs used only in dire emergencies, sir.
GERONTE	Have you ever seen such insolence?
SGANARELLE	Girls can be obstinate at times.
GERONTE	You could never imagine how madly in love she is with that Leandre.
SGANARELLE	Hotness of blood causes that in young minds.
GERONTE	As for me, as soon as I discovered the fierceness of her love, I kept her constantly under lock and key.
SGANARELLE	You did the wise thing.
GERONTE	And I prevented any possible communication between them.
SGANARELLE	Very good.
GERONTE	Something very foolish would have occurred had I permitted them to see each other.
SGANARELLE	Without a doubt.
GERONTE	And I believe she would not have been above running off with him.
SGANARELLE	What a rascal!
GERONTE	But he is wasting his time.
SGANARELLE	Haha!
GERONTE	And I shall prevent him from ever seeing her.

SGANARELLE   He shall discover that he is not dealing with a fool, and that there are many tricks to be learned from a man as clever as you.

Scene 8: Sganarelle, Geronte, Lucas

LUCAS   (In a frenzy) Ah! Sir! Something terrible has happened! Your daughter has run off with her Leandre. It was him who was the apothecary, and our good doctor over there was the one who did this fine operation!

GERONTE   What? Stab me in the back like that? (He turns to Lucas) Quickly now, see that he does not leave the premises while I get the magistrate. Ah, traitor, I shall see that you pay for your crimes!

Geronte exits to call for the magistrate.

LUCAS   By jingo. Doctor! You'll hang for this! (As Sganarelle starts to move off) Stay right where you are!

Scene 9:   Sganarelle, Lucas, Martine

Martine enters looking around the courtyard.

MARTINE   Good heavens! How much trouble I had trying to find this place! Could you tell me what happened to the doctor I gave you?

LUCAS   There he be; the one who's gonna hang.

MARTINE   What's that? My husband hanged? Alas! And what did he do to deserve that?

LUCAS	Our master's daughter eloped, and it was all his doin's.
MARTINE	Alas! My dear husband, is it really true that they are going to hang you?
SGANARELLE	See for yourself **(Sighing)** Ah!
MARTINE	Must you let yourself die in the presence of so many people?
SGANARELLE	What do you expect me to do?
MARTINE	If only you had finished cutting our wood, that would at least have given me some consolation.
SGANARELLE	Please leave; you're breaking my heart.
MARTINE	No, I'd rather stay and give you the courage you'll need to face death, and I shall not leave until I've seen you hanged.
SGANARELLE	**(Sighing)** Aaah.

Scene 10: Sganarelle, Martine, Lucas, Geronte

Geronte, still outraged, returns.

GERONTE	The magistrate will soon be here, and you will be brought to a place where I shall receive satisfaction for the wrong you did me.
SGANARELLE	**(Hat in hand)** Alas! You wouldn't settle for just having them beat me with a stick, would you?
GERONTE	No, no. Justice will prevail... but what is this I see?

Leandre, leading Lucinde by the hand, returns to the courtyard.

Scene 11: Geronte, Sganarelle, Martine, Lucas, Jacqueline, Lucinde, Leandre

LEANDRE	Sir, I have come to have Leandre appear before you, and to place Lucinde once more in your charge. We had originally planned to run off and get married but we ultimately decided upon another, more proper course of action. I have no attention to steal your daughter and it is only with your blessing that I would take her. What I shall say to you, sir, is that I have just received word that my uncle has died, and that I am heir to his entire fortune.
GERONTE	Sir, I regard you as a man of outstanding virtue, and I give you my daughter with the greatest joy in the world.
SGANARELLE	(Aside) Whew! That was a close call for medicine!

Hand in hand, Lucinde and Leandre are led away by an overjoyed Geronte. Lucas and Jacqueline follow, leaving Sganarelle and Martine alone in the courtyard.

MARTINE	Well, now that you're not going to be hanged, don't you think you should thank me for your title as doctor? After all, it was I who procured that honor for you.
SGANARELLE	Yes, and you also procured for me more beatings than I can count.
MARTINE	The outcome is too wonderful for you to bear resentment, sir.
SGANARELLE	So be it. In consideration of the dignity that you bestowed upon me, I forgive you for the beatings. But henceforth, you shall

show me the great respect due a man of my station, and shall always keep in mind how greatly one must fear...the wrath of a doctor!

THE END

The Affected Damsels

(LES PRECIEUSES RIDICULES)

CHARACTERS

MAGDELON, A Parisian Maiden
CATHOS, Her Cousin
LA GRANGE, A Suitor
DU CROISY, A Suitor
GORGIBUS, Father of Magdelon & Uncle of Cathos
MASCARILLE, La Grange's Valet
JODELET, Du Croisy's Valet
MAROTTE, Gorgibus' Servant
ALMANZOR, Gorgibus' Servant
TWO CHAIR CARRIERS
TWO TOUGHS
NEIGHBORS

The scene takes place in a suburb of Paris, at the home of Gorgibus.

Scene 1: LaGrange, Du Croisy

DU CROISY	La Grange…
LA GRANGE	What is it?
DU CROISY	Look at me and give me a serious answer.
LA GRANGE	Well?
DU CROISY	Were you pleased with the reception we received here?
LA GRANGE	Frankly, no.
DU CROISY	Do you think we have grounds to be?
LA GRANGE	For my part, I was outraged. Did you ever see two female bumpkins put on such airs, or two gentlemen treated in a more contemptible fashion? They could hardly bring themselves to offer us chairs. Never have I seen so many whispered exchanges, such continual yawning, such incessant demands for the time of day as they rubbed their eyes in boredom and fatigue. No matter what we asked, the reply was never more than a yes or no. We couldn't have been received more shabbily were we the lowliest creatures on earth.
DU CROISY	It appears that this matter has deeply affected you.
LA GRANGE	Indeed, it has, and I'll not allow such impertinence to go unavenged. I know the reason for our rejection. It seems that the blight of pretentiousness that is presently infecting Paris has spread as far as the provinces, and that those two snobbish nincompoops have succumbed to it completely. I know now what it takes to be well received here, and you and I are

going to put on a little charade that will show them for the nitwits that they are.

DU CROISY   How?

LA GRANGE   I have a certain valet named Mascarille who can depict himself convincingly as a gentleman of elegance and wit, qualities that cater perfectly to the prevailing vogue in Paris. He's nothing but an imbecile with aristocratic pretensions. He plays the gallant, writes verses, and constantly denigrates the other valets whom he considers crude and beneath his station.

DU CROISY   Well, what do you plan to do?

LA GRANGE   What do I plan to do? We must...wait, let us first withdraw from here.

Scene 2: Gorgibus, Du Croisy, La Grange

GORGIBUS   Well, gentlemen, how did your visit with my niece and daughter turn out?

LA GRANGE   I suggest that you ask them rather than us about it. All we can do, sir, is to express our appreciation for your courtesy and tell you that we remain your most humble servants. **(He bows and exits with Du Croisy.)**

GORGIBUS   Hmm, they left in quite a huff. I wonder why... I'm going to get to the bottom of this. Hey there!

Scene 3: Gorgibus, Marotte

MAROTTE   What is it, sir?

GORGIBUS   Where are your mistresses?

MAROTTE   In their chamber.

GORGIBUS	Doing what?
MAROTTE	Making pomade for their lips.
GORGIBUS	I'll pomade them! Tell them to come down.

Marotte exits.

GORGIBUS   Those hussies with their pomades are out to bankrupt me. All I see around here are egg whites, "virgin's milk," and a thousand other concoctions that I never heard of. Since our stay here they've used up the lard of at least a dozen pigs, and I could feed four servants daily just on the lambs' feet they grind up.

Scene 4: Magdelon Cathos, Gorgibus

GORGIBUS   Must you really spend so much money greasing your faces? Tell me what happened between you and those gentlemen to cause them to leave so coldly. Didn't I tell you to receive them as prospective husbands?

MAGDELON   And in what esteem, my good father, would you have us hold people of such grossly inappropriate behavior?

CATHOS   And how, uncle, would you expect a girl of reason to adjust to such comportment?

GORGIBUS   And what was their great fault, pray tell?

MAGDELON   They are devoid of any sense of gallantry. Imagine! Starting right off with marriage proposals!

GORGIBUS   And just how would you have them begin? By seducing you? Shouldn't a gesture like that make us all proud? Could anything be more honorable than that? Doesn't this sacred bond to which they aspire testify to the honesty of their intentions?

MAGDELON   Oh, father, what you're saying is so outrageously bourgeois. I am ashamed to hear you speak thus, and you would do well to familiarize yourself with courtly manners.

GORGIBUS   All that fancy claptrap means nothing to me. I tell you that marriage is something holy and sacred, and that's where all decent folk ought to begin.

MAGDELON   God heavens! If everyone were like you, everything would be over hardly before it started. A fine thing were Cyrus to begin by marrying Mandane and if there were no obstacles in the path of Aronce's marriage to Clelie!

GORGIBUS   What the deuce are you telling me?

MAGDELON   Father, my cousin here will back me when I say that marriage must be the last in the series of events. A proper suitor must know how to express himself beautifully...to be gentle, tender and passionate. His courtship must proceed according to the rules. First, there is the matter of the first meeting of his love to be. This can take place at church, or at some public ceremony, or simply while taking a walk. He might also be brought fortuitously to her home by a relative or a friend, only to emerge from there in a state of ecstasy and melancholia. During his frequent initial visits, he does not reveal his feelings to his beloved, but never misses the opportunity to pose a question on courtly love that challenges the minds of those assembled. When the time comes for the declaration, it usually takes place on some secluded garden path. The lady resists this declaration with an abrupt display of anger and blushing, and banishes the suitor from her sight. Finally, he succeeds in appeasing her, and gradually she responds to his passionate discourse. He ultimately succeeds in eliciting that avowal of love that is so fraught with pain. After that, the adventure begins; rivals who deter the course of an established love, the persecution of the fathers, unfounded bursts of jealousy, accusations, fits of despair and so forth. This is the mandatory sequence of events for those versed in the ways of courtly love. But to start right off with a proposal of marriage is to put the cart before the horse, so to speak; to the heart this constitutes the ultimate venality.

GORGIBUS What the devil kind of gobbledygook am I hearing? This is really high-class talk!

CATHOS Indeed, uncle, my cousin has delved into the very essence of the matter. How else can one be expected to receive men so devoid of gallantry? I would wager that they are totally unfamiliar with the Map of Tenderness that plots the course of courtly love, with its landmarks of love letters, thoughtful little gestures, gallant expressions of love and pretty verses. Could you not perceive that in their entire demeanor, there was not the slightest indication of true worth? To come courting without a ribbon about their knees, with hats without plumes, with their hair in a disheveled state and with outfits bereft of appropriate adornment. Good heavens, what kind of suitors are they? What frugality of dress, what dryness of conversation! Utterly unbearable! Their shirt fronts were of inferior quality and their breeches were a good six inches too narrow.

GORGIBUS   **(Aside)** They've gone balmy, they have, the two of them. **(Aloud)** I can't understand a word of this gibberish, Cathos, and you, Magdelon...

MAGDELON   Oh, I beseech you, father, to desist from calling us by those strange names.

GORGIBUS   What do you mean, "strange names?" Are not these the names with which you were baptized?

MAGDELON   Good heavens, how can you be so uncouth? I am truly astonished that someone like you could have produced a daughter of such elegance and wit. Cathos and Magdelon are completely devoid of style, and won't you concede that names of that ilk could by themselves desecrate the most beautiful of literary expression?

CATHOS   It is true, uncle, that our names virtually assault the sensitive ear, and the name of Polyxène that my cousin has chosen, and that of Aminte which I have given to myself possess a certain elegance that even you must acknowledge.

GORGIBUS   Listen, there is only one thing I have to say: Why you have changed the names given to you by your godparents is beyond me, and as far as these gentlemen are concerned, I know their families and their financial situations, and I insist that you accept them as husbands. I'm tired of having to support you both; the responsibility of two girls is a bit much for a man of my years.

CATHOS   As for me, uncle, all I can tell you is that I find the thought of marriage completely shocking.

MAGDELON   Won't you please stop rushing us and allow us some exposure to the high society of Paris? Give us the chance to be courted in a manner befitting our station and sophistication.

GORGIBUS   (**Aside**) No doubt about it...they're completely daft. (**Aloud**) Listen again; I'll hear no more of this nonsense. I'm the master here and I'm telling you to end all this blabbering right now. Either the two of you get married shortly or, by Jupiter, I'll make nuns of you both. On that I give you my solemn oath! (**Exits**)

Scene 5: Cathos, Magdelon

CATHOS   Good heavens, my dear, there are three words to describe your father: plebeian, dull-witted and insensitive.

MAGDELON   What can I do, my dear? He confuses me. It's difficult to persuade myself that I'm really his daughter, and I would not be surprised to learn some day that I am the issue of a far more illustrious source.

CATHOS   I am inclined to agree with you. I, too, have similar feelings.

Scene 6: Magdelon, Cathos, Marotte

MAROTTE   There's a lackey outside asking if you are at home, and says that his master wishes to see you.

MAGDELON   Will you ever learn to announce yourself in a less vulgar fashion, idiot! Say instead: "Here is an importunate who asks if you are amenable to a visitation."

MAROTTE   By the saints! I don't know any of that there Latin... I didn't have no learnin' about that there filosofy stuff that you see in them fancy books.

MAGDELON   Such impertinence! Do you see what I have to endure? And just who is the master of this lackey?

MAROTTE   He says it was the Marquis de Mascarille.

MAGDELON   **(To Cathos)** Ah, my dear, a marquis. **(To Marotte)** Yes, go tell him that he may come in. **(To Cathos)** It is undoubtedly some worldly gentleman who has heard of us.

CATHOS   Most assuredly, my dear.

MAGDELON   We'll have to receive him here rather than in our room. Let's at least tidy up our hair and live up to our reputation. (To Marotte) Quickly, render us our charm counselor.

MAROTTE   By the saints, I got no idea what the devil you're talkin' about. You'll have to speak more clear if you want me to understand you.

MAGDELON   Fetch us the mirror, idiot that you are, and make sure you don't sully the glass with the reflection of your image.

(They exit.)

Scene 7: Mascarille, Two Porters

The Two Porters carry Mascarille its a sedan chair.

MASCARILLE   Hey there, porters, gently now. Oops! Watch it! Stop bumping against the threshold. Are you two rogues planning to break me in two the way you're banging this thing against every wall and curbstone?

1ST PORTER   Hell, it's a narrow doorway, and you insisted in being brought all the way in.

MASCARILLE   I should say so! Would you good-for-nothings have me expose the delicate state of my plumes to the inclemency of the rainy season, and that I imprint my footwear in mud? Off with you now, and bring your chair with you.

2ND PORTER   We'd like to be paid now, sir.

MASCARILLE   Eh?

2ND PORTER   I said, sir, that we'd like you to kindly give us some money.

MASCARILLE   **(Slapping him)** How's that, you rogue? How dare you ask for money of a person of my quality!

2ND PORTER   Is this the way poor people are paid? And does your quality put bread on our table?

MASCARILLE   Hah! I'll teach you your place. How dare this rabble trifle with me?

1ST PORTER	**(Removing a pole-handle front his chair, rather threateningly)** See this? Pay up, now.
MASCARILLE	What's that?
1ST PORTER	I said we want our money right now.
MASCARILLE	That's reasonable.
1ST PORTER	Quickly now.
MASCARILLE	Yes, yes, of course. You have the most admirable way of expressing yourself, but I'm afraid that your partner is a rogue who doesn't know what he's talking about. **(Paying him)** There now, are you content?
1ST PORTER	No, I am not content. You slapped my friend, and... **(Raising the pole)**
MASCARILLE	Gently now. **(Paying more money)** Here you are. That's for the slap. One can get anything out of me if he goes about it the right way. Go now, and come back later to take me to the Louvre in time to watch the King as he prepares for bed.

Scene 8: Marotte, Mascarille

MAROTTE	Sir, my mistresses will be with you in a moment.
MASCARILLE	Tell them not to hurry; I am comfortably installed to await them.
MAROTTE	Here they are.

Scene 9: Magdelon, Cathos, Mascarille, Almanzor

MASCARILLE	**(After bowing graciously)** Ladies, the audacity of my visit most undoubtedly surprises you, but it is your reputation that is responsible for this inexcusable imposi-

	tion. For you see, I am so dazzled by the allure of excellence that I would pursue it to the ends of the earth.
MAGDELON	Ah, sir, your quest for excellence will be fruitless in this household.
CATHOS	Whatever excellence exists here is by dint of your presence.
MASCARILLE	Ah! I must protest the readiness of your wit. It is obvious that the renown you have achieved is well-deserved, and the world of Paris, with all its elegance notwithstanding, will be no match for you.
MAGDELON	Your graciousness is exceeded only by the lavishness of your praise, and my cousin and I would do well to be on guard against the genteel flow of your flattery.
CATHOS	We must have chairs brought in, my dear.
MAGDELON	Almanzor, hither!
ALMANZOR	**(Arriving promptly)** Madame?
MAGDELON	Quickly now, array the accoutrements of conversation.

Almanzor exit.

MASCARILLE	Tell me, is it safe for me to be here?
CATHOS	Of what might you be afraid?

Almanzor returns with chairs.

| MASCARILLE | Of the theft of my heart! Of the deprivation of my liberty! I see before me eyes of devastating charm, eyes capable of cruel and unsuspecting enslavement I have only to glance at them to sense their power to ensnare me. By my soul, I do not trust |

	them, and I shall flee from here unless you promise they will not harm me.
MAGDELON	What a scintillating personality he has, my dear!
CATHOS	He possesses all the effervescence of a true Hamilcar.
MAGDELON	Be not afraid, for our eyes have no wicked designs on you, and your heart may relinquish all concern as to their intention.
CATHOS	But I beseech you, sir, do not be so insensitive to the feelings of that chair which, for the past quarter hour, has been extending its arms in hope of embracing you.
MASCARILLE	**(After combing his hair and adjusting his breeches)** Well, now, ladies, what have you to say about Paris?
MAGDELON	Alas, sir, what can we say? It would be the antithesis of reason not to confess that Paris is the focal point of marvels and the center of good taste, fine wit and gallantry.
MASCARILLE	As for myself, I contend that beyond the gates of Paris there is no sustenance for people of discernment.
CATHOS	That is an uncontestable truth.
MASCARILLE	The streets are somewhat muddy, but fortunately there is always the sedan.
MAGDELON	It is true that the sedan provides us with a marvelous refuge against the insults of mud and inclement weather.
MASCARILLE	Do you receive many visitors? What outstanding personalities are included in your guest list?
MAGDELON	Alas, our reputation is not as yet sufficiently widespread, but we are making

encouraging headway in this regard. We have one friend in particular who has promised to bring here all the distinguished poets who recently published a collection of their selected works.

CATHOS As well as certain other gentlemen who have been referred to us as sovereign arbiters of literary accomplishments.

MASCARILLE There is no one in a better position than I to assist you in this matter, for I am visited by all these scholarly gentlemen. In fact, there are at least a half dozen of them about me every morning when I wake up.

MAGDELON Good heavens, we would be infinitely obliged to you for such a gracious and friendly gesture; for after all, the acquaintance of these gentlemen is an indispensable stepping stone to the highest echelons of society. For it is through them that reputations are established, as you know. A single visit from any of them could suffice to attain renown; but aside from this, it is the intellectual nourishment that one derives from such visits that gives them particular value. Through them one learns the innumerable things so vital in the development of a worldly mind. They keep you abreast of the news of the social world and of the delightful prose and verse currently being written by its constituents. You are able to recount offhand things like: "Monsieur So-and-So has just composed the most beautiful work in the world on such-and-such a topic," or "a certain lady has just matched the lyrics for a song,'' or "Monsieur X has composed a joyful madrigal," while some other gentleman has completed a poem bewailing infidelity, or how "last night a certain gentleman wrote a six-line poem to a Mademoiselle X, only to receive her response by eight o'clock of the following morning," while various other authors are either sketching, writing or publishing their respective works. It is the knowledge of all things of this nature that promotes one's stature among the genteel and, if you are ignorant of these things, whatever intelligence you might have amounts to nothing.

CATHOS   Indeed, anyone who lays claim to a modicum of wit and who does not keep apprised of the most insignificant quatrains being written each day, merely accentuates his ridiculousness, and I would be mortified were I to be shown something new with which I was not familiar.

MASCARILLE   Yes, it is truly shameful not to be up on everything that is being written but, be not concerned, for I am going to establish at this residence a veritable Academy of Fine Minds. I promise you that there will not be a line of verse written in all of Paris that you will not have memorized before anyone else in Paris has even seen it. As for myself, I must confess that I, myself, dabble a bit in poetry, which is read and discussed in the more elegant Parisian circles. To date, I have written two hundred songs, an equal number of sonnets, four hundred epigrams, more than a thousand madrigals, not to mention the enigmas and profiles.

MAGDELON I must confess that I have a furious attraction for profiles; to me they are the epitome of elegance.

MASCARILLE Profiles are difficult and require a keen intellect. You shall see some of mine, which I'm sure you will not find displeasing.

CATHOS As for me, I'm terribly fond of enigmas.

MASCARILLE Yes, they really exercise the mind. As a matter of fact, I just wrote four of them this morning that I'll have you figure out.

MAGDELON Madrigals are so delightful when they are all well turned.

MASCARILLE Now that's my specialty. I am presently at work writing the entire history of Rome in madrigal form.

MAGDELON Oh! That will be the ultimate in beauty! You must reserve me a copy when you publish it.

MASCARILLE Of course. I promise each of you a copy in the finest binding. I recognize that it is somewhat beneath my station to publish in my name. I do it only to appease the money-hungry booksellers who are constantly hounding me.

MAGDELON I would imagine that it must be a great pleasure to be published.

MASCARILLE Undoubtedly, but while on this subject, I simply must read to you an impromptu that I composed yesterday while visiting a

	duchess friend of mine, for my gift for impromptu borders on the diabolical.
CATHOS	Oh! The impromptu is the veritable touchstone of wit!
MASCARILLE	Listen to this...
MAGDELON	We are all ears.
MASCARILLE	Aha! I was caught completely off my guard. When, quite innocently, I did your face regard. Then, your sly little eye promptly stole my heart and, in the remaining void, left naught but grief. Stop, thief! Stop, thief! Stop, thief! Stop, thief!
CATHOS	Ah! That is gallantry raised to its ultimate expression.
MASCARILLE	Everything I do has a certain air of spontaneity... completely devoid of pedantry.
MAGDELON	Nothing could be more true.
MASCARILLE	Did you notice my opening? "Aha!" Now, that's really extraordinary... "Aha!" Like a man made suddenly aware of something. "Aha!" Like a surprise. "Aha!"
CATHOS	Yes, I find that "Aha!" truly admirable.
MASCARILLE	Oh, it's really nothing.
CATHOS	How can you say such a thing? That is something beyond price.
MAGDELON	No doubt about it; I would have written that "Aha!" than an entire epic poem!
MASCARILLE	The plague take me if you both have not been blessed with excellent taste.
MAGDELON	Well, let's say that I am not completely devoid of it.
MASCARILLE	But don't you also find admirable the phrase "I was caught completely off my guard," as if to say "I was caught napping;" a rather natural form of expression,

"I was caught completely off my guard." While "quite innocently," without malice aforethought like a poor lamb being led to slaughter, "I did your face regard..." that is to say, I gazed upon you, I observed you, I contemplated you. "Your sly little eye..." Notice the rhyming meter..." sly little eye." Wasn't that cleverly chosen?

CATHOS   Very cleverly.

MASCARILLE   "Sly..." that is to say, sneakily... like a cat that has just caught a mouse... "Sly!"

MAGDELON   Nothing could have been expressed more eloquently.

MASCARILLE   "Promptly stole my heart..." Absconds with it, ravishes it. "Stop, thief! Stop, thief. Stop thief! Stop, thief... Doesn't that conjure the image of a man shouting after a thief whom he wishes to have arrested? Stop, thief! Stop, thief! Stop, thief! STOP THIEF!"

MAGDELON   A truly gallant and witty turn of speech.

MASCARILLE   I would like you to hear the song I have written to go with that.

CATHOS   You've learned music as well?

MASCARILLE   I? Not a note.

CATHOS   How, then, can that be?

MASCARILLE   People of quality know everything without having learned a thing.

MAGDELON   Most assuredly, my dear.

MASCARILL   I would like your reaction to the melody. Heh, heh, la, la, la, la, la, ahem. The brutality of the season has furiously outraged the delicacy of my voice. But, no matter, for it is the substance that counts. **(He sings)**

CATHOS   Oh! Could there ever be a more enthrall-
              ing melody? It's beauty is absolutely
              devastating!

MAGDELON   It possesses a definite chromatic quality.

MASCARILLE   Did you remark how cleverly I matched
              thought with music? Stop, thief! and then
              a series of abrupt, breathtaking shouts...
              Stop! Stop! Stop! Stop! Stop! Stop! Stop,
              thief! And suddenly the decrescendo, like
              a person's ultimate gasp for breath... Stop,
              thief!

MAGDELON   Oh! I tell you that it is the zenith of attain-
              ment. The absolute zenith. The zenith of
              zeniths Everything is superb, I assure you,
              and I am overwhelmed by both music and
              lyrics.

CATHOS   This is my first experience with such
              forceful expression.

MASCARILLE   Everything I do comes naturally to me. I
              require no mental exertion whatsoever.

MAGDELON   You are indeed the spoiled child of mother
              Nature, and I marvel at the degree to
              which she showered her gifts upon you.

MASCARILLE   At what do you spend your time here?

CATHOS   At absolutely nothing.

MAGDELON   Up to now, we have been enduring a
              frighthtful dearth of aesthetic diversion.

MASCARILLE   May I offer, then, to escort you both to
              the theater one of these days? There is a
              new play being put on, and I think it
              would be delightful if we were to see it
              together.

MAGDELON   How could we possibly refuse?

MASCARILLE   However, I must ask that when you are
              there that you applaud appropriately. It

was only this morning that the author himself visited me and I feel, consequently, a certain commitment to the success of his play. You see, it is the custom among we people of condition to have authors read their new plays to us so that we might find them beautiful and work toward their recognition. If, during a performance, we acclaim a particular work, the people in the cheaper seats wouldn't dare contradict us, as you might imagine. As for me,. I am a man of principle, and once I am committed to a certain work, I invariably shout "How beautiful that is!" and that's even before the curtain rises.

MAGDELON   No need for further discussion. Paris is truly a wonderful place. Hundreds of things take place there every day about which we in the provinces are completely oblivious, irrespective of whatever aesthetic sensitivities we might possess.

CATHOS   So be it; now that you have advised us, we will make it our duty to applaud appropriately whatever is being done or said on stage.

MASCARILLE   I may be mistaken, but I get the distinct impression that you also have written a play.

MAGDELON   Well, there might be something in what you say.

MASCARILLE   Aha! Good heavens, you must show it to me. Listen, just between us, I have just written one that I plan to have staged.

CATHOS	How wonderful! And by which theater group do you plan to have it produced?
MASCARILLE	What a question! By the great actors of the Burgundian Theater, of course. They are the only ones capable of demonstrating the true merit of a particular work. All the others are incompetents who deliver lines as one would do in normal conversation. They know nothing about the dynamic delivery nor the well-placed pauses for effect. After all, how can the audience know when to applaud if the actor does not stop to advise them?
CATHOS	Indeed, there is technique involved in making the audience aware of the beauty of a particular work. And the value of a work lies solely in the way it is presented on stage.
MASCARILLE	How does this little trimming strike you? Don't you find it in congruence with my ensemble?
CATHOS	Utterly.
MASCARILLE	The ribbon is well-chosen?
MAGDELON	Furiously well-chosen. It is pure Paris.
MASCARILLE	And what say you of my knee ruffles?
MAGDELON	Strikingly chic.
MASCARILLE	I take pride in the fact that they are a good thirty centimeters wider than the run-of--the-mill variety.
MAGDELON	I must avow that my eyes have never caressed such a high level of elegance in the realm of personal attire.
MASCARILLE	Allow your olfactory organs to be caressed by the scent of these gloves.
MAGDELON	A frightfully delicate fragrance.

CATHOS   Never have I encountered anything as exquisite.

MASCARILLE   Now, smell my wig.

They smell his powdered wig.

MAGDELON   An essence of undeniable quality, with a delectable mind-swaying effect.

MASCARILLE   You haven't said a word about my plumes. How do you like them?

CATHOS   Devastatingly beautiful.

MASCARILLE   Would you believe that this headpiece alone cost an entire gold piece? The fact is that I'm virtually a slave to things of beauty.

MAGDELON   I assure you that we are as one in this regard, for I am furiously fastidious about whatever I wear. Even my under stockings must be of impeccable quality.

MASCARILLE   **(Shouting suddenly)** Ah! Oh! Oh! Gently! May God forsake me, ladies, but you're treating me unfairly. I must complain of your tactics...they are unworthy of you.

CATHOS   What is it? What is wrong?

MASCARILLE   How's that? Both of you against my heart simultaneously. Attacking me from the left and right. The situation is unfair; the match is unequal. I must cry "Murder!"

CATHOS   I must confess that he does have a rather original form of expression.

MAGDELON   A most admirable turn of phrase.

CATHOS   Your fear exceeds your injury, and your heart bleeds before it's wounded.

MASCARILLE   The devil take me if it's not wounded to the core.

Scene 10: Marotte, Mascarille, Magdelon, Cathos

MAROTTE	Someone to see you, madame.
MAGDELON	Who?
MAROTTE	The Viscomte de Jodelet.
MASCARILLE	The Viscomte de Jodelet?
MAROTTE	Yes, sir.
CATHOS	Do you know him?
MASCARILLE	He's only my best Friend.
MAGDELON	(**To Marotte**) Have him enter at once.
MASCARILLE	It's been some time now since I've seen him, and I'm delighted by this opportunity.
CATHOS	Here he is.

Scene 11: Marotte, Mascarille, Magdelon Cathos, Viscomte de Jodelet, Almanzor

MASCARILLE	Viscomte (**They kiss each other on the cheek.**)
JODELET	Marquis!
MASCARILLE	Such a pleasure meeting you!
JODELET	Such a joy seeing you here!
MASCARILLE	One more kiss, I beseech you.
MAGDELON	(**To Cathos**) Well, now, my dear, it seems that our reputations are becoming established. Society is now beating a path to our door.
MASCARILLE	Ladies, allow me to present this gentleman. I assure you he is deserving of your acquaintance.
JODELET	It is fitting that I come here to pay you the respect you so richly deserve, for your charms demand lordly dominion over people of all stations.

MAGDELON	Your compliments attain the highest echelons of flattery.
CATHOS	This day must be noted on our calendar as one of exceptional fortune.
MAGDELON	**(To Almanzor, who is just off stage)** Come now, little boy, must everything be repeated to you? Don't you see that the supplementation of another chair is needed? Almanzor obeys.
MASCARILLE	You must not be surprised to see the Viscomte in his present condition. He has just gotten over an illness which, as you see, has left him somewhat pale.
JODELET	The fruit of long nights at the court and of the fatigues of war.
MASCARILLE	Are you aware, ladies, that you see before you in the Viscomte one of the most valiant men of the century? The walking embodiment of courage!
JODELET	My dear Marquis, where courage is concerned, we are as one. We are fully aware of your capacity in this regard.
MASCARILLE	It is true that we've seen each other in combat.
JODELET	And in places where it was hot, indeed.
MASCARILLE	**(Looking at Magdelon and Cathos)** Yes, but not as hot as here. Ha ha ha!
JODELET	We met in the army. At the time, he was the commander of a cavalry regiment stationed on a Maltese convict ship.
MASCARILLE	That is true. However, you enlisted before I did and were already commanding two thousand cavalrymen, while I was merely an officer of minor rank.

JODELET	War is such a beautiful thing. Unfortunately, there is little recognition at court today for men-of-arms of our capacity.
MASCARILLE	I'm tempted to hang up my sword.
CATHOS	As for myself, I must confess that I have a furious attraction for men of the sword.
MAGDELON	I as well; however, I prefer that their bravery be seasoned with wit.
MASCARILLE	Do you recall the siege of Arras where we overtook that fortress shaped like a half--moon?
JODELET	What do you mean "half-moon?" that fortress was the size of a full moon, if anything.
MASCARILLE	I believe you're right.
JODELET	I ought to remember it, by Jupiter, for it was there that a grenade burst got me in the leg. I still bear the scars. Touch it gently and you'll realize what a wound it was.
CATHOS	**(After having touched the spot)** The scar is indeed enormous.
MASCARILLE	**(To Magdelon)** Give me your hand and feel this one. Right here in the back of my head. Do you feel it?
MAGDELON	Yes, I feel something.
MASCARILLE	It's a bullet wound I received during my last campaign.
JODELET	**(Baring his chest)** And here you see where a bullet went right through me during the attack of Gravelines *(A small town near Dunkerque whre the Spaniards defeated the French in 1558, about 100 years prior to the time of the alleged bullet would of Jodelet).*

MASCARILLE	**(About to drop his breeches)** Now ready yourselves for a truly frightful wound!
MAGDELON	That won't be necessary; we'll take your word for it.
MASCARILLE	These are marks of honor that show a man's mettle.
CATHOS	We have no doubts concerning your substance.
MASCARILLE	Viscomte, did you bring your carriage?
JODELET	Why?
MASCARILLE	We could take the ladies for a ride and refreshments.
MAGDELON	But we can't go today.
MASCARILLE	Well then, let's get some musicians for dancing.
JODELET	By Jupiter, an excellent idea.
MAGDELON	Agreed; however, don't we need more people than that?
MASCARILLE	Hey there! Lackeys! Champagne! Picardy, Burgundy, Cascaret, Basque, La Verdure, Lorraine, Provence, La Violette! May the devil take all lackeys! In all of France I don't think there's a nobleman more poorly attended than I. Those lowlifes constantly abandon me!
MAGDELON	Almanzor, go out and tell the marquis' men to find some violinists, and then invite some ladies and gentlemen of our quarter to dissipate the solitude of our ball.

Almanzor exits.

MASCARILLE	Viscomte, what say you about those eyes?

JODELET	What about you, marquis? How do they strike you?
MASCARILLE	I? I say that we'll be lucky to leave this place with our freedom intact. There's a strange thumping with me, and my heart is hanging on by a thread.
MAGDELON	What a natural flow of speech! Such a masterful turn of phrase!
CATHOS	He certainly dispenses a furious abundance of wit.
MASCARILLE	As proof of my sincerity, I'm going to compose an impromptu on that very theme. **(He meditates briefly.)**
CATHOS	Ah! To hear something composed especially for us would elicit our deepest appreciation.
JODELET	I would do likewise, but my poetic veins have been somewhat drained by the numerous bloodlettings I've gotten recently.
MASCARILLE	What the deuce is wrong with me? The first line of verse pours out freely, but I have a devil of a time with the others. I seem unable to write under the pressure of time However, I shall write you the most beautiful impromptu in the world…as soon as I'm not rushed.
JODELET	He has the wit of a demon.
MAGDELON	To say nothing of his chivalry and turn of speech.
MASCARILLE	Viscomte, tell me, has it been a long time since you've seen the Countess?
JODELET	More than three weeks.
MASCARILLE	Do you know that the Duke visited me this morning and invited me to go deer hunting with him?

MASCARILLE   Here come our friends.

Scene 12: Local neighbors, Magdelon, Cathos, Mascarille, Viscomte, Almanzor

MAGDELON   My dear friends, we beg your pardon, but these gentlemen fancied providing us with the foot-stirring accoutrements, and we sent for you to populate the voids of our dancing assemblage.

NEIGHBOR   We are most obliged.

MASCARILLE   This is merely an impromptu dance; however, one of these days we'll put on a full-fledged ball with all the trappings. Have the violinists arrived?

ALMANZOR   **(As Musicians enter)** Yes, sir. They are here.

CATHOS   Well, then ladies, let's take our places.

MASCARILLE   **(Dancing alone, providing a solo prelude)** Lalalalalalala.

MAGDELON   Such elegant stature.

CATHOS   And such appropriate flourishes to his dancing.

MASCARILLE   **(Taking Magdelon)** You'll notice my spontaneity never conflicts with the dictates of vogue. Ugh! **(To the Musicians)** Will you watch the tempo, nincompoops? Do they expect us to dance to that? To the devil with you all! Can't you maintain the beat? Lalalala. Steady now, you gut-scraping bumpkins!

JODELET   **(Dancing in turn)** Not so fast, I beseech you! I'm barely out of a sick bed.

Scene 13: La Grange, Du Croisy, Jodelet, Mascarille

LA GRANGE	**(Suddenly beating Mascarille with a stick)** Aha! You scoundrels! What are you doing here? We've been looking for you for three hours!
MASCARILLE	Ouch! Oooh! Ouch! You didn't mention a beating like this!
JODELET	**(Being beaten by Du Croisy)** Ouch! Ouch! Oooooh!
LA GRANGE	**(To Mascarille)** This is the just reward for your brazen impression of a person of quality.
DU CROISY	**(To Jodelet)** This will teach you your place!
MAGDELON	What is the meaning of this?
JODELET	It's ...a ... Ouch! wager!
CATHOS	How's that? To allow yourselves to be beaten like that?
MASCARILLE	Good heavens! I preferred to simply overlook the matter rather than unleash my violent temper.
MAGDELON	To tolerate such an affront and, in our presence!
MASCARILLE	It's really nothing, I tell you. Let's ignore it and resume the dance. We've known each other for a long time, and among friends such trifles are no cause for anger.
LA GRANGE	I can promise you, rogues that you are, that you'll find little cause for laughter. You there, come in.

Two "Toughs" enter.

DU CROISY	So then, ladies, you would have us endure seeing our lackeys being better received

	than us?... Seeing them court you and provide dancing at our expense?
MAGDELON	Your lackeys?
LA GRANGE	Yes, our lackeys. And it was not very decent of you to corrupt them as you did.
MAGDELON	Good heavens! What insolence!
LA GRANGE	But they'll no longer have our clothes to dazzle you, and if they still appeal to you, it will be for their pretty faces. Strip them instantly!
JODELET	Adieu, my beautiful adornments.
MASCARILLE	Sic transit gloria Marquis and Viscomte.
DU CROISY	Ah! Villains! To dare to walk in our footsteps! You'll have to search elsewhere for trappings to seduce your lady friends, I assure you.
LA GRANGE	It was bad enough impersonating us, but to do so with our own clothes!
MASCARILLE	Ah, destiny! How fickle you are.
DU CROISY	Quickly now, strip them down to their last rag.
LA GRANGE	Take all those clothes outside. Now, ladies, in their present condition, you may court them to your hearts' content without running the slightest risk of our jealousy.

Du Croisy and La Grange exit.

CATHOS	Ah! Such confusion!
MAGDELON	I shall die of vexation!
VIOLINISTS	**(To Mascarille)** What's going on here? Who's going to pay us?
MASCARILLE	Ask the Viscomte.
JODELET	Ask the marquis.

Scene 16: Gorgibus enters.

GORGIBUS   Ah! Vixens that you are! From what those gentlemen told me on their way out, you've really created a fine state of affairs.

MAGDELON   Oh, father, we have been the victims of the most cruel of tricks.

GORGIBUS   Yes, it was a cruel trick, but it was brought on by your own stupidity. They were offended by the way you treated them, and now I'm the one who must bear the brunt of all this.

MAGDELON   Ah! I swear to you that I shall either be avenged or die of shame. And as for you two impostors, how dare you remain here after such insolence?

MASCARILLE   Imagine treating a marquis in such a fashion! So this is the level to which society has sunk. The slightest misfortune turns affection into scorn. Come, my friend, let us seek fortune elsewhere, for it is obvious that in this shrine to sham, true worth goes unrecognized, even in it most extreme state of exposure.

Mascarelle and Jodelet exit.

VIOLINISTS   Sir, in view of their default of payment, we insist that you compensate us for playing.

GORGIBUS   **(Beating them)** Yes, yes, I'll compensate you, all right, and this is the form of currency. (To Magdelon and Cathos) And as for you two scatterbrains, I don't know what keeps me from giving you the same treatment. Your shenanigans will make us the laughingstock of the neighborhood. Go find a place to hide and never come out! And finally, to all those destructive amusements of idle minds, which are at the root of their folly...novels, verses, songs, sonnets... MAY YOU ALL BURN IN HELL!

THE END

The Miser

(L'AVARE)

(Regular Edition)

CHARACTERS:

HARPAGON, Father of Cleante and Elise, and in love with Mariane.

CLEANTE, Son of Harpagon, and in love with Mariane

ELISE, Daughter of Harpagon, and in love with Valere.

VALERE, Son of Anselme, and in love with Elise.

MARIANE, In love with Cleante, and courted by Harpagon.

ANSELME, Father of Valere and Mariane.

FROSINE, Adventuress.

MASTER SIMON, Usurer.

JACQUES, Harpagon's cook and coachman.

LA FLECHE, Cleante's valet.

CLAUDIA, Harpagon's servant.

BRINDAVOINE, Harpagon's first lackey.

LA MERLUCHE, Harpagon's second lackey.

OFFICER

OFFICER'S CLERK

ACT I

Scene 1: Valere, Elise

VALERE Come now, my charming Elise, after providing such gracious assurances of your love, why are you suddenly sad? In the midst of my joy, alas, I see you sigh. Tell me, are you sorry to have made me so happy? Do you regret being compelled by my love for you to sign those papers of engagement?

ELISE No, Valere. I regret nothing that I do for you. I feel myself being swept along by a force so delectable as to melt whatever resolve I might have to change things but, to speak truthfully, I am uneasy about the outcome of all this, and I fear that I may love you more deeply than I should.

VALERE What is there to fear, Elise, in your kindness toward me?

ELISE A hundred things at once: a father's anger, a family's reproaches, the censure of society, but above all, Valere, I fear a change of heart on your part, as well as that criminal coldness with which those of your sex repay excessive displays of innocent love.

VALERE Please don't wrong me by judging me by others. You may question anything but my resolve to honor my indebtedness to you. My love for you is eternal and far too intense for me to ever fail you.

ELISE Oh, Valere, all men are alike; they all make the same speeches, and it is only through their actions that they show their differences.

VALERE   Since actions alone reveal our true selves, at least give me a chance to act before you judge me. Don't allow unfounded suspicion to cause you to accuse me unjustly. Do not, I beseech you, destroy me with such harsh speculation, but allow me instead the time to prove to you the indisputable sincerity of my love.

ELISE   Ah, how easily are we persuaded by those we love. Yes, Valere, I believe that it is not in you to deceive me. I feel that your love for me is true, and that you will be faithful to me. It is not my wish to doubt you; my only concern is how I might be blamed for all of this.

VALERE   But why should this bother you?

ELISE   I would have nothing to fear if everyone saw you as I do, for my faith in you justifies whatever I might do for you. In its defense, my heart can only proffer a belief in your goodness--a belief reinforced by a spiritual confirmation within me. My mind reverts constantly to that terrifying moment during which our destinies were joined, to the selfless heroism you displayed in risking your life to save mine from the fury of the waves, to the tenderness you showed me once we were safely ashore, to the unfailing homage of a love that neither time nor hardship has dampened, a love that compels you to deny both family and country to conceal your true social position, and to work as a domestic for my father solely for the opportunity to be near me. I am deeply moved by all of this, and I feel that it justifies my signing the engagement; however, I am concerned that others may misinterpret my actions in this matter.

VALERE   Of everything you have said, it is only my love for you that is deserving of mention; and as for your qualms, I contend that your father's comportment provides whatever justification is necessary to shield you from the possible misinterpretation of others; his shameful avarice, particularly with regard to his children, would warrant conduct of a far more extravagant nature. Forgive my bluntness, charming Elise, but when I speak of your father, there is very little good that comes to mind. In any event, should God grant that I find my parents, we will have little difficulty obtaining his blessing. I am waiting impatiently for news of them, and, if word doesn't arrive soon, I shall go in search of them myself.

ELISE   Do not leave, Valere, I beg of you. Remain here and concentrate on winning the blessing of my father.

VALERE   Are you not aware of all my efforts in that direction? Recall, if you will, the obsequious demeanor with which I gained entrance to his service and how, in order to please him, I constantly feign agreement with his every sentiment. I am making admirable progress, for I feel that the best way to win men over is to mirror their proclivities, to abide by their maxims, to praise their shortcomings, and to applaud their every gesture. Man's susceptibility to flattery is without bounds, and there is never the danger of an overdose; for no matter how obvious your method of praise might be, it will not fail to dupe even the cleverest of men. There is nothing so absurd that when seasoned with a little praise, can't be digested. My work here sorely compromises my sense of integrity, but this is the price I must pay, for adaptation is the sole path to his confidence.

The fault here lies not with flattery, but rather with those who relish it.

ELISE Why don't you try to win the approval of my brother as well so that, should the maidservant decide to reveal our secret, we may rely on his support.

VALERE I cannot manage them both simultaneously; the divergence of temperament is so great as to render futile any ingratiating efforts on my part. You, however, are in a better position to gain your brother's support by virtue of the good relationship that exists between you. Here he comes. I must go. This would be a good time to discuss our relationship, but reveal to him only what you deem appropriate.

ELISE I don't know if I'll have the courage to tell him our secret.

Scene 2: Cleante, Elise

CLEANTE I'm so glad to find you alone, my sister, for there is a matter of extreme importance that I must discuss with you.

ELISE I am listening, my brother. What do you have to tell me?

CLEANTE Many things wrapped into one small sentence-- I'm in love.

ELISE You're in love?

CLEANTE Yes, I'm in love; but before going any further, let me say that I am aware of my dependence upon my father, and how, as his son, I must submit to his will. We must not pledge our love without the consent of those to whom we owe the light of day. Heaven has given them dominion over our will and we must accept it. Unaffected by the blinding passions of youth, they are in a better position to determine what is best for us. I'm saying all this to you to forestall any reproaches you may feel inclined to voice, for I'm too much in love to heed them.

ELISE   Are you and your loved one engaged, dear brother?

CLEANTE   No, but I am determined that this shall come to pass, and I implore you once again not to try to dissuade me.

ELISE   My dear brother, do you believe me to be so insensitive?

CLEANTE   No, but you are not in love, and know nothing of the sweet violence that tender love enkindles in our hearts, and I won't allow the wisdom of your arguments to affect the ardor I feel within me.

ELISE   Alas, my dear brother, don't speak of my wisdom, for it does not exceed that of any other, and if I were to reveal to you what is in my heart, you would perhaps think me more foolish than yourself.

CLEANTE   Oh, if only your heart, like mine, were torn by....

ELISE   Let us first discuss your situation; tell me who it is that you love.

CLEANTE   A young lady who recently moved here and whose beauty captivates all who see her. She is indeed one of Nature's most desirable creations, and I am enraptured by the mere sight of her. Her name is Mariane, and she lives under the charge of an elderly mother, who is nearly always ill, but who enjoys the unbounded affection of her charming daughter. She tends to her every need with touching devotion. Her innumerable charms are reflected in whatever she does; her appealing tenderness, her enchanting demeanor, her angelic goodness, her...ah, dear sister, if you could only see her.

ELISE I see her clearly enough in the exuberance of your description, and the fact that you love her is, in itself, proof of her worthiness.

CLEANTE I have learned secretly that they are not particularly affluent and, consequently, are having difficulty maintaining their household. Imagine, my sister, what a pleasure it would be to help my beloved out of her financial distress, to discreetly provide some small measure of assistance to a virtuous family; and now, consider my displeasure at being denied this joy as well as the means to lavish upon that beautiful creature a continuing testimony of my love--and all this because of the avarice of a father.

ELISE Yes, Cleante, I can readily understand your displeasure.

CLEANTE Ah, sister, it is greater than can be imagined, for what is there to match in cruelty the unbounded niggardliness to which we are subjected--this barren milieu where we must languish? As it stands, we have to borrow simply to survive, even to the point where, for the very clothes on our backs, we must suffer the humiliation of relying on the generosity of merchants. Finally, I wanted to ask your help in discussing this matter with our father. If he opposes me, I am determined to depart with my beloved and enjoy whatever happiness Heaven deigns to offer. To accomplish this, I have been looking everywhere in the hope of obtaining a loan, and if your situation resembles mine, that is to say, if you are confronted with the same opposition, we shall both leave this place, thereby liberating ourselves from the tyranny of his insufferable avarice to which we have been subject for so long.

ELISE It is true that with each day that passes, he provides us with more reason to regret the death of our mother and that...

CLEANTE I hear his voice. Let us withdraw from here and continue our discussion in private; afterwards, we shall join forces to better confront the obduracy of his nature.

Scene 3: Harpagon, La Fleche

HARPAGON Off with you this instant, and not a word out of you! Get out of my house, you first-class, swindling gallows bird!

LA FLECHE (**Aside**) I have never seen anything to match the wickedness of this cursed old man. I truly feel he is possessed by the devil.

HARPAGON What are you mumbling?

LA FLECHE Why are you dismissing me?

HARPAGON You've got your nerve asking me for reasons, you scoundrel. Get out quickly before I thrash you.

LA FLECHE What have I done?

HARPAGON Enough to warrant your dismissal.

LA FLECHE My master, your son, ordered me to wait for him.

HARPAGON Wait for him in the street. I'll not have you snooping about my house, and using what you see to your advantage, nor will I tolerate a traitor whose damnable eyes scrutinize my every deed, devour my possessions, and probe every recess of my household with thieving intent.

LA FLECHE How the devil can anyone possibly steal from you? Everything you own is locked and guarded night and day.

HARPAGON What I feel should be locked, I lock; and what I feel should be guarded, I guard. Are you not just another spy who watches everything I do? **(aside)** I shudder to think he might know something about my money. **(aloud)** Are you not the sort of man who would spread rumors of my hidden wealth?

LA FLECHE You have hidden wealth?

HARPAGON No, knave that you are, I didn't say that. **(aside)** I could kick myself! **(aloud)** No, I am merely asking if there is sufficient malice in you to spread rumors to that effect.

LA FLECHE What does it matter whether you do or don't, since it doesn't affect me either way?

HARPAGON Any more of your back talk and I'll box your ears. **(He raises his hand as if to slap L.F.)** Again I say, get out of here!

LA FLECHE Very well, I'm leaving.

HARPAGON Hold on! Are you taking anything with you?

LA FLECHE What could I take from you?

HARPAGON Come here and let me see. Hold out your hands.

LA FLECHE There you are.

HARPAGON The others.

LA FLECHE The others?

HARPAGON Yes.

LA FLECHE There you are.

HARPAGON **(pointing to his breeches)** Did you put anything in there?

LA FLECHE Look for yourself.

HARPAGON **(feeling the bottoms of his breeches)** These large breeches are excellent receptacles for stolen articles, and I would love to hang the man who designed them.

LA FLECHE **(aside)** Oh, how a man like this deserves what he fears, and what a joy it would be to rob him.

HARPAGON Eh ?

LA FLECHE What?

HARPAGON What did you say about robbing?

LA FLECHE I said that you're groping everywhere to see if I robbed you.

HARPAGON That's what I want to do. **(He gropes in L.F.'s pockets)**

LA FLECHE **(aside)** A plague on greed and those who live by it.

HARPAGON How's that? What did you say?

LA FLECHE What did I say?

HARPAGON Yes. What did you say about greed?

LA FLECHE I said, "A plague on greed and those who live by it."

HARPAGON To whom do you refer?

LA FLECHE The greedy.

HARPAGON And just who are the greedy?

LA FLECHE Misers and skinflints.

HARPAGON But whom do you have in mind when you say that?

LA FLECHE Why are you so concerned?

HARPAGON I am concerned when I need to be.

LA FLECHE Do you think I'm referring to you?

HARPAGON I think what I think; but I insist that you name the party to whom you were addressing those remarks.

LA FLECHE I was speaking...I was speaking to myself.

HARPAGON Is that so? **(showing his clenched fist)** Perhaps you can use a helping hand?

LA FLECHE You forbid me to curse the greedy?

HARPAGON   No, but I forbid you to continue blabbing and
being insolent. Not another word out of you.

LA FLECHE   I am not naming anyone.

HARPAGON   I'll thrash you if you speak.

LA FLECHE   If the shoe fits, wear it.

HARPAGON   Will you be still?

LA FLECHE   Yes, in spite of myself. **(shows Harpagon one
of the pockets of his jerkin)**

HARPAGON   Aha!

LA FLECHE   Here's another pocket for you. Are you satisfied?

HARPAGON   Come on, hand it over without my having to
search you.

LA FLECHE   How's that?

HARPAGON   What you took from me.

LA FLECHE   I haven't taken a thing from you.

HARPAGON   Are you sure?

LA FLECHE   I assure you.

HARPAGON   Off with you then, and may the devil take you.

LA FLECHE   How cordially do you dismiss me. **(Exit)**

HARPAGON   May you suffer the pangs of a guilty conscience!
That rogue of a valet really grates me, and I
take great pleasure in the thought of never again
having to see that wretched cripple!

Scene 4: Harpagon, Elise, Cleante

HARPAGON   Oh, what a burden it is to keep a large sum of
money in one's house, and lucky is the man who
is blessed with a hiding place which is not only
secure, but also accessible in times of financial
need. I have no faith in strong boxes, for they
are the prime target of thieves. Nevertheless, I
don't know if it was wise of me to have buried
in the garden the ten thousand gold pieces that

I received yesterday. Ten thousand gold pieces in one's house is a rather large...**(Elise and Cleante enter, speaking softly)** Good Heavens! My emotions loosened my tongue and I nearly betrayed myself. What is it?

CLEANTE   Nothing, father.

HARPAGON   Have you been there for a long time?

ELISE   We just arrived.

HARPAGON   Did you hear...

CLEANTE   Hear what, father?

HARPAGON   Come now...

ELISE   How's that?

HARPAGON   What I just said.

CLEANTE   No.

HARPAGON   Yes you did! Yes you did!

ELISE   I beg your pardon.

HARPAGON   I am certain that you overheard something. The fact is that I was merely talking to myself about the difficulty of obtaining money today, and I was envying the man who can have ten thousand gold pieces in his house.

CLEANTE   We were reluctant to approach you for fear of interrupting you.

HARPAGON   I am anxious to clarify this so that you won't mistakenly believe that I am the one with the ten thousand gold pieces.

CLEANTE   It is not for us to meddle in your affairs.

HARPAGON   Oh, would to God I had those ten thousand gold pieces!

CLEANTE   I don't believe...

HARPAGON   Ah, that really would be something.

ELISE   These are things that...

HARPAGON   I could certainly use them.

CLEANTE   I think that...

HARPAGON   That would indeed improve my financial status.

ELISE	You are...
HARPAGON	And you wouldn't hear me complain so much about these hard times.
CLEANTE	Good Heavens, father, you have no grounds for complaint, for it is a known fact that you're a man of sufficient means.
HARPAGON	Of sufficient means you say? Only liars and scoundrels would say that of me. Nothing could be more false.
ELISE	Please don't get angry.
HARPAGON	How strange it is to have my own children betray me and become my enemies.
CLEANTE	Does my reference to your money make me your enemy?
HARPAGON	Yes, and if you keep talking like that and continue your spendthrift ways, one of these days someone will come here and cut my throat, thinking that my clothes are stuffed with money.
CLEANTE	In what way am I a spendthrift?
HARPAGON	In what way? Could anything be more scandalous than that extravagant outfit in which you parade about town? I was scolding your sister yesterday, but you are worse than she. This situation literally screams for heavenly retribution, and I could have made a profitable investment with the money I spent decking you out like that from head to toe. I've told you time and again that I find your behavior displeasing. You strut about dressed like a marquis, and it's only by robbing me that you could do so.
CLEANTE	How am I robbing you?
HARPAGON	Who knows? How else could you afford those fancy clothes?
CLEANTE	I, father? The fact is that I gamble, and since I'm very lucky, I can afford to dress in style.

HARPAGON That's bad business. If you are lucky at gambling, you should invest in something that will yield a profitable return. Aside from everything else, I would like to know the purpose of all those ribbons you have dangling from head to toe. Would not a half dozen laces suffice to secure a pair of breeches, and is it really necessary to spend money on wigs when one's own hair would do as well? I'll wager that in wigs and ribbons alone you've squandered a veritable fortune in potential interest.

CLEANTE I agree.

HARPAGON Let's change the subject. Eh? **(aside)** I think that they're signaling each other to steal my purse. **(aloud)** What was the meaning of all that gesturing?

ELISE Both my brother and I have something to say to you, and we were trying to decide who would be the first to speak.

HARPAGON And I, too, have something to say to you.

CLEANTE We wish to speak to you of marriage, father.

HARPAGON And I'd like to speak to you on the same subject.

ELISE Ah, father!

HARPAGON Why this sudden emotion? Is it the idea or the reality that frightens you?

CLEANTE We are concerned about any plans you might have made regarding our marriages, and how such plans might conflict with our own wishes.

HARPAGON A little patience. Do not be alarmed. I know what you both need, and neither of you will have reason to complain about my intentions. Let's begin with you, Cleante. Are you acquainted with a young lady named Mariane, who lives nearby?

CLEANTE   Yes, father.

HARPAGON **(to Elise)** And you?

ELISE   I've heard of her.

HARPAGON What are your impressions of this young lady, my son?

CLEANTE   A truly charming person.

HARPAGON Her face?

CLEANTE   Sincere and decidedly intelligent.

HARPAGON Her demeanor?

CLEANTE   Admirable beyond a doubt.

HARPAGON Don't you feel that such a girl deserves consideration?

CLEANTE   Yes, father.

HARPAGON That she would make a highly desirable partner?

CLEANTE   Very desirable.

HARPAGON That she gives every indication of being a good housekeeper?

CLEANTE   Undoubtedly.

HARPAGON And that a husband would be very satisfied with her?

CLEANTE   Assuredly.

HARPAGON There's only one minor drawback. I fear that her financial situation leaves something to be desired.

CLEANTE   Ah, father! When it comes to marrying a person of such quality, money means nothing.

HARPAGON Pardon me! But the fact remains that if the money falls short of one's expectations, one should expect other forms of compensation.

CLEANTE   That's understandable.

HARPAGON I'm glad that you agree with me, for her genteel bearing and affectionate nature have captured my heart, and I have decided to marry her...providing of course that a dowry, however modest, is in the offing.

CLEANTE What's that?

HARPAGON Eh?

CLEANTE You say that you have decided...

HARPAGON To marry Mariane.

CLEANTE Who? You, you?

HARPAGON Yes, me, me, me! What do you mean by that?

CLEANTE Excuse me, but I suddenly feel a little faint, and I must withdraw from here.

HARPAGON That's nothing. Go to the kitchen and drink a large glass of water. **(Exit Cleante)** There goes another of those weak-kneed fops whose virility couldn't match that of a chicken! Well, my daughter, this is what I have planned for myself. As for your brother, I have chosen for him a certain widow I heard about this morning; and as for you, I shall give you to Lord Anselme.

ELISE To Lord Anselme?

HARPAGON Yes, a mature man, prudent and wise, who is not more than fifty, and who is reputed to be quite wealthy.

ELISE **(curtsying)** If you please, father, I do not wish to marry.

HARPAGON **(curtsying in turn)** And I, my little daughter, my dearest, I wish that you do, if you please.

ELISE I beg your pardon, father.

HARPAGON I beg your pardon, daughter.

ELISE I am the most humble servant of Lord Anselme; but, with your permission, I shall not marry him.

HARPAGON And I am your most humble valet; but with your permission, you shall marry him this very evening.

ELISE This very evening?

HARPAGON This very evening.

ELISE That will never happen, father.

HARPAGON Yes it will, daughter.

ELISE   No.
HARPAGON Yes.
ELISE   No, I tell you.
HARPAGON And I tell you yes.
ELISE   This is something you shall not force me to do.
HARPAGON This is something I will force you to do.
ELISE   I will kill myself rather than marry such a man!
HARPAGON You shall not kill yourself, and you shall marry
            him---brazen creature that you are! Has ever a
            daughter spoken thus to her father?
ELISE   Has ever a father forced such a marriage on his
            daughter?
HARPAGON The matter is settled as far as I'm concerned,
            and I'll wager that my choice will be approved
            by everyone.
ELISE   And I'll wager that no reasonable person could
            condone such a match.
HARPAGON Here comes Valere. Shall we seek his opinion in
            this matter?
ELISE   Very well.
HARPAGON Will you submit to his judgment?
ELISE   Yes, I'll abide by what he says.
HARPAGON So be it.

Scene 5: Valere, Harpagon, Elise

HARPAGON Over here, Valere. My daughter and I have
            chosen you to decide which of us is right in a
            certain matter.
VALERE   It is you, sir, without question.
HARPAGON Do you know what we are discussing?
VALERE   No, but you could never be wrong, for you are
            reason personified.
HARPAGON I wish to marry her off this very evening to a
            man who is as rich as he is wise, and the hussy

has the audacity to defy me. What do you say to that?

VALERE What do I say to that?

HARPAGON Yes.

VALERE Well, er, ...

HARPAGON What?

VALERE I say that essentially I share your feelings, for it could never be that you are wrong; however, I submit that she also is not completely wrong, and...

HARPAGON How's that? Seigneur Anselme is a man of importance--a gentleman who is noble, considerate, poised, wise and very rich, and whose first marriage left him with no children. Could she possibly make a better match?

VALERE That is true; but she might feel that you are rushing things somewhat, and that she at least needs time to develop feelings for this man that concur with...

HARPAGON This is an opportunity that calls for fast action. It's not every day that such an advantageous situation presents itself and, if he agrees to take her without a dowry...

VALERE Without a dowry?

HARPAGON Yes.

VALERE Ah! There is no argument against such reasonable terms. Therefore, I have nothing more to say.

HARPAGON This will save me a lot of money.

VALERE Assuredly, there is no denying that. It is true that your daughter may claim that marriage is nothing to take lightly, that it can result in a lifetime of happiness or misery, and that a commitment unto death must only be made with great precaution.

HARPAGON   Without a dowry!

VALERE   You are right. That is the determining factor; but there are people who contend that in such situations, a girl's feelings should be respected, and that a great disparity of age and temperament often leads to much dissension in a marriage.

HARPAGON   Without a dowry!

VALERE   Ah! A truly incontestable argument. Nevertheless, there are many fathers who are more concerned with their daughters' happiness than with the amount of the dowry---fathers who wouldn't sacrifice their daughters at the altar of money---fathers who strive for marriages where both parties are suited to each other and where an atmosphere of honor, tranquillity and joy might prevail, and...

HARPAGON   Without a dowry!

VALERE   That's true. There's no rebuttal to that. Without a dowry! An utterly irrefutable argument.

HARPAGON   (aside, looking at the garden) Aha! I think I hear a dog barking. Could someone be after my money? (To Valere) Stay right here; I'll be back in a moment. (Exit)

ELISE   Valere, did you mean what you said to him?

VALERE   What I said was meant to placate him, thereby furthering our cause; to contradict him would court disaster. With certain people, it is necessary to appear obsequious; any form of resistance, however logical and justified, would only aggravate their natural inflexibility. Therefore, when dealing with people of this nature, if you wish to achieve your ends, you must feign agreement with whatever they say, and...

ELISE   But this marriage, Valere?

VALERE   We'll find a way to stop it.

ELISE   But how can we, since it is to take place this
             evening?

VALERE   You must request a postponement and pretend to
             be ill.

ELISE   But if they call the doctors, they'll discover the
             pretense.

VALERE   You jest. What do doctors know? Come now,
             with them you can choose any sickness you wish
             and those idiots will come up with all sorts of
             reasons to explain its origin.

HARPAGON   **(aside)** It was nothing, thank God.

VALERE   In any event, we can always resort to flight,
             which will solve all our problems, and if your
             love, beautiful Elise, is sufficiently intense...**(he
             notices Harpagon)**. Yes, a daughter must obey
             her father. She must not concern herself with a
             husband's appearance; and when there is no
             dowry involved, she must accept whoever is
             offered.

HARPAGON   Excellently put, my boy!

VALERE   Sir, I most humbly beg your pardon for the
             liberty I took in speaking to your daughter as I
             did.

HARPAGON   How's that? I am delighted, and it is my wish
             that you have absolute power over her. **(to Elise)**
             No use trying to run away. I bestow upon him
             the authority that Heaven gave me over you, and
             you are to comply with his every wish.

VALERE   **(to Elise)** Did you hear that? Enough of your
             protests! **(to Harpagon)** Sir, I shall follow her
             constantly and continue to counsel her in this
             matter.

HARPAGON   Yes. I shall be much obliged. Assuredly...

VALERE   It's good to keep a tight rein on her.

HARPAGON   That is true. One must...

VALERE   Be not concerned, for I believe I shall succeed.
HARPAGON Go to it. I've some business in town, but I'll be
            back shortly.
VALERE   **(to Elise)** Yes, money is more precious than
            anything in the world, and you should thank
            Heaven for giving you such a wonderful father.
            He has a flawless sense of value. When one
            offers to take a daughter without a dowry, it is
            something to accept without hesitation, for the
            absence of a dowry takes precedence over
            beauty, youth, station, honor, wisdom, and
            integrity.
HARPAGON Spoken like a prophet! What a fine lad! Fortu-
            nate the man with a servant like this!

ACT II

Scene 1: Cleante, La Fleche

CLEANTE   Ah, you wretch! Where have you been hiding? Did I not order you to...?

LA FLECHE   Yes, sir, I came here and was waiting for you faithfully when your father, ungracious man that he is, drove me out threatening to beat me.

CLEANTE   What news have you of our business affair? The situation is more urgent than ever, for since our last meeting, I have learned that I have none other than my father as a rival.

LA FLECHE   Your father in love?

CLEANTE   Yes, and I had a devil of a time trying to conceal from him my shock at this news.

LA FLECHE   Him, meddling in love? Where the deuce did he get such a notion? Is this some type of joke? Is love anything for the likes of him?

CLEANTE   This passion of his must be some type of penance for my sins.

LA FLECHE   But why do you conceal from him your own love?

CLEANTE   I don't want to arouse his suspicions, and in order to prevent this marriage, I'd like to hold in reserve any course of action that might be needed. What answer did they give you?

LA FLECHE   In faith, sir, those who borrow are truly unfortunate and, when you are in the grip of usurers, as in your case, there are some rather strange things to which you must subject yourself.

CLEANTE   The deal will not go through?

LA FLECHE   I beg your pardon. Master Simon, the agent they gave us, an active and zealous man, says that he has done wonders for you, and he assured me that it was your face alone that won his confidence.

CLEANTE Will I have the fifteen thousand francs I am asking for?

LA FLECHE Yes, but under certain conditions that you must accept for the deal to go through.

CLEANTE Did you speak directly to the lender?

LA FLECHE Ah, that's not the way it's done. He is even more anxious to remain anonymous than you; in fact, the entire transaction is carried out in a manner more mysterious than you can imagine. Under no circumstance is his name ever to be mentioned; you are to meet with him in a house borrowed expressly for this purpose so that he might learn from you directly about your family and financial situation, and I do not doubt that your father's name alone will facilitate matters.

CLEANTE The inheritance of our deceased mother should also work in my favor.

LA FLECHE Here are some clauses that he dictated to our go-between that are to be shown to you as the first order of business: "Provided that the lender see all the securities of the borrower, and that the borrower be of age, and of a family whose wealth is ample, solid, secure and free of all encumbrance, a binding and precise document shall be drawn up by a notary of the highest repute, which notary shall be chosen by the lender."

CLEANTE That leaves nothing to be said.

LA FLECHE So as not to burden his conscience, the lender will loan the money at the legal rate of five and one-half percent interest.

CLEANTE Five and one-half percent? Good heavens, that's fair enough!

LA FLECHE That is true. "But since the said lender does not have at his disposal the sum in question, and since, to accommodate the borrower, he is obliged to borrow said sum from another party at the rate of twenty percent, it shall be agreed that the said first borrower shall pay this interest in addition to the rest, since it is only to oblige the first borrower, that the said lender is undertaking this loan."

CLEANTE What usurious monster are we dealing with here? That's more than twenty-five per cent!

LA FLECHE That's true. It is something you must consider.

CLEANTE What good would that do? I need the money, and I must consent to everything.

LA FLECHE That's the answer I gave him.

CLEANTE Is there anything else?

LA FLECHE Just one small article: "Of the fifteen thousand francs in question, the borrower will only receive twelve thousand in cash; as for the remaining three thousand, the borrower must accept the equivalent in used clothing, jewelry, and various miscellaneous items which are listed in the attached memorandum and for which the said lender has established the most moderate prices possible."

CLEANTE What does all that mean?

LA FLECHE Listen to the memorandum: "First, a four-poster bed, draped with Hungarian lace against a decorative backing of olive colored cloth, with six chairs and a matching counterpane lined with taffeta in shades of red and blue. The bed comes with a canopy of good Aumale serge in pale rose fringed in silk. All items mentioned are in very good condition."

CLEANTE And what am I to do with all that?

LA FLECHE Wait, there's more: "Plus a tapestry depicting the loves of Gombaud and Macée. Plus a large walnut table with twelve sculpted legs, which can be opened from either end and which comes with six stools."

CLEANTE What possible use...?

LA FLECHE Be patient. "Plus three large muskets inlaid with mother-of-pearl and their accompanying rests. Plus a brick furnace equipped with two retorts and three flasks, very useful for those with a bent for distilling."

CLEANTE This is too much!

LA FLECHE Gently now. "Plus a lute from Bologne furnished with nearly all of its strings. Plus a game of troll-madame, and a checkerboard with a game of goose restored from the Greeks, very suitable for whiling away leisure time. Plus one lizard skin, three and one-half feet long, stuffed with hay--a delightful curio to hang from the ceiling. The total value of all this actually amounts to four thousand five hundred francs; but, as a gesture of consideration, the lender is reducing the value to three thousand francs.

CLEANTE May the plague choke him with his "consideration", throat-cutting scoundrel that he is! Did anyone ever hear of such usury? You would think that the outrageous interest he's charging me would satisfy him...but no; he wants to extort an additional three thousand francs from me for some junk he's accumulated! Out of all that, I'm only getting two hundred crowns, and I've got to accept his terms for the scoundrel has a dagger at my throat.

LA FLECHE Now please don't take offense, sir, but you remind me of how Panurge went bankrupt-taking money in advance, buying dear and selling cheap and spending his money before he got it.

CLEANTE   What do you expect me to do? This is the level to which young people are reduced by the accursed avarice of fathers, and after such treatment, it's no wonder that sons relish the demise of their fathers.

LA FLECHE   Well, I must admit that the avarice of your father would infuriate the most complacent of men. However, unlike some of my friends, I am by nature a very cautious man and have assiduously avoided any form of financial transaction that might result in a confrontation with the hangman. But in your father's case, I am sorely tempted to ignore all precautions --for robbing him would not only be a source of personal gratification, it would also afford me the opportunity to perform an admirable service for mankind.

CLEANTE   Let me have another look at that cursed document.

Scene 2: Simon, Harpagon, Cleante, La Fleche

SIMON   Yes, sir, he's a man in such a financial bind that he will abide by any demands you might make of him.

HARPAGON   But are you certain, Master Simon, that there are no risks involved? Can you advise me of the name, financial status and family background of this party?

SIMON   No, there is nothing further I can say, for it is only by chance that I was referred to him. But he personally will answer any questions you may have, and his agent assures me that once you

know him you will be satisfied. All I can tell
you is that he comes from a very rich family,
that he has already suffered the loss of his
mother and, should you wish, he would guarantee that within eight months his father, too, will
go on to his reward.

HARPAGON There is something to that, for we are bound by
the dictates of charity to be of service to people
whenever the occasion arises.

SIMON That goes without saying.

LA FLECHE (softly, to Cleante) What's the meaning of this?
Our Master Simon speaking to your father?

CLEANTE (softly, to La Fleche) Has someone revealed to
him my identity? Are you capable of such a
treasonable act?

SIMON Aha! You're really rushing things, aren't you?
Who told you it was to be here in this house?
(To Harpagon) I'll have you know, sir, that it
was not I who revealed your name and place of
residence. But since you are both people of
discretion, I don't feel there is any harm done
and I don't see why the two of you can't settle
this affair directly.

HARPAGON How's that?

SIMON This is the gentleman who wishes to borrow the
fifteen thousand francs in question.

HARPAGON Aha! So you're the rogue given to such shameful extremes!

CLEANTE And you are the culprit responsible for these
shameful demands! (**Exit Simon and La Fleche**)

HARPAGON It's you who is trying to bankrupt himself by
such condemnable borrowing!

CLEANTE And it's you who enriches himself by such
criminal usury!

HARPAGON   How dare you show your face to me after that?

CLEANTE   How dare you show your face to anyone after that?

HARPAGON   Are you not ashamed to sink to such a level of irresponsibility? To rush headlong into such horrendous expenditures? And to dissipate so disgracefully the money earned by the sweat of your parents' brows?

CLEANTE   Are you not disturbed by the dishonor that your business tactics heap upon you? Doesn't it bother you to see your reputation destroyed by your insatiable lust for riches, by your infamous lending conditions which would put to shame the most diabolical of usurers?

HARPAGON   Away with you, rogue that you are! Be gone, I say!

CLEANTE   Who is the greater rogue, I ask you -- the one who borrows out of need, or he who steals without need?

HARPAGON   Withdraw from here, I tell you -- I'll hear no more of your insolence! **(Alone)** I'm rather glad this distasteful episode took place. It served as a warning to intensify my scrutiny of his every action.

Scene 3: Frosine, Harpagon

FROSINE   Sir...

HARPAGON   I'll be with you in a moment. **(Aside)** I must first check my money.

Scene 4: La Fleche, Frosine

LA FLECHE   **(Not seeing Frosine)** This entire affair is getting more comical by the moment. Somewhere he must have a warehouse amply stocked with all kinds of bric-a-brac, for there is nothing recognizable in the memorandum we have.

FROSINE Well, well, my poor La Fleche, what on earth brings you here?

LA FLECHE Why, hello Frosine, and what, might I ask, are you doing here?

FROSINE The same as I do everywhere: namely, serving those in need of a liaison. Since my celestial endowments are unfortunately limited to those of shrewdness and a flair for intrigue, I must utilize them to their fullest in order to survive in this world where one must live by one's wits.

LA FLECHE Are you conducting some business with the proprietor here?

FROSINE Yes. It's a small affair for which I expect payment.

LA FLECHE From him? It will take whatever guile you might possess to squeeze a sou out of him: I warn you that money does not flow freely in this household.

FROSINE There are ways and there are ways.

LA FLECHE Perhaps. After all, who am I but a mere valet? But I know Harpagon, the lord of this manor, and you as yet have been denied the pleasure. I tell you that of all humans, he is the least human, of all mortals, the most hardened and tightfisted. There is no service you might render that will gain access to his purse. Should you desire praise, esteem or benevolent lip-service, he's your man -- a veritable oasis -- his cup runneth over. But mention money, and you'll find yourself on arid ground -- he'd let you die of thirst. Nothing exceeds the hollowness of his gesture of goodwill, and his aversion for the word "give" is so great that he can never say "I give you my blessing", but rather "I lend you my blessing".

FROSINE   Come, come, I'm quite familiar with the art of cajoling men. I know the secret of winning their affection, of playing upon their vanity and of finding and exploiting their weaknesses.

LA FLECHE That will get you nowhere here. I defy you to wrangle a sou out of the party in question. Unflinchingly, he will watch you die rather than open his purse. In a word, he loves money more than reputation, honor, virtue, and he is revolted by the mere sight of a would-be borrower. To separate him from his money is to tear out his entrails, to thrust a dagger through his heart; and if...but here he comes; I must go.

Scene 5: Harpagon, Frosine

HARPAGON **(Aside)** All is well. **(To Frosine)** Well, Frosine, what can I do for you?

FROSINE   My, my, you look exceptionally well! A veritable picture of health.

HARPAGON Who, me?

FROSINE   Never have I seen you look so hale and hearty

HARPAGON Really?

FROSINE   I know some twenty-five year-olds who look older than you do.

HARPAGON Nevertheless, Frosine, I'm still a good sixty years old.

FROSINE   Come now, what's sixty years? Actually, you're at the prime of life, the mellowest phase of existence.

HARPAGON That's true, but I'd still like to shave off about twenty years.

FROSINE   That is hardly necessary, for with your constitution, you'll live to be a hundred.

HARPAGON   You think so?

FROSINE   Certainly. You have all the indications. Hold still for a moment. Yes, of course -- there it is right between your eyes, a sign of long life.

HARPAGON   Is this a specialty of yours?

FROSINE   Indeed it is. Show me your hand. Ah! Good heavens! What a life line!

HARPAGON   How's that?

FROSINE   Don't you see how far this line extends?

HARPAGON   And just what does that mean, pray tell?

FROSINE   A life span of a hundred years...but my feeling is that you'll reach one hundred twenty.

HARPAGON   Is that possible?

FROSINE   I tell you that it would take the knife of an assassin to terminate your earthly stay, and that you will have to bury not only your children, but your grandchildren as well.

HARPAGON   Splendid! What news have you of our little business matter?

FROSINE   Must you ask? Have you ever seen me involved in anything I did not successfully conclude? I am particularly gifted when it comes to matchmaking. The party does not exist for whom I could not readily find a suitable partner, and I believe that if I set my mind to it, I could pair off the Grand Turk with the Duomo of Venice. In your case, however, the difficulties were minimal. Since I have dealings with both ladies, I was in a position to tell them all about you. I advised the mother of your intentions regarding Mariane, which were prompted by your chance meetings with her on the street and by her window.

HARPAGON   And her answer was...

FROSINE   She received the proposal with joy, and when I expressed your strong desire to have Mariane attend the signing of your daughter's marriage contract this evening, she consented willingly and asked that I make the necessary arrangements.

HARPAGON   The fact is, Frosine, that I am obliged to give Anselme a dinner, and I would like to have Mariane share in the treat.

FROSINE   You are right. Her plans are to visit your daughter after lunch and then go to the fair; she will then return here for the dinner.

HARPAGON   Very well. I could then loan them my carriage so that they might go together.

FROSINE   That would do quite nicely.

HARPAGON   However, Frosine, have you discussed with the mother the matter of dowry? After all, when it comes to marrying off a daughter, she should realize her motherly obligation to impoverish herself, if necessary, to heighten her daughter's desirability.

FROSINE   How's that? We are discussing here a girl who will provide you with an income of twelve thousand francs.

HARPAGON   An income of twelve thousand francs!

FROSINE   Yes. First of all, she was raised in a household where expenditures on food were minimal. She is accustomed to a diet of salad, milk, cheese and apples; consequently, you will be spared the expense of fancy table service, exquisite consommés, endless recipes of peeled barley, as well as all the other delicacies that many women require. This alone will result in a substantial yearly saving on your part of at least three thousand francs. In addition, her tastes are extremely modest; she has little use for fancy clothes, expensive jewelry or sumptuous furnishings -- things to which other women are highly attracted. We have here an additional saving of more than four thousand francs. Furthermore, unlike her present-day counterpart, she has an intense dislike for gambling which enhances her virtue all the more, since I knew a woman in this town whose losses at card playing for this year alone amounted to twenty thousand francs. But let us be modest and assume that the average woman would expend one-fourth of that -- that is to say five thousand francs -- and let us determine what this means in terms of total yearly savings. First, there is the saving of three thousand francs on food, then the four thousand francs on clothes and diamonds, and finally the five thousand francs on gambling -- which comes to a grand total of twelve thousand francs!

HARPAGON   That's not bad; but your accounting is rather fanciful.

FROSINE   I beg your pardon, but is there nothing substantial in the acquisition through marriage of great sobriety, of the inheritance of a great love of simplicity in adornment, and of a great fund of hatred for gambling?

HARPAGON   I wish you would stop insulting my intelligence by speaking of a dowry consisting of expenses she will not incur. Speak to me instead of more tangible assets.

FROSINE   Good heavens, you'll have your fill of tangible assets, among which are included certain properties abroad to which you will have title.

HARPAGON   I'll believe that when I see it. However, Frosine, there is still something that troubles me. As you are aware, the girl is young, and as is usually the case with people of her age, she may prefer the company of her peers. I fear that a man of my advanced years might be distasteful to her. Such a situation in my house could occasion some rather irksome repercussions.

FROSINE   Ah! How little do you know of her! I realize that I have failed to advise you of still another unique facet of her personality. The young lady in question despises young people and is irresistibly attracted to the elderly.

HARPAGON   She?

FROSINE   Yes, she. I only wish you could hear her speak on that subject. She is revolted by the mere sight of a young man. Let her see, however, a handsome, mature gentleman with a majestic beard and her pulse quickens with delight. The older they are the more charming she finds them, and I warn you not to try to present yourself as being younger than you are for she will consider no one who is not at least sixty. Did you know that less than four months ago she called off a marriage at the very last minute upon learning that her suitor was only fifty-six years old and could sign the marriage contract without the use of spectacles?

HARPAGON   Just because of that?

FROSINE   Yes. She contends that she could never be happy with a man of fifty-six, especially if he doesn't wear eye glasses.

HARPAGON   I find what you say most extraordinary.

FROSINE   More extraordinary than you might think. In her bedroom there are some pictures and prints, and what do you think they are? Adomises, Cephaluses, Parises and Apollos? Not at all. They are instead fine portraits of Saturn, of King Priam, of old Nestor, and of good father Anchises on the shoulders of his son.

HARPAGON That is truly admirable! Never would I have supposed such a thing, and I'm delighted to learn that she is thus inclined. Indeed, were I a young woman, I wouldn't like young men either.

FROSINE I believe it. Young men are not worthy of a woman's love. They're nothing but pretentious bumpkins who strut about with woefully exaggerated notions of their irresistibility. How any woman could derive pleasure from such company, I am at a loss to explain.

HARPAGON My sentiments exactly; and yet there are women for whom they hold a fatal attraction.

FROSINE They are either mad or devoid of common sense. How could such young fops be classified as men? How could a woman seek any form of attachment with such base creatures?

HARPAGON This is what I say every day with their girlish ways, their three strands of turned up cat whiskers they call a mustache, their cottony wigs, their droopy breeches unbuttoned at the stomach!

FROSINE How ludicrous do they appear when compared to a man like you. Your mode of dress and overall appearance would devastate any woman alive.

HARPAGON Am I really that attractive?

FROSINE Why, you're absolutely irresistible, I tell you! Just look at that face...an artist's dream! Turn that way, if you please. Perfect! Let me see you walk. What an excellent physical specimen! Such stature, such fluidity of movement...the veritable quintessence of masculine charm.

HARPAGON Aside from my occasional fits of coughing, I do pretty well, thank you.

FROSINE Even your coughing has a certain charm about it.

HARPAGON Tell me, has Mariane seen me yet?

FROSINE No, but in the course of our discussion, I described you in great detail, and emphasized the advantages of marrying a man of your merits.

HARPAGON You did well, and I thank you for it.

FROSINE Sir, there's a small favor I'd like to ask of you. **(Harpagon frowns)** I'm involved in a lawsuit that I'm about to lose because of a shortage of funds. However, were you to be gracious enough to extend a helping hand in this matter, I could easily win the case...You can't imagine how pleased she'll be to see you. **(Harpagon smiles)** How irresistible will you appear to her, especially with that old-fashioned ruff of yours. But what will dazzle her the most are your breeches, attached as they are to your doublet with laces. One look at those laced-up breeches and she will be yours!

HARPAGON I'm delighted to hear this.

FROSINE In truth, sir, this lawsuit is of extreme importance to me. **(Harpagon frowns)** If I lose it, I shall be ruined, and all it would take to rectify matters is just a small measure of assistance, and ....er ....Ah, if you could only have seen how delighted she was to hear me speak of you. **(Harpagon smiles)** When I spoke of your qualities, her eyes glowed with joy, and consequently, she is extremely impatient to marry you.

HARPAGON You have made me very happy, Frosine, and I must admit that I am most indebted to you.

FROSINE I beseech you, sir, to give me the little assistance I ask of you. **(Harpagon frowns)** It would put me back on my feet and I would be extremely grateful to you.

HARPAGON Goodbye. I've got some letters to write.

FROSINE I assure you, sir, that you could never help me out of a greater difficulty.

HARPAGON I shall order my carriage to take you to the fair.

FROSINE I would not impose upon you were I not forced to.

HARPAGON And I'll see that dinner is served early to spare you any hunger pangs.

FROSINE Please don't refuse me the favor I ask...You can't believe the pleasure...

HARPAGON I've got to go. Someone's calling me. See you later.

FROSINE **(Alone)** May the fever send you choking to Hell, wretched dog that you are! That skinflint has held firm against all my attacks, but I'll not give up that easily, for there is another course of action that will most assuredly lead to a more rewarding conclusion.

ACT III

Scene 1: Harpagon, Cleante, Elise, Valere, Dame Claudia, Jacques, Brindavoine, La Merluche

HARPAGON   All right, everyone gather round for his assignment this evening. Come here, Claudia, we'll begin with you. **(Claudia is holding a broom)** Good, I see you're armed and ready. Your task is to clean everywhere, and you are to be especially careful not to rub the furniture too hard for fear of wearing it out. In addition, I'm placing you in charge of the bottles during the dinner service; if one is missing or broken, I'll hold you responsible and will deduct it from your wages.

JACQUES   **(Aside)** A suitable punishment.

HARPAGON   Off you go. **(Exit Claudia)** You, Brindavoine, and you, La Merluche, will be in charge of rinsing the glasses and serving the drinks, but you are to do so only when the guests are thirsty. Despite the custom of certain impertinent lackeys, I'll not have you coaxing my guests into drinking a drop more than they wish. Finally, don't serve anyone until he's asked you more than once, and make doubly sure that there's always plenty of water available.

JACQUES   **(Aside)** Yes, pure wine goes to your head.

MERLUCHE   Do we take off our aprons, sir?

HARPAGON   Yes, when the guests arrive -- but make sure you don't spoil your clothes.

BRIND'INE   You know, sir, that one of the front flaps of my doublet is covered with a big spot of lamp oil.

MERLUCHE   And me, sir, I got a big hole in the backside of my breeches and, no disrespect, sir, but people can see my....

HARPAGON   Enough! **(to La Merluche)** Be clever; walk so that your backside always faces the wall. **(Harpagon places his hat in front of his doublet to show Brindavoine how to conceal the oil spot)** And you, always hold your hat like this when you serve. **(To Elise)** And as for you, my daughter, you will watch as they clear the table and see that nothing is wasted. That's a suitable task for a daughter. You will now prepare to greet my fiancee, who will be visiting you and taking you with her to the fair. Have you understood my instructions?

ELISE   Yes, father.

HARPAGON   And as for you, my fine fop of a son, I shall graciously forgive your behavior of a while ago, but I will not tolerate any more of those sullen looks.

CLEANTE   I, father, sullen looks? And for what reason?

HARPAGON   Good heavens, we all know how children feel when the father remarries, and the jaundiced eye with which they behold their step-mother; but if you want me to forget your latest offense, I strongly advise you to greet her as cordially as you can. I want smiles, not frowns.

CLEANTE   To tell you the truth, father, I find it difficult to adjust to the idea of her becoming my step-mother; I would be lying if I told you otherwise. However, you have my word that I shall receive her most cordially, and that there will be a continual smile on my face.

HARPAGON   I shall hold you to that.

CLEANTE   You will have no grounds for complaint.

HARPAGON   I'd better not. Valere, help me with this. And, oh yes, come here Jacques, I saved you for the last.

JACQUES   Are you addressing me as your coachman or as your cook, sir, for both jobs are mine.

HARPAGON   As both.

JACQUES   But which one in particular?

HARPAGON   As my cook.

JACQUES   Then wait, please. **(He removes his coachman's coat and appears dressed as a cook.)**

HARPAGON   What the deuce was that all about?

JACQUES   I await your orders.

HARPAGON   I am committed to giving a dinner this evening, Jacques.

JACQUES   **(Aside)** Do my ears deceive me?

HARPAGON   Tell me, will you prepare a fancy dinner?

JACQUES   Yes, if you give me lots of money.

HARPAGON   Blast it all! Always money! Is there nothing else to say? Money, money, money! They're always mouthing the same word...MONEY Always the same topic...MONEY! It's their protective weapon...MONEY!

VALERE   Never have I heard a more impertinent response. What skill is there in preparing a fancy meal with plenty of money? Any simpleton could accomplish that. It's the ability to prepare a fancy meal with little money that determines the true measure of a cook.

JACQUES   A fancy meal with little money.

VALERE   Yes.

JACQUES   In faith, Mr. Steward, I would be deeply obliged to you if you would tell me the secret of how that is done. Since you seem to know everything about everything, perhaps you'd like to take over my job as cook.

HARPAGON   Hold your tongue! What do we need?

JACQUES   You'll need your steward here, who says he can prepare a fancy meal with little money.

HARPAGON Enough I want you to answer me!

JACQUES How many will we have to feed?

HARPAGON Eight or ten; but you must count on eight, for when there is food for eight, there's food for ten.

VALERE Of course.

JACQUES Well, we'll need four large soups and five courses...Soups...entrees...

HARPAGON What the devil! You're talking as though we're feeding an entire town.

JACQUES Roasts...

HARPAGON (Covering Jacques' mouth with his hand) Ah, traitor! You're eating everything I have!

JACQUES Side dishes...

HARPAGON Still?

VALERE Are you planning to burst their stomachs? It is not our master's intent to have his guests gorge themselves to death. You really ought to familiarize yourself with the rules of good health. As any doctor will tell you, there is no greater detriment to health than the act of over-eating; thus, the more frugal the meals you serve, the more friendship you display. To quote an ancient philosopher, one must eat to live, and not live to eat.

HARPAGON Beautifully put, my lad! Come here and let me hug you. Never have I heard a more beautiful sentence: "One must live to eat, and not eat to li..." No, that's not it...How does it go again?

VALERE "One must eat to live and not live to eat."

HARPAGON Yes, yes! Did you hear that? Who's the great man who said that?

VALERE The name escapes me for the moment.

HARPAGON Remember to put these words in writing, for I'm going to have them engraved in gold letters on the mantelpiece in my dining room.

VALERE Certainly, and with regard to the dinner, I shall assume full responsibility. Leave everything to me.

HARPAGON Go to it.

JACQUES That's even better -- less work for me.

HARPAGON You must select foods that are very filling, like a fatty mutton stew and a potted pie stuffed with chestnuts. That'll cut their appetites at the outset.

VALERE Rely on me.

HARPAGON Now, Jacques, you must clean my carriage.

JACQUES Wait a minute. You're now speaking to me as your coachman. **(He puts his coat on again.)** You were saying...?

HARPAGON I was saying that my carriage must be cleaned, and that my horses must be readied for the trip to the fair.

JACQUES Your horses, sir? In faith, they're hardly in any condition to walk. Mind you, I'm not saying that they're sick, it's just that you've been putting them on such severe fasts that they look more like scarecrows than horses.

HARPAGON They must be sick. They lie about doing nothing!

JACQUES Even if they do nothing, sir, they've still got to eat. It would be better for those poor beasts to have more work to do and to get fed for it. It breaks my heart to see their ribs stick out as they do, for I really like my horses. When I see them suffer, I suffer with them. Every day I feed them out of my own mouth because nice people should have pity on their fellow creatures.

HARPAGON Having them walk to the fair won't strain them that much.

JACQUES No, no. I don't have the courage to drive them there. I wouldn't have the heart to whip them in their condition. How could they drag a carriage when they can hardly drag themselves?

VALERE Sir, I shall ask our neighbor, Le Picard, to drive them there, and we could also call upon him to serve in the preparation of the dinner.

JACQUES So be it. If anyone's going to kill them, I'd rather it not be me.

VALERE Jacques is acting very reasonable.

JACQUES Our good steward is acting very indispensable.

HARPAGON Enough of this!

JACQUES Sir, if there's one thing I can't stand it's a back-scratcher. He don't fool me with all his checking on the bread, wine, wood, salt and candles. All that's just to get on your good side. He makes me mad, he does, and I also get mad when I hear the things people say about you every day. For in spite of everything, I still happen to like you...in fact, I would say that I like you more than anyone else in the world...after my horses, of course.

HARPAGON Of course, but may I ask you, Jacques, just what it is that people say of me?

JACQUES Yes, sir, if I was sure that you would not get mad at me.

HARPAGON In no way.

JACQUES I beg to differ, sir, for I know you will get mad.

HARPAGON Not at all. On the contrary, it would give me great pleasure to learn how they speak of me.

JACQUES All right, sir, since you insist. I shall tell you frankly that you are the laughing-stock of the neighborhood. Everywhere I go I hear people making jokes about your stinginess. Some say that you have special almanacs printed where the days of fasting are doubled, thereby cutting down on your food bills. There are others who say that at New Year's, or at any other time for gift-giving, you always have a quarrel ready so that you can send people packing empty-handed. There is a man who says that you brought your neighbor's cat to court for having eaten the remains of a leg of lamb. Another man says that he caught you stealing oats out of the mouths of your own horses, and that your previous coachman, not recognizing you in the dark, whacked the daylights out of you. They say you don't like to talk about this incident, and I can't say that I blame you. In short, sir, you are the butt of everyone's jokes, and the only words I hear to describe you are "miser", "skinflint", "money-grubber" and "usurer".

HARPAGON   **(Beating him)** And you, sir, are a fool, a rogue, a scamp and an impudent numbskull!

JACQUES   Ouch! I told you that you'd get mad at the truth and that you wouldn't believe me.

HARPAGON   I'll teach you to speak properly!

Scene 2: Jacques, Valere

VALERE   From where I stand, Jacques, you paid dearly for your frankness. **(Laughing)**

JACQUES   Mind your own business! You just started work here and already you're trying to take over. Laugh at your own beatings and not mine.

VALERE   Ah, Jacques, please don't be angry, I beseech you. **(trying to restrain his laughter.)**

JACQUES	(aside) He's sweet-talking me. I'm going to act tough and if he's fool enough to fall for it, I'll give him a little beating. (Aloud) Have you noticed, Mr. Laughingboy, that I don't find this funny at all, and that if you make me mad enough, I'll give you something that will really make you howl. (Jacques pushes Valere to the end of the stage in a threatening fashion.)
VALERE	Ah, gently now.
JACQUES	What do you mean "gently"? You get on my nerves, you do.
VALERE	I beseech you.
JACQUES	And I don't like your impertinence.
VALERE	Sir Jacques!
JACQUES	Don't give me any of that "sir" business. I've a good mind to pick up a stick and give you a sound thrashing.
VALERE	What's that you say? A stick? (Valere now pushes Jacques to opposite end of stage)
JACQUES	Eh? Well, I really didn't mean a stick.
VALERE	I'll have you know, Sir Numbskull, that I'm quite capable of using a stick on you.
JACQUES	Without a doubt.
VALERE	And as far as cooks go, you are among the worst.
JACQUES	I certainly am.
VALERE	You still know nothing about me.
JACQUES	I certainly don't
VALERE	You'd thrash me, would you?
JACQUES	It was only in jest.
VALERE	Your manner of jest does not please me. (Valere-starts beating Jacques with a stick) This will teach you to do so with more finesse. (Valere exits)

JACQUES To hell with the truth...it hurts too much. From now on, you'll never hear a word of it from me. What right does that high-falutin steward have to beat me? He's not my master. He'd better watch his step, for the first chance I get, I'll make him pay.

Scene 3: Frosine, Mariane, Jacques

FROSINE Is the master at home, Jacques?
JACQUES I'll say he is!!
FROSINE Please tell him that we are here.

Scene 4: Mariane, Frosine

MARIANE Ah, Frosine, I feel very strange coming here, and I shudder at what I'm about to see.
FROSINE Why? What disturbs you?
MARIANE Alas! How can you ask? Have you no understanding of the terror that precedes the moment of torture?
FROSINE I understand that Harpagon is not your preferred source of torture, and from the expression on your face, I can tell that the blond youngster of whom you spoke is definitely on your mind.
MARIANE Yes, Frosine, I'll not deny it. In the course of his respectful visits to our home, I have come to regard him tenderly.
FROSINE But do you know who he is?
MARIANE No, I don't. But there is an attractiveness about him that would make me choose him above all others, were I to have my choice. Imagine my torment, Frosine, when I compare him with the man they wish to foist upon me.

FROSINE   Good heavens! I admit that those pretty boys have their charm and have a way with words; however, most of them are poor as church mice and could never provide for you as would a rich, older man. I am aware of the sensual deprivation and the other distasteful things you would have to endure with an older husband, but that would only be for a short time. Once he dies, you'll be free to choose whomever you like.

MARIANE   What a strange state of affairs! Having to wait until someone dies to be happy...and since when does death always conform to our wishes?

FROSINE   Are you serious? You shall marry him only on condition that you be widowed shortly. This must definitely be stipulated in the contract. How impertinent it would be on his part not to die within three months! Here he comes in the flesh.

MARIANE   Ah, Frosine! Just look at that face!

Scene 5: Harpagon, Frosine, Mariane

HARPAGON   Please don't be offended, my beauty, if I appear before you wearing my spectacles. I know that your charms are so striking, so visible unto themselves that one hardly needs spectacles to perceive them; but, after all, it is with lenses that one observes the stars, and I assure you that you are indeed a star, the most beautiful of stars in the universe of stars...Frosine, she does not answer me, and she doesn't seem to be very pleased to see me.

FROSINE   It's just that she's still in a state of surprise; besides, girls are always reluctant to express at first hand what they feel in their hearts.

HARPAGON   You're right. There now, my pretty one. Here comes my daughter to greet you.

Scene 6:   Elise, Harpagon, Mariane, Frosine

MARIANE   Kindly excuse my delay in visiting you, Madame.

ELISE   It is I who should ask pardon for not having visited you first.

HARPAGON   See what a big girl she is; but, then again, weeds always do grow fast.

MARIANE   **(Aside to Frosine)** Oh, how he revolts me!

HARPAGON   What did that beauty say?

FROSINE   That she finds you truly admirable.

HARPAGON   You do me too much honor, my adorable morsel.

MARIANE   **(Aside)** What an animal!

HARPAGON   I am much obliged to you for these sentiments.

MARIANE   **(Aside)** I can't stand this any longer.

HARPAGON   Here, too, is my son, who comes to pay his respects.

MARIANE   **(Softly to Frosine)** Ah, Frosine! There he is in the flesh! The man of whom I spoke!

FROSINE   **(To Mariane)** A marvelous turn of events.

HARPAGON   I see that you are astonished that my children should be so grown-up; but don't worry, I'll soon be rid of them both.

Scene 7:   Cleante, Harpagon, Elise, Mariane, Frosine

CLEANTE   Madam, I can assure you that this is a most unexpected encounter. I was also surprised somewhat earlier when my father advised me of his intentions.

FROSINE   I share in your surprise...I was not prepared for this.

CLEANTE   Truly, my father could not have made a better choice, and I am deeply pleased and honored to see you. However, I must admit that I derive little pleasure from the prospect of having you as a step-mother. It would be difficult for me to wish such a title on you. There are some who might be offended by the brutal frankness of what I am saying, but I am sure I can rely on your understanding nature. The fact is, Madame, that the very thought of this marriage repulses me. You cannot fail to realize, Madame, the destructive impact this will have upon me. Indeed, with my father's permission, I would like to say that were it up to me, this marriage would never take place.

HARPAGON   Just listen to the impertinence of that compliment. What a beautiful confession, indeed, to make to her.

MARIANE   And may I say, in turn, that the thought of having you as my step-son is no less repugnant to me than my being your step-mother is to you; that I would never willingly cause you the slightest distress, and that this marriage that grieves you thus would never take place were I not bound to it by an absolute power.

HARPAGON   She is right... one stupid compliment deserves another. I beg your pardon, my beauty, for my son's impertinence. He's a young fool, too stupid to realize the effect of what he says.

MARIANE   I found nothing offensive in what he said. On the contrary, I enjoyed hearing him express his true feelings. Were he not to have done so, my respect for him would have diminished.

HARPAGON   It's so good of you to excuse his faults. He's young and foolish now, but in time he'll grow wiser.

CLEANTE   No, father. It's not in me to change, and I implore Madame to believe me.

HARPAGON   Listen to that crazy ranting. He gets worse and worse.

CLEANTE   Would you rather have me betray my heart?

HARPAGON   Enough! You'll speak no more of this.

CLEANTE   Very well, since you wish that I change the subject, allow me to serve as my father's spokesman and confess that I have never known anyone as charming as you, that nothing makes me more happy than the opportunity to please you, and that the joy of being your husband would excel that of being the greatest prince on earth. Yes, Madame, to possess you would be the ultimate ecstasy, and for such a conquest there is nothing I wouldn't or couldn't do, no obstacle I could not surmount, no ...

HARPAGON   Gently now, my son, if you please.

CLEANTE   I'm only complimenting her on your behalf.

HARPAGON   I have my own tongue to express myself, and I don't need you as an intermediary. Quickly now, **(to the servants)** some chairs.

FROSINE   No. It would be preferable to leave now for the fair so that we'll return early enough for a lengthy discussion.

HARPAGON   **(To the servants)** Harness the horses to the carriage. Please excuse me, my beauty, for neglecting to provide you with some refreshment before leaving.

CLEANTE   That's already been arranged, father. I'm having some mandarin oranges, sweet lemons and preserves sent up on your behalf.

HARPAGON (Aside to Valere) Valere!

VALERE (To Harpagon) He's lost his senses.

CLEANTE Do you feel that I should have offered more, father? I'm sure Madame will graciously overlook my error.

MARIANE That really wasn't necessary.

CLEANTE Just look at that ring my father is wearing on his finger, Madame. Have you ever seen a diamond shine like that?

MARIANE It certainly does sparkle.

CLEANTE (Removing it from his father's finger and giving it to Mariane) You must look at it closely.

MARIANE Such marvelous reflections! It's truly beautiful.

CLEANTE (Stands in front of Mariane, who tries to return it) No, Madame, your hands form too beautiful a setting. Keep it as a gift from my father.

HARPAGON From me??

CLEANTE Is it not true, father, that you wish to give it to her as a token of your love?

HARPAGON (Aside to Cleante) How's that?

CLEANTE A fine question, indeed. (To Mariane) He's gesturing his approval.

MARIANE I don't want to...

CLEANTE You jest, Madame. He wouldn't dream of taking it back.

HARPAGON (Aside) This is outrageous!

MARIANE But this would be...

CLEANTE (Still preventing Mariane from returning the ring) No, I tell you, you would offend him.

MARIANE Please...

CLEANTE In no way.

HARPAGON (Aside) May the plague...

CLEANTE   Just look how you have wounded him by your refusal.

HARPAGON   **(Aside to Cleante)** Ah! Traitor!

CLEANTE   Now he's getting desperate.

HARPAGON   **(Aside to Cleante in menacing tones)** Conniving brigand that you are!

CLEANTE   It's not my fault, father. I'm doing my best to convince her to keep it, but she's very obstinate.

HARPAGON   **(Aside to Cleante furiously)** Scoundrel!

CLEANTE   It's because of you that my father is cross with me.

HARPAGON   **(Aside to Cleante, maintaining his fury)** Rogue!

CLEANTE   Resist no more, Madame, I beseech you, lest you make him ill.

FROSINE   Good heavens, why such ceremony? Keep the ring and make him happy.

MARIANE   Very well. Since I have no wish to upset you, I shall accept the ring, but only temporarily.

Scene 8: Harpagon, Mariane, Frosine, Cleante, Brindavoine, Elise

BRIND'INE   Sir, there's a man out there who'd like to speak to you.

HARPAGON   Tell him I'm busy and to come some other time.

BRIND'INE   He says that he's got some money for you.

HARPAGON   Excuse me. I'll be right back.

Scene 9: Harpagon, Mariane, Cleante, Elise, Frosine, La Merluche, Valere

MERLUCHE   **(Enters running and topples Harpagon)** Sir...

HARPAGON   Ah!. I'm dying!

CLEANTE   What is it, father? Did you hurt yourself?

HARPAGON   I'll wager anything that my debtors paid that traitor to make me break my neck.

VALERE   No cause for alarm.

HARPAGON   What are you doing here, you assassin?

MERLUCHE   I'm here to tell you that both your horses have lost their shoes.

HARPAGON   Bring them to the smithy at once.

CLEANTE   While they're being shod, father, I'll do the household honors for you and escort Madame to the garden, where I'll have the refreshments served.

HARPAGON   Valere, see that he serves as sparingly as possible, and send back whatever you can to the food merchant.

VALERE   Understood. **(Exits)**

HARPAGON   **(Alone)** Impertinent son that you are Do you want to bankrupt me?

ACT IV

Scene 1: Cleante, Mariane, Elise, Frosine

CLEANTE   Let us return here where we can speak freely.

ELISE   Yes, Madame, my brother has spoken to me of his love for you, and I'm familiar with the anguish that such an obstacle can engender. You may be assured of my extreme interest and concern.

MARIANE   How consoling it is to have the support of a person like you. I pray that I'll always have your friendship to rely on when fortune frowns upon me.

FROSINE   It's unfortunate that you did not consult me before this. I could have certainly avoided this unpleasant turn of events.

CLEANTE   To what end? This is my cruel destiny; but in any event, my beautiful Mariane, what have you decided?

MARIANE   Alas! My state of subservience does not allow for any decision on my part. All I can do is wish.

CLEANTE   Is wishing the only solace your heart can offer? No assuaging pity? No helpful kindness? No relieving affection?

MARIANE   What can I say? Were you in my position, you would comprehend the futility of my situation. Advise me. Command me. I place myself in your hands, for I know that you would never suggest anything that would compromise my honor or my sense of propriety.

CLEANTE   Alas! Why must I always be constrained by the dictates of honor and propriety?

MARIANE   What would you have me do? Even if I were inclined to ignore the restrictions imposed upon those of my sex, I still have my mother to consider. She raised me with extreme kindness, and I could never displease her. You, however, have my permission to do your utmost to win her over. Do and say whatever you must, and should the situation demand that I reveal to her my love for you, I shall do so freely.

CLEANTE Frosine, my poor Frosine, would you help us?

FROSINE With the greatest of pleasure. When it comes to serving love's true cause, I'm really quite sentimental. How may I be of service?

CLEANTE Think of something, I beseech you.

MARIANE Show us a way out of this.

CLEANTE Find a way to undo what you have wrought.

FROSINE This will pose quite a challenge. **(To Mariane)** Since your mother is not a totally unreasonable person, I may be able to persuade her to transfer to the son the gift she planned for the father. **(To Cleante)** However, the problem stems from the fact that your father is none other than your father.

CLEANTE I understand.

FROSINE What I mean is that to reject him is to incur his wrath, and this would hardly incline him to consent to your marriage. Therefore, we must find a way to have you appear less desirable in his eyes so that it will be he, and not you, who does the rejecting.

CLEANTE You are right.

FROSINE Yes, I know, but the problem is how to go about it. Wait! Suppose we found an older woman with a talent equivalent to mine, capable of playing the role of a lady of quality. For the sake of believability, she could engage a quickly improvised retinue and adopt some exotic title, such as Marchioness or Viscountess, and could originate from, let us say, lower Brittany...I could then easily convince your father that she is a woman of enormous wealth, hopelessly in love with him, and willing to transfer all her possessions to him in a contract of marriage. I am certain that your father would be receptive to such a proposal, for his love of money surpasses his love for you. Subsequently, after he takes the bait and provides you with the consent you seek, it matters little what he does upon learning the true worth of a "Marchioness".

CLEANTE   A thoroughly ingenuous plan!

FROSINE   Let me handle this. I've just thought of a friend of mine who'll make a perfect marchioness.

CLEANTE   If your plan succeeds, Frosine, I'll be deeply grateful to you. However, my charming Mariane, preventing this marriage will be no small task, and you must do what you can from your end. You can begin by trying to win your mother over to our side. Make liberal use of the eloquent graciousness, the irresistibility that Heaven has placed in your eyes and lips, and take care not to forget those harmonious words, those gentle bequests and those endearing caresses which can never be denied.

MARIANE   I'll do whatever I can and shall forget nothing.

Scene 2: Harpagon, Cleante, Mariane, Elise, Frosine

HARPAGON   **(Aside and still unseen)** Aha! My son kisses the hand of his future stepmother, and she does little to discourage it. Is there more to this than meets the eye?

ELISE   There's my father.

HARPAGON The carriage is ready. You may leave when you wish.
CLEANTE Since you're not going, father, I'll take them myself.
HARPAGON No. You stay. They can go quite nicely by themselves; besides, I have need of you. **(The ladies exit.)**

Scene 3: Harpagon, Cleante

HARPAGON Aside from the fact that she's to be your step-mother, what have you to say of the lady?
CLEANTE What have I to say?
HARPAGON Yes, of her manner, her figure, her beauty, her intelligence.
CLEANTE They'll do, I guess.
HARPAGON Nothing more than that?
CLEANTE To speak frankly, she fell far short of my expectations. I find her demeanor blatantly coquettish, her figure ill-proportioned, her facial attributes mediocre, and her wit far from spectacular. However, you must not feel that I'm trying to downgrade her in your eyes, for as far as step-mothers go, I suppose I like this one as well as I would any other.
HARPAGON But you were just saying to her that...
CLEANTE I was speaking gallantly on your behalf merely to please you.
HARPAGON You are, therefore, not attracted to her?
CLEANTE I? In no way.
HARPAGON I'm sorry to hear that, for it spoils an idea that came to me when she was here. Looking at her, I became painfully aware of the difference in our ages, and got to thinking about what people would say about my marrying such a youngster.

I was about to give up the whole idea, but since
I had already pledged my word, I decided to
have her marry you instead. But now with this
aversion you have for her, I don't...

CLEANTE   You'd give her to me?

HARPAGON Yes, to you.

CLEANTE   In marriage?

HARPAGON Yes, in marriage.

CLEANTE   Hear me; while it is true that I don't find her
terribly attractive, I would somehow force
myself to marry her, if only to please you, my
dear father.

HARPAGON No, no. I'll derive no pleasure in forcing you
into this, for I'm not as unreasonable as you
might think.

CLEANTE   But I'd gladly make this sacrifice out of love for
you.

HARPAGON No, no; without love, no marriage is happy.

CLEANTE   But that's something that may come with time,
for it is said that love is often a fruit of marriage.

HARPAGON No, no. From a man's standpoint, it's a risky
business that could lead to much unpleasantness.
If you loved her, so be it, I'd have let you marry
her; but since you don't, I'll stick to my original
plan and marry her myself.

CLEANTE   Well, father, I am compelled by the present turn
of events to inform you that I have loved Mariane at first sight, and were it not for your feelings
toward her and my fear of displeasing you, I
would have already asked for your consent to
marry her.

HARPAGON Have you visited her?

CLEANTE   Yes, father.

HARPAGON Several times?

CLEANTE	Rather frequently, considering the short time I've known her.
HARPAGON	Were you well received?
CLEANTE	Very well; but they did not know who I was, which accounts for Mariane's surprise a moment ago.
HARPAGON	Have you declared your love for her and your intention to marry her?
CLEANTE	Of course, and I even broached the subject with her mother.
HARPAGON	And did she listen to your intentions concerning her daughter?
CLEANTE	Yes, very civilly.
HARPAGON	And does the daughter love you in return?
CLEANTE	Judging from appearances, I am convinced that she cares for me.
HARPAGON	**(Aside)** Aha! Just what I wanted -- to worm that secret out of him. **(To Cleante)** My son, there are three things you must do: first, purge yourself of this love; second, you must discontinue the courtship of a lady whom I claim for myself; and finally, you must get married soon to a girl chosen for you.
CLEANTE	So this was all a little game you were playing with me. Very well, father, since this is how things stand, I shall tell you flatly that I will never renounce my love for Mariane, that I shall stop at nothing to prevent your having her, despite the mother's consent that you possess.
HARPAGON	How's that, impertinent wretch that you are, you'd dare to intrude in my domain?
CLEANTE	It is you who are intruding in mine, for it is I who knew her first.
HARPAGON	Am I not your father? And do you not owe me respect?

CLEANTE   Love reigns supreme even over a father's authority.

HARPAGON   Yes, and I'll rain some supremely fine blows on your head!

CLEANTE   All your threats will be to no avail.

HARPAGON   You shall give up Mariane!

CLEANTE   Never!

HARPAGON   **(To Jacques)** Fetch me a stick immediately!

Scene 4: Jacques, Harpagon, Cleante

JACQUES   Now, now, gentlemen. What is all the commotion?

CLEANTE   To hell with his stick.

JACQUES   Ah, sir, gently now.

HARPAGON   How dare he address me with such impudence?

JACQUES   **(To Harpagon)** Ah, sir, I beseech you.

CLEANTE   I will not yield an inch.

JACQUES   How's that? To your father?

HARPAGON   Let me at him.

JACQUES   How's that? At your son?

HARPAGON   Jacques, to show how right I am in this matter, I'll let you be the judge.

JACQUES   I agree. **(To Cleante)** Move back a little.

HARPAGON   I love a girl whom I wish to marry, and this scoundrel has the audacity to love her, too, and to seek her hand in marriage despite my orders.

JACQUES   Ah, he is wrong.

HARPAGON   Is it not a shameful display of disrespect for a son to compete with his father in a matter of love?

JACQUES   Without a doubt. Stay here and let me speak to him. **(Crosses to Cleante)**

CLEANTE   If he wants you to act as judge, so be it, for I care little whom he might choose.

JACQUES	You do me too much honor, sir.
CLEANTE	I am in love with a young lady who returns my affection most tenderly. My father, however, intends to destroy our affair by claiming for himself the hand of the lady in question.
JACQUES	He is most assuredly wrong.
CLEANTE	Should he not be ashamed at his age to think of marriage? Is it appropriate for a relic like him to be in love? Should he not leave affairs of the heart to the young?
JACQUES	You are right. He can't be serious. Let me have a word with him. **(He returns to Harpagon)** Well, your son is not as strange as you say, and he is acting most reasonably. He says that he is aware of the respect he owes you, and he regrets his prior outburst of anger. He is now willing to submit to your demands, provided you treat him better than previously and provide him with a marriage partner to his liking.
HARPAGON	Ah! Well, in that case, Jacques, tell him that he can expect anything from me and that, with the exception of Mariane, he can marry anyone he wants.
JACQUES	Let me handle this. **(Cross to Cleante)** Well, now, your father is far less unreasonable than you make him out to be. He told me that it was your outbursts that angered him, and were it not for the way you act, he would be far more receptive to your requests. You must treat him more civilly and display the respect and submissiveness that a son owes his father.
CLEANTE	Ah! Jacques, you can assure him that if he gives me Mariane, I will be the most submissive of men and would never do anything against his will.

JACQUES   **(To Harpagon)** It is done. He agrees to everything you say.

HARPAGON   Excellent!

JACQUES   **(To Cleante)** Everything is settled. He is satisfied with your promises.

CLEANTE   Heaven be praised!

JACQUES   Gentlemen, your previous quarreling was due to
a misunderstanding on both your parts. Howev-
er, now that you are in agreement, the way is
cleared for amicable discussion.

CLEANTE   Jacques, all my life I will be indebted to you for
this.

JACQUES   Your servant, sir.

HARPAGON   Jacques, you have pleased me greatly, and for
that you deserve a reward. **(He reaches into his
pocket, giving Jacques the impression that he
is about to receive something. All that emerges, however, is a handkerchief.)** Off with you
now, and be assured that I will remember this.

JACQUES   I kiss your hands.

Scene 5: Cleante, Harpagon

CLEANTE   I beg you to forgive my display of anger, father.

HARPAGON   That was nothing.

CLEANTE   I assure you that I could not regret it more
deeply.

HARPAGON   And as for me, I cannot express my joy at
seeing you so reasonable.

CLEANTE   How good of you to be so quick to forgive my
transgression.

HARPAGON   The faults of a repentant child are easy to forgive.

CLEANTE   How's that? You don't bear me any resentment
for my outburst?

HARPAGON	How can I, with a son who's so submissive and respectful?
CLEANTE	I promise you, father, that to my dying day I shall never forget your kindness in this affair.
HARPAGON	And I promise <u>you</u> that there will be nothing from me you shall not obtain.
CLEANTE	Ah, father, I shall ask for nothing more. What more can I ask of you after your giving me Mariane?
HARPAGON	What did you say?
CLEANTE	I said that you have pleased me greatly, father, and that when you granted me Mariane you granted my every wish.
HARPAGON	Who said anything about granting you Mariane?
CLEANTE	Why you, father.
HARPAGON	I?
CLEANTE	Most assuredly.
HARPAGON	How's that? Why, it's you who promised to give her up.
CLEANTE	I? Give her up?
HARPAGON	Yes.
CLEANTE	Never!
HARPAGON	You have not renounced your pursuit of her?
CLEANTE	On the contrary, I am more resolved than ever.
HARPAGON	How's that? You gallows bird. You still persist?
CLEANTE	Nothing will change what I feel.
HARPAGON	I'll fix you, you traitor!
CLEANTE	Do whatever you like.
HARPAGON	I forbid you to see me again.
CLEANTE	How refreshing.
HARPAGON	I abandon you.
CLEANTE	Please do.
HARPAGON	I'll disown you.
CLEANTE	So be it.
HARPAGON	I'll disinherit you.

CLEANTE   Whatever you wish.
HARPAGON   And I give you my curse.
CLEANTE   I've no need of your gifts.

Scene 6: La Fleche, Cleante

LA FLECHE   **(Entering from the garden, money box in hand)** Ah! Sir! How glad I am to find you. Follow me quickly.
CLEANTE   What is it?
LA FLECHE   Follow me, I tell you, we're in luck.
CLEANTE   How's that?
LA FLECHE   This is it.
CLEANTE   What?
LA FLECHE   I've been guarding this all day.
CLEANTE   What is it?
LA FLECHE   Your father's treasure .... I filched it.
CLEANTE   How did you do it?
LA FLECHE   I'll explain everything, but I can hear him shouting. Let's withdraw.

Scene 7: Harpagon

HARPAGON   **(Shouting "Stop! thief" from the garden and entering hatless)** Stop thief! Stop thief! Assassin! Murderer! Justice, just Heaven! I am lost; I am assassinated! They've cut my throat; they've stolen my money. Who can it be? What has become of him? Where is he? Where is he hiding? How can I find him? Where shall I run? Where shall I not run? Isn't he there? Isn't he here? Who is it? Stop! **(Grabbing his own arm)** Give me back my money, you scoundrel! Oh, it's me. I'm so confused I don't even know where I am, who I am or what I'm doing. Alas, my poor money, my poor money, my dear friend, they have deprived me of you, and since they've taken you from me, I've lost my support, my consolation, my joy. All is finished for me, and there's nothing left for me to do in this world. Without you, life is impossible. It's done; I can't go on; I'm dying. I'm dead. I'm buried. Is there no one to resuscitate me by returning my dear money, or at least to tell me who took it? Eh? What's that you say?...It's no one. Whoever did this timed it craftily to coincide with that conversation I had with that traitorous son of mine. Let's go out. I shall go to the police and have the entire household put to the torture...maidservants, valets, son, daughter, and myself as well. **(To the audience)** So many people! And you all look suspicious to me. Any one of you could pass for my thief. Eh? What are you talking about there? About my robber? What's that commotion over there? Is my thief there? Please, if any of you knows who he is, I implore you to tell me. Perhaps he's hiding somewhere there among you? They all look at me and laugh. I'll wager they're all accomplices in this crime. Let's get on with it. Quickly now: policemen, archers, provosts, judges, racks, gallows and hangmen. I'll have everybody hanged, and after that, if I still don't find my money, I'll hang myself.

ACT V

Scene 1: Harpagon, the Officer, his Clerk

OFFICER   Leave it to me. Thank God, I know my job. I've been solving thefts for so long that I'd like to have a thousand francs for every man I've had hanged.

HARPAGON   This affair should be the concern of every magistrate, and if they don't recover my money, I'll demand justice from justice itself.

OFFICER   We must proceed in the prescribed manner. Now then, how much money did you say was in the money box?

HARPAGON   Ten thousand crowns in cash.

OFFICER   Ten thousand crowns?

HARPAGON   Ten thousand crowns.

OFFICER   That's quite a theft.

HARPAGON   There is no torture horrible enough to meet the enormity of this crime, and if the culprit is not punished, nothing will be safe, no matter how sacred it might be.

OFFICER   The money was in what denominations?

HARPAGON   In good louis d'or and pistoles of full weight.

OFFICER   Whom do you suspect of the theft?

HARPAGON   Everybody; and I want you to arrest the entire town and suburbs.

OFFICER   In our quest for evidence we must not allow intemperance to frighten people away. We must instead pursue a course of quiet diligence leading to the recovery of your money.

Scene 2: Maitre Jacques, Harpagon, Officer, Clerk

JACQUES   **(Speaking to someone offstage while entering)**
I'll be right back. Have his throat cut, his feet

grilled, his body immersed in boiling water, and then hang him from the rafters.

HARPAGON   Who? The man who stole my money?

JACQUES   No, that suckling pig your steward just sent me. I'm having it prepared for you my way.

HARPAGON   We're not concerned about that. Right now there is another matter to discuss with this gentleman.

OFFICER   Don't be alarmed. It is not my intent to promote scandal. All will be gentleness and discretion.

JACQUES   Is the gentleman one of the dinner guests?

OFFICER   My dear friend, you must not hide anything from your master.

JACQUES   In faith, sir, I'll show you all I know and will treat you as well as I can.

HARPAGON   That's not the point.

JACQUES   If my dinner is not what I would have it be, it's the fault of the niggardly steward.

HARPAGON   Traitor! We're not talking about the dinner. You must tell me what you know about the money they took from me.

JACQUES   They took money from you?

HARPAGON   Yes, scoundrel, and if you don't cough it up, I'll have you hanged!

OFFICER   Good heavens! You must not mistreat him. I can tell by his face that he's an honest man and that he would much rather reveal what he knows than be sent to prison. Yes, my friend, if you confess, not only will you be spared any punishment, but you will also receive appropriate compensation from your master. His money was stolen today, and I'm sure you must know something about it.

JACQUES   **(Aside)** This is the chance I've been waiting for to get back at that steward. He was the favorite since the day he came. His advice is the only one they heed -- and then there's that beating he just gave me.

HARPAGON What's going on in that mind of yours?

OFFICER Leave him be. He's preparing to give you satisfaction. I told you he was a gentleman.

JACQUES Sir, since it is your wish that I be forthright, I shall tell you that the guilty party in this affair is none other than your steward.

HARPAGON Valere?

JACQUES Yes.

HARPAGON The one who appeared so faithful to me?

JACQUES The very one. He's your thief, I believe.

HARPAGON On what do you base this?

JACQUES On what?

HARPAGON Yes.

JACQUES I base it on....on what I base it on.

OFFICER But you must produce evidence.

HARPAGON Did you see him loitering where I kept my money?

JACQUES Indeed I did! Er....where was your money?

HARPAGON In the garden.

JACQUES Precisely. I saw him loitering in the garden. What was the money put in?

HARPAGON In a money box.

JACQUES That's it! I saw him with a money box.

HARPAGON And this money box...describe it to me. I'll tell you in a second if it's mine.

JACQUES Describe it to you?

HARPAGON Yes.

JACQUES Well, it....er....looks like a money box.

OFFICER Most of them do. Can you give a more detailed description?

JACQUES It's a large money box.

HARPAGON The one stolen from me is small.

JACQUES	Oh yes, it's small if you're talking about size; when I said "large", I was talking about the contents.
OFFICER	And what color was it?
JACQUES	What color?
OFFICER	Yes.
JACQUES	It's color was...It had a certain color...Perhaps you might help me describe it?
HARPAGON	Eh?
JACQUES	Wasn't it red?
HARPAGON	No, gray.
JACQUES	Ah, yes, grayish-red, that's exactly what I meant.
HARPAGON	That's the one! No doubt about it Take down his statement, sir, word for word. Lord above, whom can I trust now? There's nothing left to believe in, and after this, I think I could be my own thief.
JACQUES	Sir, here he comes now. Please don't tell him that I'm the one who revealed his guilt.

Scene 3: Valere, Harpagon, Officer, Clerk, Maitre Jacques

HARPAGON	Come here! Come and confess the foulest action, the most horrible offense ever committed.
VALERE	What is it, sir?
HARPAGON	How is it, traitor, that you do not blush from your crime?
VALERE	To what crime do you refer?
HARPAGON	To what crime do I refer? You scoundrel, as if you didn't know what I was talking about! Don't put on that act with me. The truth is out and I know everything. How could you abuse my goodness, gain entry to my household solely to betray me, and do me such an evil turn?

VALERE	Sir, since they've told you everything, I shall not deny the matter.
JACQUES	(**Aside**) Aha! Could I have guessed right without even knowing it?
VALERE	I intended to discuss it with you, but was waiting for the proper moment. However, things being what they are, I implore you to control your temper and to listen to my explanation.
HARPAGON	And what possible explanation can you proffer, infamous thief that you are?
VALERE	Ah, sir, I hardly deserve those names. It is true that I wronged you, but what I did was excusable.
HARPAGON	Excusable? An ambush, a murder like that?
VALERE	I beseech you, sir, not to get angry. When you've heard me out, you'll realize that the wrong is not as great as you're making it.
HARPAGON	Not as bad as I'm making it? It's my very flesh and blood, you scoundrel!
VALERE	Your blood has not fallen into bad hands, and I am in a position to preclude any irreparable injury.
HARPAGON	That's exactly what I want...return what you've stolen from me!
VALERE	There'll not be the slightest offense to your honor, sir.
HARPAGON	This is not a matter of honor; but tell me, who made you do this?
VALERE	Alas, do you really wish to know?
HARPAGON	I certainly do.
VALERE	A god who excuses everything done in his name...Love.
HARPAGON	Love?
VALERE	Yes.

HARPAGON There's a fine kind of love, indeed -- the love of my gold pieces!

VALERE You are mistaken, sir. I am neither dazzled nor tempted by your wealth, and I make no claim on any of your possessions, if only you leave me with the one I have.

HARPAGON Never in a million years! You compound your insolence by asking to keep what you've stolen from me!

VALERE Do you call that a theft?

HARPAGON Do I call that a theft? A treasure like that?

VALERE A treasure, indeed, undoubtedly the most precious you have; but you would not lose it by giving it to me. For this treasure so endowed with charm, I plead on my knees, and you are bound by decency to acquiesce.

HARPAGON I'll do nothing of the sort. Just what do you mean?

VALERE We are bound by our promise of mutual faithfulness and by our vow never to part.

HARPAGON How admirable a vow and how pleasing a promise.

VALERE Yes, we are eternally pledged to each other.

HARPAGON I'll put a stop to that, I assure you.

VALERE Nothing but death can separate us.

HARPAGON How you lust for my money!

VALERE I have already told you, sir, that what I did was not out of self-interest. My motives were far more noble than you might imagine.

HARPAGON Next you'll be telling me that taking my money was an act of Christian charity. But I'll set things straight, brazen gallows bird; you'll have the law after you and I'll have my satisfaction.

VALERE You may do as you wish. I am prepared to suffer whatever punishment may please you. I implore you to believe, however, that if any wrong has been done, it is I who is solely responsible. Your daughter shares none of the blame.

HARPAGON I can truly believe that since it would be against her nature to be involved in such a crime. But I want back what is mine! Confess the hiding place!

VALERE What hiding place Your treasure is still in your house.

HARPAGON (Aside) Oh, my darling money box! (Aloud) Still in my house?

VALERE Yes, sir.

HARPAGON Hah! Tell me, you haven't laid your hands upon ....

VALERE Laid my hands upon....Ah! You wrong us both, sir. The passion burning within me is completely pure and respectful.

HARPAGON (Aside) A passion for my money box.

VALERE I would rather die than evoke the suggestion of offensive thought. Too much goodness and decency are involved for that.

HARPAGON (Aside) My money box is too decent!

VALERE The sight of her fulfills my every desire, and nothing unwholesome has ever tarnished the tender love that those beautiful eyes have inspired within me.

HARPAGON (Aside) The beautiful eyes of my money box! You'd think he's speaking of a sweetheart!

VALERE Mrs Claudia knows the truth of this matter and she can verify to you...

HARPAGON How's that? My servant is an accomplice in this affair?

VALERE Yes, sir, she served as witness to our engagement. Once convinced of the sincerity of my love, it was with her persuasion that we pledged our troth to one another.

HARPAGON (Aside) Eh? Is his fear of the law affecting his senses? (To Valere) What's my daughter got to do with this?

VALERE And I say to you, sir, that, because of her sense of modesty it was not without considerable difficulty that she complied with the dictates of my heart.

HARPAGON Whose modesty?

VALERE Your daughter's! It was not until yesterday that she finally agreed to sign the engagement papers.

HARPAGON My daughter signed a promise of marriage to you?

VALERE Yes, sir, just as I to her.

HARPAGON By the saints, another disaster!

JACQUES (To the officer) Start writing ..sir, start writing.

HARPAGON Despair piled upon despair! Misfortune at every turn. Come sir, do your duty and draw up an indictment of him as a thief and...

VALERE I am not deserving of those names, and once my identity is known...

SCENE 4: Elise, Mariane, Frosine, Harpagon, Valere, Jacques, Officer and Clerk

HARPAGON Ah! Shameless daughter! Daughter unworthy of a father like me! So this is the result of my teachings? You fall in love with an infamous thief and pledge your troth without my consent. You're both mistaken if you think you'll get away with this. (To Elise) The four walls of a convent will provide the restraint you need; (To

	Valere) and as for you, the gallows will cure your audacity!
VALERE	We will not be judged by your anger. I shall be heard before being condemned.
HARPAGON	Did I say "gallows"? I'll have you alive on the wheel with your bones broken!
ELISE	**(On her knees)** Open your heart, father, I beseech you. Do not crush us with the weight of your paternal authority. Instead of making decisions in the heat of passion, allow yourself time to reflect upon a proper course of action. Try, at least, to better acquaint yourself with the man by whom you feel offended. You have a completely false impression of him. You will easily understand why I accepted him once you learn that were it not for him, I would have died long ago. Yes, father, it was he who, on that day of peril, rescued me from a watery grave, and it is to him, therefore, that you owe the life of the very daughter whom ....
HARPAGON	So what? I would have him let you drown rather than do what he did to me.
ELISE	Father, I call upon your love for me as my father to ....
HARPAGON	No, no, I'll listen to none of this. Let justice take its course.
JACQUES	(Aside) You'll pay me for that beating you gave me.
FROSINE	Now, this is a strange kettle of fish!

SCENE 5: Anselme, Harpagon, Elise, Mariane, Frosine, Valere, M. Jacques, Officer and Clerk

ANSELME	What is it, Lord Harpagon? You seem quite upset.

HARPAGON Ah! Lord Anselme! Observe before you the most pitiful of men. That contract you have come to sign is in a state of confusion and disorder. I am a dead man stripped of my wealth and honor, and there you see a traitor, a scoundrel, a violator of the most sacred rights, who wormed his way into my household posing as a domestic for the purpose of stealing my money and seducing my daughter.

VALERE Your money is no concern of mine. Why do you subject me to this tirade?

HARPAGON Yes, and they are engaged to be married. This is also an affront to you, Lord Anselme, and it therefore behooves you to prosecute to the full extent of the law .... at you own expense, of course.

ANSELME I do not intend to marry a woman against her will, nor would I lay claim to a heart already promised to another. However, in this matter I am prepared to protect your interests as well as mine.

HARPAGON This is an honest officer who assures me that nothing prevails over the pursuit of his duty. **(To the officer)** Charge him for the criminal that he is, sir.

VALERE What is criminal about loving your daughter? And once my identity is known, any punishment to which you feel I am liable for having engaged your daughter...

HARPAGON Enough of this claptrap! The world today is full of these nobility thieves --these impostors who use their obscurity to assume the first illustrious name that pops into their heads.

VALERE I'll have you know, sir, that I would consider it unworthy of me to claim anything that was not mine, and that all Naples can bear witness to my station.

ANSELME Hold on, sir. Consider what you're about to say, for you are running a far greater risk than you think. You happen to be speaking to someone who is totally familiar with...someone in a position to challenge what you may say.

VALERE **(Proudly putting on his hat)** I have nothing to fear, and if, as you claim, you are thoroughly familiar with Naples, you must be acquainted with the name of Don Thomas d'Alburcy.

ANSELME I most certainly am...probably better than anyone else.

HARPAGON I don't give a hoot about Don Thomas nor of Don Martin, for that matter.

ANSELME Please allow him to speak. Let's hear what he has to say.

VALERE What I have to say is that Don Thomas d'Alburcy is my father.

ANSELME He is your ....

VALERE Yes.

ANSELME Come now, sir, you jest, of course, to exonerate yourself. You'll have to come up with a better story than that. There's no salvation in playing the impostor.

VALERE May I ask that you weigh your words more carefully, sir. I am not an impostor and can verify whatever I claim.

ANSELME How's that? You dare pretend to be the son of Don Thomas d'Alburcy?

VALERE Yes, and I can prove it.

ANSELME I marvel at your audacity. May I advise you that the gentleman of whom you speak died at sea with his wife and children at least sixteen years ago in an attempt to flee the persecution of the nobility during the Neopolitan uprising.

VALERE Yes, but I must inform you that his seven-year-old son, along with a servant, were both rescued by a Spanish ship, and it is that very son who stands before you now. The ship's captain, moved by my plight, raised me as his son. As soon as I was of age, I joined the military. I recently learned that, contrary to my long-held belief, my father was not dead. It was while passing through here in search of him that heaven ordained that I should meet the charming Elise, and her beauty completely overwhelmed me. Indeed, my love for her was so intense that I decided to have someone else continue the search for my father so that I might be free to enter the service of this household, where I enjoy her proximity and protect her from the severity of her father.

ANSELME But what evidence can you provide other than words?

VALERE The Spanish captain, a ruby signet ring once belonging to my father, an agate bracelet given to me by my mother and, finally old Pedro, the servant who, with me, was spared from the shipwreck.

MARIANE You speak the truth, and what you say convinces me that you are my brother.

VALERE You, my sister?

MARIANE Yes. I have been deeply moved by everything you have said. Our mother has spoken to me at length of our family's misfortune, and how great will be her joy in seeing you! Our lives were spared during that shipwreck, but only at the expense of our liberty. While clinging to some floating debris, your mother and I were picked up by a pirate ship, and after ten years of slavery, by a stroke of luck, we regained our liberty. Upon our return, we found that all our possessions were sold, and we were unable to locate Father. We then went to Genoa, where Mother collected the remnants of a depleted inheritance. From there, fleeing the inhumanity of her relatives, she came here to a life of continual languish.

ANSELME   O Lord, how wondrous is thy power. You alone can perform such miracles! Come, my children, let us embrace and share this moment of joy!

VALERE   You are our father?

MARIANE   Is it for you that my mother has grieved for so long?

ANSELME   Yes, my daughter; yes, my son. I am Don Thomas d'Alburcy. Heaven decreed that I should survive that shipwreck with the money I had on my person. For sixteen years, believing both of you to be dead, I have been traveling extensively in quest of a gentle and wise woman with whom I might experience once again the joys of family life. The situation in Naples remained too hazardous for me to ever return; thus, I arranged to sell my possessions there and decided to settle here under the name of Anselme. My other name was too painful a reminder of past sorrows.

HARPAGON   That is your son?

ANSELME   Yes.

HARPAGON   I shall, therefore, sue you for the ten thousand gold pieces he stole from me.

ANSELME   He stole from you?

HARPAGON   Yes, he did.

VALERE   Who told you that?
HARPAGON   Jacques.
VALERE   **(To Jacques)**You told him that?
JACQUES   You know I'd never say a thing like that.
VALERE   Do you really believe me capable of such a foul act?
HARPAGON   Capable or incapable, I want my money back.

SCENE 6:   Cleante, Valere, Mariane, Elise, Frosine, Harpagon, Anselme, Officer, Jacques

CLEANTE   Stop tormenting yourself and making such wild accusations, Father. I know about your money, and I can tell you that if you allow me to marry Mariane, you'll have your money back.
HARPAGON   Where is it?
CLEANTE   No need for concern. It is totally under my control. Your choice is quite simple. You either give me Mariane or lose your money box.
HARPAGON   Nothing has been taken from it?
CLEANTE   Nothing at all. Do you intend to agree to this marriage and add your consent to that of her mother?
MARIANE   **(To Cleante)** But don't you realize now that this consent is no longer sufficient and that you must now address yourself to my father and brother, whom God has returned to me?
ANSELME   Heaven has not reunited us, my children, for me to counter your wishes. Lord Harpagon, surely you must realize that a young girl would prefer the son over the father. Come now, don't force us to say what you don't need to hear, and consent with me instead to this double marriage.
HARPAGON   Before I decide anything, I must first see my money box.

CLEANTE You will find it filled to the brim and in excellent health.

HARPAGON I've not the money to spend on the marriage of my children.

ANSELME You need not be concerned; I've enough for them.

HARPAGON Are you saying that you shall pay all costs for both marriages?

ANSELME Yes, I will. Does that satisfy you?

HARPAGON Yes, providing you have new clothes made for me for the wedding.

ANSELME Agreed. Now let us rejoice in the glorious events of the day.

OFFICER Hold on, gentlemen, I beg of you! Who'll pay for my depositions?

HARPAGON We don't need your depositions.

OFFICER Yes, but I do not intend to have drawn them up for nothing.

HARPAGON **(Pointing to Jacques)** As a form of payment, I offer you this man to hang.

JACQUES What is a man to do? If I tell the truth, I get beaten, and if I lie, I get hung.

ANSELME Lord Harpagon, we forgive his deception.

HARPAGON So then, you'll pay the officer?

ANSELME So be it. **(To Valere and Mariane)** Let us go quickly to your mother so that she might share our joy.

HARPAGON And I with haste, to my beloved money box.

The Miser

(L'AVARE)

(Short Edition)

CHARACTERS

HARPAGON, Father of Elise and Cleante
CLEANTE, Son of Harpagon
ELISE, Daughter of Harpagon
VALERE, Harpagon's Steward
MARIANE, Young Lady and Lover of Cleante
FROSINE, A Matchmaker and Adventuress
LORD ANSELME, A Neighbor
LA FLECHE, Valet to Cleante
SIMON, A Usurer
JACQUES, Harpagon's Cook and Coachman
BRINDAVOINE, LA MERLUCHE,
and CLAUDIA, Harpagon's Servants
OFFICER and OFFICER'S CLERK

The play takes place in the Parisian countryside, at the home of Harpagon.

ACT I

Scene 1: **Valere, Elise**

VALERE   Come now, my beloved Elise, why this sadness in the midst of my joy? Do you regret being compelled by my love for you to sign those papers of engagement?

ELISE   No, Valere, but I fear that I may love you more deeply than I should.

VALERE   What is there to fear?

ELISE   A hundred things at once: a father's anger, a family's reproaches, the censure of society but above all, Valere, I fear a change of heart on your part, as well as that criminal coldness with which men repay displays of innocent love.

VALERE   Please don't judge me by others. My love for you is eternal and far too intense to ever fail you.

ELISE   Oh, Valere, all men are alike; it's not what they say but how they act that counts.

VALERE   Since actions alone reveal our true selves, at least give me the chance to act before you judge me. Don't allow unfounded suspicion to cause you to accuse me unjustly. Let me prove to you the sincerity of my love.

ELISE   Ah, how easily are we persuaded by those we love. Yes, Valere, I believe that it is not in you to deceive me. I feel that your love for me is true, and that you will be faithful to me. It is not my wish to doubt you; my only concern is how I might be blamed for all this.

VALERE   But why should this bother you?

ELISE   I would fear nothing if everyone saw you as I do. My mind reverts constantly to that terrifying moment during which our destinies were joined, to the heroism you displayed in risking your life to save mine from the fury of the waves, to the tenderness you showed me once we were safely ashore, to the unfailing homage of a love that neither time nor hardship has dampened...a love that compels you to deny both family and country, to conceal your true social position, and to work as a domestic for my father solely for the opportunity to be near me. I am deeply moved by -all of this, and I feel that it justifies my signing the engagement; however, I am concerned that others may misinterpret my actions in this matter.

VALERE   Of everything you have said, it is only my love for you that is deserving of mention. Forgive my bluntness, charming Elise, but when I speak of your father, there is very little good that comes to mind. In any event, should God grant that I find my parents, we will have little difficulty obtaining his blessing. I am waiting impatiently for news of them and, if word doesn't arrive soon, I shall go forth in search of them myself.

ELISE   Do not leave, Valere, I beg of you. Remain here and concentrate on winning the blessing of my father.

VALERE   Are you not aware of all my efforts in that direction? Recall, if you will, the obsequious demeanor with which I gained entrance to his service and how, in order to please him, I constantly feign agreement with his every sentiment. Man's susceptibility to flattery is

	without bounds, and there is never the danger of an overdose. My work here sorely compromises my integrity, but this is the price I must pay.
ELISE	Why don't you try to win the approval of my brother as well so that, should the maidservant decide to reveal our secret, we may rely on his support?
VALERE	I cannot manage them both simultaneously... Here he comes. I must go. This would be a good time to discuss our relationship, but reveal to him only what you deem appropriate.

Scene 2: Cleante, Elise

CLEANTE	I'm so glad to find you alone, my sister, for there is a matter of extreme importance that I must discuss with you.
ELISE	What is it, Cleante?
CLEANTE	I'm in love.
ELISE	You're in love?
CLEANTE	Yes, I'm in love. But, before going any further, let me say that I am aware of my dependence upon my father and how, as his son, I must submit to his will.
ELISE	Are you and your loved one engaged, dear brother?
CLEANTE	No, but I am determined that this shall come to pass, and I implore you once again not to try to dissuade me.
ELISE	My dear brother, do you believe me to be so insensitive?
CLEANTE	No, but you are not in love, and know nothing of the sweet violence that tender love enkindles in our hearts.

ELISE   Let us first discuss your situation. Tell me who it is that you love.

CLEANTE   A young lady who recently moved here and whose beauty captivates all who see her. She is indeed one of Nature's most desirable creations, and I am enraptured by the mere sight of her. Her name is Mariane, and she lives under the charge of her elderly mother who is nearly always ill. She tends to her every need with touching devotion. Her innumerable charms are reflected in whatever she does; her appealing tenderness, her enchanting demeanor, her angelic goodness, her...ah, dear sister, if you could only see her.

ELISE   Your descriptions are clear enough and the fact that you love her is, in itself, proof of her worthiness.

CLEANTE   I have learned that they are having difficulty maintaining their household. Imagine, my sister, what a pleasure it would be to help my beloved out of her financial distress, to discreetly provide some small measure of assistance to a virtuous family; and now, consider my displeasure at being denied this joy because of a father's avarice.

ELISE   Yes, Cleante, I can readily understand your displeasure.

CLEANTE   Ah, sister, it is greater than can be imagined, for what is there to match in cruelty the unbounded niggardliness to which we are subject -- this barren milieu where we must languish? As it stands, we have to borrow simply to survive, even to the point where, for the very clothes on our backs, we must suffer the humiliation of relying on the generosity of merchants.

Finally, I wanted to ask you to help me in discussing this matter with our father. If he opposes me, I am determined to depart with my beloved and enjoy whatever happiness Heaven deigns to offer. To accomplish this, I have been looking everywhere in the hope of obtaining a loan, and if your situation resembles mine, that is to say, if you are confronted with the same opposition, we shall both leave this place, thereby liberating ourselves from the tyranny of his insufferable avarice to which we have been subject for so long.

ELISE It is true that with each day that passes, he provides us with more reason to regret the death of our mother and that...

CLEANTE I hear his voice. Let us withdraw from here and continue our discussion in private.

Scene 3: Harpagon, La Fleche

HARPAGON Off with you this instant, and not a word out of you! Get out of my house, you first class, swindling gallows bird!

LA FLECHE (**Aside**) I have never seen anything to match the wickedness of this cursed old man. I truly feel he is possessed by the devil.

HARPAGON What are you mumbling?

LA FLECHE Why are you dismissing me?

HARPAGON You've got your nerve asking me for reasons, you scoundrel. Get out quickly before I thrash you.

LA FLECHE Very well, I'm leaving.

HARPAGON Hold on! Are you taking anything with you?

LA FLECHE What could I take from you?

HARPAGON Come here and let me see. Hold out your hands.

LA FLECHE There you are.

HARPAGON The others.

LA FLECHE The others?

HARPAGON Yes

LA FLECHE There you are

HARPAGON (**Pointing to his breeches**) Did you put anything in there?

LA FLECHE Look for yourself

HARPAGON (**Feeling the bottoms of his breeches**) These large breeches are excellent receptacles for stolen articles, and I would love to hang the man who designed them.

LA FLECHE (**Aside**) Oh, how a man like this s deserves what he fears, and what a joy it would be to rob him... Here's another pocket for you. Are you satisfied?

HARPAGON Come on, hand it over without my having to search you.

LA FLECHE How's that?

HARPAGON What you took from me

LA FLECHE I haven't taken a thing from you.

HARPAGON Are you sure?

LA FLECHE I assure you

HARPAGON Off with you, then, and may the devil take you.

LA FLECHE How cordially you dismiss me. (**EXIT**)

Scene 4: Harpagon, Elise, Cleante

HARPAGON Oh, what a burden it is to keep a large sum of money in one's house, and lucky is the man who is blessed with a hiding place which is not only secure, but also accessible in times of financial need. I have no faith in strong boxes, for they are the prime target of thieves. Nevertheless, I don't know if it was wise of me to have buried in the garden the ten thousand gold pieces that I received yesterday. **(Elise and Cleante enter, speaking softly)** Good Heavens! I nearly betrayed myself What is it?

CLEANTE   Nothing, father.

HARPAGON   Have you been there for a long time?

ELISE   We just arrived.

HARPAGON   Did you hear...

CLEANTE   Hear what, father?

HARPAGON   Come now...

ELISE   How's that?

HARPAGON   What I just said.

CLEANTE   No.

HARPAGON   Yes you did! Yes you did!

ELISE   I beg your pardon.

HARPAGON   Oh, would to God I had those ten thousand gold pieces!

CLEANTE   Good Heavens, father! You have no grounds for complaint. You're a man of sufficient means.

HARPAGON   Of sufficient means, you say? Only liars and scoundrels would say that of me. Nothing could be more false.

ELISE   Please don't get angry.

HARPAGON   How strange it is to have my own children betray me and become my enemies.

CLEANTE   Does my reference to your money make me your enemy?

HARPAGON   Yes, and if you keep talking like that and continue your spendthrift ways, one of these days someone will come and cut my throat, thinking that my clothes are stuffed with money.

CLEANTE   In what way am I a spendthrift?

HARPAGON In what way? Could anything be more scandalous than that extravagant outfit in which you parade about town? You strut about dressed like a marquis, and it's only by robbing me that you could do so.

CLEANTE How am I robbing you?

HARPAGON Who knows? How else could you afford those fancy clothes?

CLEANTE I, father? The fact is that I gamble, and since I'm very lucky, I can afford to dress in style.

HARPAGON Let's change the subject. Eh? **(Aside)** I think they're signaling each other to steal my purse. **(Aloud)** What was the meaning of all that gesturing?

ELISE Both my brother and I would say something to you, and we were trying to decide who would be the first to speak.

HARPAGON And, I too, have something to say to you.

CLEANTE We wish to speak to you of marriage, father.

HARPAGON And I'd like to speak to you on the same subject.

ELISE Ah, father!

HARPAGON Why this sudden emotion? Is it the idea or the reality that frightens you?

CLEANTE We are concerned about any plans you might have regarding our marriages, and how such plans might conflict with our own wishes.

HARPAGON A little patience. I know what you both need. Let's begin with you, Cleante. Are you acquainted with a young lady named Mariane, who lives nearby?

CLEANTE Yes, father.

HARPAGON **(To Elise)** And, you?

ELISE I've heard of her.

HARPAGON   What are your impressions of this young lady, my son?

CLEANTE   A truly charming person.

HARPAGON   Her face?

CLEANTE   Sincere and decidedly intelligent.

HARPAGON   Her demeanor?

CLEANTE   Admirable beyond a doubt.

HARPAGON   Don't you feel that such a girl deserves consideration?

CLEANTE   Yes, father.

HARPAGON   That she would make a highly desirable partner?

CLEANTE   Very desirable.

HARPAGON   That she gives every indication of being a good housekeeper?

CLEANTE   Undoubtedly.

HARPAGON   And that a husband would be very satisfied with her?

CLEANTE   Assuredly.

HARPAGON   There's only one minor drawback. I fear that her financial situation leaves something to be desired.

CLEANTE   Ah, father! When it comes to marrying a person of such quality, money means nothing.

HARPAGON   Pardon me! But the fact remains that if the money falls short of one's expectations, one should expect other forms of compensation.

CLEANTE   That's understandable.

HARPAGON   I'm glad that you agree with me, for her genteel bearing and affectionate nature have captured my heart, and I have decided to marry her...-providing, of course, that a dowry, however modest, is in the offing.

CLEANTE   Eh?

HARPAGON   What's that?

CLEANTE   You say that you have decided

HARPAGON   To marry Mariane.

CLEANTE   Who? You, you?

HARPAGON   Yes, me, me, me. What do you mean by that?

CLEANTE   Excuse me, but I suddenly feel a little faint, and I must withdraw from here. (Exit)

HARPAGON   What a weak-kneed fop! Well, my daughter, this is what I have planned for myself As for your brother, I have chosen for him a certain widow I heard about this morning; and as for you, I shall give you to Lord Anselme.

ELISE   Lord Anselme?

HARPAGON   Yes, a mature man, prudent and wise, who is not more than fifty, and who is reputed to be quite wealthy.

ELISE   **(Curtsying)** If you please, father, I do not wish to marry.

HARPAGON   **(Curtsying in turn)** And I, my little daughter, my dearest, I wish that you do.

ELISE   I beg your pardon, father.

HARPAGON   I beg your pardon, daughter.

ELISE   I am the most humble servant of Lord Anselme, but, with your permission, I shall not marry him.

HARPAGON   And I am your most humble valet, but with your permission, you shall marry him this very evening.

ELISE   This very evening?

HARPAGON   This very evening.

ELISE   That will never happen, father.

HARPAGON   Yes, it will, daughter.

ELISE   I will kill myself rather than marry such a man.

HARPAGON   You shall not kill yourself, and you shall marry him--brazen creature that you are! Here comes Valere. Shall we seek his opinion in this matter?

ELISE   Very well.

HARPAGON Will you submit to his judgment?
ELISE Yes, I will abide by what he says.
HARPAGON So be it.

Scene 5: Valere, Harpagon, Elise

HARPAGON Over here, Valere. My daughter and I have chosen you to decide which of us is right in a certain matter.
VALERE It is you, sir, without question.
HARPAGON Do you know what we are discussing?
VALERE No, but you could never be wrong, for you are reason personified.
HARPAGON I wish to marry her off this very evening to a man who is as rich as he is wise, and the hussy has the audacity to defy me. What do you say to that?
VALERE What do I say to that?
HARPAGON Yes.
VALERE Well, er...
HARPAGON What?
VALERE I say that essentially I share your feelings, for it could never be that you are wrong; however, I submit that she also is not completely wrong, and...
HARPAGON How's that? Lord Anselme is a man of importance--a gentleman who is noble, considerate, poised, wise, and very rich, and whose first marriage left him with no children. Could she possibly make a better match?
VALERE That is true; but she might feel that you are rushing things somewhat.
HARPAGON This is an opportunity that calls for fast action. It is not every day that such an advantageous

situation presents itself, and if he agrees to take her without a dowry...

VALERE Without a dowry?

HARPAGON Yes.

VALERE Ah! There is no argument against such reasonable terms. Therefore, I have nothing to say.

HARPAGON This will save me a lot of money.

VALERE True, but your daughter may claim that marriage is nothing to take lightly, that it can result in a lifetime of happiness or misery, and that a commitment unto death must only be made with great precaution.

HARPAGON Without a dowry!

VALERE You are right. But there are people who claim that a girl's feelings should be respected, and that a great disparity of age and temperament often leads to much dissension in a marriage.

HARPAGON Without a dowry!

VALERE Ah! A truly incontestable argument. Nevertheless, there are many fathers who are more concerned with their daughters' happiness than with the amount of the dowry.

HARPAGON Without a dowry!

VALERE That's true. There's no rebuttal to that. Without a dowry! An. Utterly irrefutable argument.

HARPAGON (Aside, looking at the garden) Aha! I think I hear a dog barking. Could someone be after my money? (To Valere) Stay right here; I'll be back in a moment. (EXIT)

ELISE Valere, did you mean what you said to him?

VALERE What I said was meant to placate him, thereby furthering our cause; to contradict him would could court disaster.

ELISE But this marriage, Valere?

VALERE We'll find a way to stop it.

ELISE	But how can we, since it is to take place this evening?
VALERE	You must request a postponement and pretend to be ill.
ELISE	But if they call the doctors, they'll discover the pretense.
VALERE	You jest. What do doctors know? Come now, with them you can choose any sickness you wish and those idiots will come up with all sorts of reasons to explain its origin.

Harpagon returns.

HARPAGON	(**Aside**) It was nothing, thank God.
VALERE	(**To Elise**) In any event, we can always resort to flight. (**Noticing Harpagon**) Yes, a daughter must obey her father, and when there is no dowry involved, she must accept whoever is offered.
HARPAGON	Excellently put, my boy
VALERE	Sir, I most humbly beg your pardon for the liberty I took in speaking to your daughter as I did.
HARPAGON	How's that? I am delighted, and it is my wish that you have absolute power over her. (**To Elise**) No use in trying to run away. I bestow upon him the authority that Heaven gave me over you, and you are to comply with his every wish.
VALERE	(**To Elise**) Did you hear that? Enough of your protests! (**To Harpagon**) Sir, I shall follow her constantly and continue to counsel her in this matter.
HARPAGON	Go to it. I've some business in town, but I'll be back shortly.

VALERE   (**To Elise**) Yes, when one offers to take a daughter without a dowry, it is something to accept without hesitation, for the absence of a dowry takes precedence over beauty, youth, honor, wisdom, and integrity.

HARPAGON Spoken like a prophet! What a fine lad! Fortunate the man with a servant like this!

ACT II

Scene 1: Cleante, La Fleche

CLEANTE Ah, you wretch! Where have you been hiding?

LA FLECHE You father drove me out threatening to beat me!

CLEANTE What news have you of our business affair? The situation is more urgent than ever, for since our last meeting, I have learned that I have none other than my father as a rival!

LA FLECHE Your father? In love?

CLEANTE Yes, and I had a devil of a time trying to conceal from him my shock at this news.

LA FLECHE Is this some type of joke? Is love anything for the likes of him? Why do you conceal from him your own love?

CLEANTE What was their answer?

LA FLECHE In faith, sir, those who borrow are truly unfortunate, and when you are in the grip of usurers, as in your case, there are some rather strange things to which you must subject yourself

CLEANTE The deal will not go through?

LA FLECHE Master Simon, the agent they gave us, assured me that it was your face alone that won his confidence.

CLEANTE Will I have the fifteen thousand francs I am asking for?

LA FLECHE Yes, but under certain conditions.

CLEANTE Did you speak directly to the lender?

LA FLECHE Ah, that's not the way it's done. Under no circumstances is his name ever to be mentioned; you are to meet with him in a house borrowed expressly for this purpose so that he might learn from you directly about your family and financial situation. Here are some clauses that he dictated to our go-between that are to be shown to you as the first order of business: "Provided that the lender see all the securities of the borrower, and that the borrower be of age, and of a family whose health is ample, solid, secure, and free of all encumbrance, a binding and precise document shall be drawn up by a notary of the highest repute, which notary shall be chosen by the lender. So as not to burden his conscience, the lender will loan the money at the legal rate of five and one-half percent interest."

CLEANTE Five and a half percent! Good heavens, that's fair enough!

LA FLECHE That is true. **(Continuing to read)** "But since the said lender does not have at his disposal the sum in question, and since, to accommodate the borrower, he is obliged to borrow said sum from another party at the rate of twenty percent, it shall be agreed that the said borrower shall pay this interest in addition to the rest, since it is only to oblige the first borrower,that the said lender is undertaking this loan."

CLEANTE What usurious monster are we dealing with here? That's over twenty-five percent!

LA FLECHE That's true. It is something you must consider.

CLEANTE What good would that do? I need the money, and I must consent to everything.

LA FLECHE That's the answer I gave him.

CLEANTE Is there anything else?

LA FLECHE Just one small article: "Of the fifteen thousand francs in question, the borrower will receive only twelve thousand in cash; as for the remaining three-thousand, the borrower must accept the equivalent in used clothing, jewelry, and various miscellaneous items which are listed in the attached memorandum and for which the said lender has established the most moderate prices possible."

CLEANTE   What does all that mean?

LA FLECHE   Listen to the memorandum: "First, a four poster bed, draped with Hungarian lace against a decorative backing of olive colored cloth with six chairs and a matching counterpane lined with taffeta in shades of red and blue. The bed comes with a canopy of good Aumale serge in pale rose fringed in silk. All items mentioned are in very good condition."

CLEANTE   And what am I to do with all that?

LA FLECHE   Wait, there's more: "Plus a tapestry depicting the loves of Gombaud and Macee. Plus a large walnut table with twelve sculpted legs which can be opened from either end and which comes with six stools."

CLEANTE   What possible use ?

LA FLECHE   Be patient. "Plus three large muskets inlaid with mother-of-pearl and their accompanying rests. Plus a brick furnace equipped with two retorts and three flasks, very useful for those with a bent for distilling."

CLEANTE   This is too much!

LA FLECHE   Gently now. "Plus a lute from Bologne furnished with nearly all of its strings. Plus a game of troll-madame, and a checkerboard with a game of goose restored from the Greeks, very suitable for whiling away leisure time. Plus a lizard skin, three and one-half feet long, stuffed with hay--a delightful curio to hang from the ceiling. The total value of all this actually amounts to four thousand five hundred francs; but, as a gesture of consideration, the lender is reducing the value to three thousand francs.

CLEANTE   What usury! He wants to extort an additional three thousand francs from me for some junk he's accumulated! Out of all that, I'm only getting twelve thousand francs, and I've got to accept his terms for the scoundrel has a dagger at my throat! I have my father's avarice to thank for him!

LA FLECHE Indeed, you have sir. Wouldn't I love to rob him! What a service to mankind it would be!

Scene 2: Simon, Harpagon, Cleante La Fleche

SIMON   Yes, sir, he's a man in such a financial bind that he will abide by any demands you might make of him.

HARPAGON But are you certain, Master Simon, that there are no risks involved? Can you advise me of the name, financial status and family background of this party?

SIMON   All I can tell you is that he comes from a very rich family, that he has suffered the loss of his mother and, should you wish, he would guarantee that within eight months his father, too, will go on to his reward.

LA FLECHE (Softly to Cleante) What's the meaning of this? Our Master Simon, speaking to your father?

CLEANTE   (Softly to La Fleche) Has someone revealed to him my identity? Are you capable of such a treasonable act?

SIMON   Aha! You're really rushing things, aren't you? Who told you it was to be here in this house? (To Harpagon) I'll have you know, sir that it was not I, sir, who revealed your name and place of residence. But since you are both people of discretion, I don't feel there is any harm done and I don't see why the two of you can't settle this affair directly.

HARPAGON How's that?

SIMON This is the gentleman who wishes to borrow the fifteen thousand francs in question.

HARPAGON Aha! So you're the rogue given to such shameful extremes!

CLEANTE And you are the culprit responsible for these shameful demands!

EXIT Simon and La Fleche.

HARPAGON It's you who is trying to bankrupt himself by such condemnable borrowing!

CLEANTE And it's you who enriches himself by such criminal usury!

HARPAGON How dare you show your face to me after that!

CLEANTE How dare you show your face to anyone after that!

HARPAGON Are you not ashamed to dissipate so disgracefully the money earned by the sweat of your parents' brows?

CLEANTE Are you not disturbed by your infamous lending conditions which would put to shame the most diabolical of usurers?

HARPAGON Away with you, rogue that you are!

CLEANTE Who is the greater rogue, I ask you? -- The one who borrows out of need, or the one who steals without need?

HARPAGON Get out! **(Cleante EXITS) (Alone)** I see that I must scrutinize his every action.

Scene 3: Harpagon, Frosine

FROSINE   Sir...

HARPAGON   I'll be with you in a moment. (Aside) I must
           first check my money.

Scene 4: La Fleche, Frosine

FROSINE   Well, well, my poor La Fleche, what on earth
           brings you here?

LA FLECHE Why, hello, Frosine. And what, might I ask,
           are you doing here? Conducting some business
           with the proprietor here?

FROSINE   Yes. It's a small affair, for which I expect
           payment.

LA FLECHE From him? It will take whatever guile you
           might possess to squeeze a sou out of him!

FROSINE   There are ways, and there are ways.

LA FLECHE Perhaps. After all, who am I but a mere valet?
           But I know Harpagon, the lord of this manor.
           You, as yet, have been denied the pleasure.
           There is no service you might render that will
           gain access to his purse.

FROSINE   Come, come. I'm quite familiar with the art of
           cajoling men.

LA FLECHE That will get you nowhere. To separate him
           from his money is to tear out his entrails, to
           thrust a dagger through his heart; and if.. But
           here he comes. I must go.

Scene 5: Harpagon, Frosine

HARPAGON   (Aside) All is well. (To Frosine) Well, Frosine,
           what can I do for you?

FROSINE   My, my, you look exceptionally well! A veritable picture of health!

HARPAGON   Who me?

FROSINE   Never have I seen you look so hale and hearty.

HARPAGON   Really?

FROSINE   I know some twenty-five year-olds who look older than you.

HARPAGON   Nevertheless, Frosine, I'm still a good sixty years old.

FROSINE   Come now, what's sixty years? Actually, you're at the prime of life, the mellowest phase of existence.

HARPAGON   That's true, but I'd still like to shave off about twenty years.

FROSINE   That is hardly necessary, for with your constitution, you'll live to be a hundred.

HARPAGON   You think so?

FROSINE   Certainly. You have all the indications. Hold still for a moment. Yes, of course...there, right between your eyes, a sign of long life.

HARPAGON   Is this a specialty of yours?

FROSINE   Indeed, it is. Show me your hand. Ah! Good heavens! What a life line!

HARPAGON   How's that?

FROSINE   Don't you see how far this line extends?

HARPAGON   And just what does that mean, pray tell.

FROSINE   A life span of a hundred years...but my feeling is that you'll reach one hundred and twenty!

HARPAGON   Is that possible?

FROSINE   I tell you that it would take the knife of an assassin to terminate your earthly stay, and that you will have to bury not only your children, but your grandchildren as well.

HARPAGON   Splendid! What news have you of our little business matter?

FROSINE   Must you ask? Have you ever seen me involved in anything I did not successfully conclude? I am particularly gifted when it comes to match-making. In your case, however, the difficulties were minimal since I have dealings with both ladies. I was in a position to tell them about you. I advised the mother of your intentions regarding Mariane.

HARPAGON   And her answer was?

FROSINE   She received the proposal with joy, and when I expressed your strong desire to have Mariane attend the signing of your daughter's marriage contract this evening, she consented willingly and asked that I make the necessary arrangements.

HARPAGON   The fact is, Frosine, that I am obliged to give Anselme a dinner, and I would like to have Mariane share in the treat.

FROSINE   You are right. Her plans are to visit your daughter after lunch and then go to the fair; she will then return here for the dinner.

HARPAGON   Very well. I could then loan them my carriage so that they might go together.

FROSINE   That would do quite nicely.

HARPAGON   However, Frosine, have you discussed with the mother the matter of a dowry? After all, when it comes to marrying off a daughter, she, as her mother, should realize her obligation to impoverish herself, if necessary, to heighten her daughter's desirability.

FROSINE   How's that? We are discussing here a girl who will provide you with an income of twelve--thousand francs.

HARPAGON   An income of twelve-thousand francs!

FROSINE   Yes! First of all, she was raised in a household where expenditures on food were minimal. She is accustomed to a diet of salad, milk, cheese, and apples; consequently, you will be spared the expense of fancy table service, exquisite consommés, endless recipes of peeled barley, as well as all the other delicacies that women may require. This alone will result in a substantial yearly saving on your part of at least three thousand francs. In addition, her tastes are extremely modest; she has little use for fancy clothes, expensive jewelry or sumptuous furnishings...things to which other women are highly attracted. We have here an additional saving of more than four thousand francs. Furthermore, unlike her present-day counterpart, she has an intense dislike for gambling, which enhances her virtue all the more, since I knew a woman in this town whose losses at card playing for this year alone amounted to twenty-thousand francs. But let us be modest and assume that the average woman would expend one-fourth of that...that is to say five thousand francs...and let us determine what this means in terms of total yearly savings. First, there is the savings of three thousand francs in food, then the four-thousand francs in clothes and diamonds, and finally the five thousand francs on gambling...which comes to a grand total of twelve-thousand francs!

HARPAGON   That's not bad ... But your accounting is rather fanciful.

FROSINE   I beg your pardon, but is nothing substantial in the acquisition through marriage of great sobriety, of the inheritance of a great love of simplicity in adornment, and of a great fund of hatred for gambling?

HARPAGON   I wish you would stop insulting my intelligence by speaking of a dowry consisting of expenses she will not incur. Speak to me instead of more tangible assets.

FROSINE   Good heavens! You'll have your fill of tangible assets, among which are included certain properties abroad to which you will have title.

HARPAGON   I'll believe that when I see it. However, Frosine, there is still something that troubles me. As you are aware, the girl is young, and as is usually the case with people of her age, she may prefer the company of her peers. I fear that a man of my advanced years might be distasteful to her. Such a situation in my house could occasion some rather irksome repercussions.

FROSINE   Ah! How little do you know of her! The young lady in question despises young people and is irresistibly attracted to the elderly.

HARPAGON   She?

FROSINE   She is revolted by the mere sight of a young man. Let her see, however, a handsome, mature gentleman with a majestic beard and her pulse quickens with delight.

HARPAGON   That is truly admirable! I'm delighted to learn that she is thus inclined. Indeed, were I a young woman, I wouldn't like young men either.

FROSINE   I believe it. Young men are pretentious bumpkins who strut about with woefully exaggerated notions of their irresistibility.

HARPAGON   My sentiments exactly; and yet there are women for whom they hold a fatal attraction.

FROSINE   How could a woman seek any form of attachment with such base creatures?

HARPAGON   This is what I say every day: with their girlish
            ways, their three strands of turned-up cat whis-
            kers that call a mustache, their cottony wigs,
            their droopy breeches unbuttoned at the stom-
            ach!

FROSINE   How ludicrous do they appear when compared
            to a man like you.

HARPAGON   Am I really that attractive?

FROSINE   Why, you're absolutely irresistible, I tell you!
            Just look at that face...an artist's dream! Turn
            that way, if you please. Perfect! Let me see you
            walk. What an excellent physical specimen!
            Such structure, such fluidity of movement...the
            veritable quintessence of masculine charm!

HARPAGON   Aside from my occasional fits of coughing, I do
            pretty well, thank you.

FROSINE   Even your coughing has a certain charm about
            it.

HARPAGON   Tell me, has Mariane seen me yet?

FROSINE   No, but I described you in great detail and
            emphasized the advantages of marrying a man
            of your merits.

HARPAGON   You did well, and I thank you for it.

FROSINE   Sir, there's a small favor I'd like to ask of you.
            (Harpagon frowns) I'm involved in a lawsuit
            that I'm about to lose because of a shortage of
            funds. However, were you to be gracious
            enough to extend a helping hand in this matter,
            I could easily win the case. You can't imagine
            how pleased she'll be to see you. **(Harpagon
            smiles)** How irresistible you will appear to her,
            especially with that old-fashioned ruff of yours.
            But what will dazzle her the most are your
            breeches, attached as they are to your doublet

with laces. One look at those laced up breeches
and she will be yours!

HARPAGON I'm delighted to hear this.

ACT III

Scene 1: Harpagon, Cleante, Elise, Valere, Claudia, Maitre
Jacques, Brindavoine, La Merluche

HARPAGON   All right, everyone gather round for his assign-
            ment this evening. Come here, Claudia, we'll
            begin with you. **(Claudia is holding a broom)**
            Good, I see you're armed and ready. Your task
            is to clean everywhere, and you are to be espe-
            cially careful not to rub the furniture too hard
            for fear of wearing it out. In addition, I'm
            placing you in charge of the bottles during the
            dinner service; if one is missing or broken, I'll
            hold you responsible and will deduct it from
            your wages.
JACQUES   **(Aside)** A suitable punishment.
HARPAGON   Off you go. **(Claudia EXITS)** You, Brinda-
            voine, and you, La Merluche, will be in charge
            of rinsing the glasses and serving the drinks, but
            you are to do so only when the guests are
            thirsty. Despite the custom of certain imperti-
            nent lackeys, I'll not have you coaxing my
            guests into drinking a drop more than they wish.
            Finally,don't serve anyone until he's asked you
            more than once, and make doubly sure that
            there's always plenty of water available.
JACQUES   **(Aside)** Yes, pure wine goes to your head.
MERLUCHE   Do we take our aprons off, sir?
HARPAGON   Yes, when the guests arrive...but make sure you
            don't spoil your clothes.
BRIND'INE   You know, sir, that one of the front flaps of my
            doublet is covered with a big spot of lamp oil.

MERLUCHE And me, sir, I got a big hole in the backside of my breeches, and people can see my... No disrespect, sir.

HARPAGON Enough! **(To La Merluche)** Be clever; walk so that your backside always faces the wall. **(Harpagon places his hat in front of Brindavoine's doublet to hide the lamp-oil stain)** And you, always hold your hat like this when you serve. **(To Elise)** And, as for you, my daughter, you will watch as they clear the table and see that nothing is wasted. That's a suitable task for a daughter. You will now prepare to greet my fiancee, who will be visiting you and taking you with her to the fair. Have you understood my instructions?

ELISE Yes, father.

HARPAGON **(To CLEANTE)** And, as for you, my fine fop of a son, I will not tolerate any more of your sullen looks.

CLEANTE I, father? Sullen looks? And for what reason?

HARPAGON Good heavens, we all know how children feel when their father re-marries, and the jaundiced eye with which they behold their new stepmother; but if you want me to forget your latest offense, I strongly advise you to greet her as cordially as you can. I want smiles not frowns!

CLEANTE You have my word that I shall receive her most cordially, and that there will be a continual smile on my face.

HARPAGON I shall hold you to that.

CLEANTE You will have no grounds for complaint.

HARPAGON I'd better not. **(To Jacques)** Maitre Jacques, I've saved you for last.

JACQUES Are you addressing me as your coachman or as your cook, sir, for both jobs are mine.

HARPAGON   As both.
JACQUES   But which one in particular?
HARPAGON   As my cook.
JACQUES   Then wait, please. (**Jacques removes his coach-man's coat and appears dressed as a cook**) I await your orders.
HARPAGON   I am committed to give a dinner this evening, Jacques.
JACQUES   Do my ears deceive me?
HARPAGON   Tell me, will you prepare a fancy dinner?
JACQUES   Yes, if you give me lots of money.
HARPAGON   Blast it all! Always money!
VALERE   Never have I heard a more impertinent response. What skill is there in preparing a fancy meal with plenty of money? Any simpleton could accomplish that. It's the ability to prepare a fancy meal with little money that determines the true measure of a cook.
JACQUES   A fancy meal with little money?
VALERE   Yes.
JACQUES   In faith, Mr. Steward, I would be deeply obliged to you if you would tell me the secret of how that is done. Since you seem to know everything about everything, perhaps you'd like to take over my job as cook.
HARPAGON   Hold your tongue! What do we need?
JACQUES   You'll need your steward here, who says he can prepare a fancy meal with little money.
HARPAGON   Enough! I want you to answer me!
JACQUES   How many will we have to feed?
HARPAGON   Eight or ten, but you must count on eight, for when there is food for eight, there's food for ten.
VALERE   Of course.
JACQUES   Well, we need four large soups and five courses

HARPAGON   What the devil! You talk as though we're feeding an entire town!

JACQUES   ...Roast...

HARPAGON   **(Covering Jacques' mouth with his hand)** Ah!
Traitor! You're eating everything I have!

JACQUES   Side dishes...

HARPAGON   Still?

VALERE   Are you planning to burst their stomachs? It is
not our master's intent to have our guests gorge
themselves to death. You really ought to familiarize yourself with the rules of good health. As
any doctor will tell you, there is no greater
detriment to health than the act of overeating;
thus, the more frugal the meals you serve, the
more friendship you display. With regard to the
dinner, I shall assume full responsibility. Leave
everything to me.

HARPAGON   Go to it.

JACQUES   That's even better... Less work for me

HARPAGON   You must select foods that are very filling, like
fatty mutton stew and a potted pie stuffed with
chestnuts. That'll cut their appetites at the
outset.

VALERE   Rely on me.

HARPAGON   Now, Jacques, you must clean my carriage.

JACQUES   Wait a minute. You are now speaking to me as
your coachman **(He puts on his coachman's
coat again)** You were saying.

HARPAGON   I was saying that my carriage must be cleaned,
and that my horses must be readied for the trip
to the fair.

JACQUES   Your horses, sir? In faith, they're hardly in any
condition to walk. It breaks my heart to see
their ribs stick out as they do.

HARPAGON Having them walk to the fair won t strain them that much.

JACQUES How can they drag a carriage when they can hardly drag themselves.

VALERE Sir, I shall ask your neighbor, Le Picard , to drive them there and we could also call upon him to serve in the preparation of the dinner.

JACQUES So be it. If anyone's going to kill them, I'd rather it not be me.

VALERE Maitre Jacques is acting very reasonably.

JACQUES Our good steward is acting very indispensable.

HARPAGON Enough of this!

JACQUES Sir, if there's one thing I can not stand it's a back scratcher! All that's just to get on your good side. It makes me angry, and I get just as angry when I hear the things people say about you every day.

HARPAGON What is it that people say about me?

JACQUES You won't get mad at me, sir...?

HARPAGON Not at all. On the contrary, it would give me great pleasure to learn how they speak of me.

JACQUES All right, sir, since you insist. I shall tell you frankly that your stinginess is the laughing-stock of the neighborhood. Some say that you have special almanacs printed where the days of fasting are doubled, thereby cutting down on your food bills. Some say you've been seen stealing the oats from the mouths of your horses, and that your previous coachman, not recognizing you in the dark, whacked the daylights out of you for it. In short, sir, you are the butt of everyone's jokes and the only words I hear to describe you are "miser," skinflint," "money-- grubber," and "usurer."

HARPAGON   (**Beating him soundly**) And you, sir, are a fool, a rogue, a scamp, and an impudent numbskull!

JACQUES   Ouch! I told you that you'd get mad at the truth and that you wouldn't believe me!

HARPAGON   I'll teach you to speak properly!

Scene 2:   Maitre Jacques, Valere

VALERE   (**Laughing**) From where I stand, Jacques, you paid dearly for your frankness.

JACQUES   Mind your own business! You just started working here and already you're trying to take over. Laugh at your own beatings and not mine.

VALERE   (**Trying to restrain his laughter**) Ah, Jacques, please don't be angry, I beseech you.

JACQUES   (**Aside**) He's sweet-talking me. I'm going to act tough and if he's fool enough to fall for it, I'll give him a little beating. (**Aloud**) Have you noticed, Mr. Laughing Boy, that I don't find this funny at all, and that if you make me mad enough, I'll give you something that will really make you howl.

Jacques pushes Valere to the end of the stage in a threatening fashion.

VALERE   Ah, gently now.

JACQUES   What do you mean "gently?" You get on my nerves, you do.

VALERE   I beseech you.

JACQUES   And I don't like your impertinence.

VALERE   Sir Jacques...

JACQUES   Don't give me any of that sir-business. I've a good mind to pick up a stick and give you a sound thrashing.

VALERE   What's that you say? A stick?

Valere now pushes Jacques to opposite end of the stage.

JACQUES   Eh? Well... I really didn't mean a stick.
VALERE   I'll have you know, Sir Numbskull, that I'm quite capable of using a stick on you.
JACQUES   Without a doubt.
VALERE   And as far as cooks go, you are among the worst.
JACQUES   I certainly am.
VALERE   You still know nothing about me.
JACQUES   I certainly don't
VALERE   You'd thrash me, would you?
JACQUES   It was only a jest
VALERE   Your manner of jest does not please me. **(Valere starts beating Jacques with a stick)** This will teach you to do so with more finesse!
Valere EXITS.

JACQUES   To hell with the truth. It hurts too much.

Scene 3: Frosine, Mariane, Jacques

FROSINE   Is the master at home, Jacques?
JACQUES   I'll say he is.
FROSINE   Please tell him that we are here.

Scene 4: Mariane, Frosine

MARIANE   Ah, Frosine, I shudder at what I'm about to see.
FROSINE   Why?
MARIANE   Alas! How can you ask?
FROSINE   I can tell that the blond youngster of whom you spoke is definitely on your mind.

MARIANE   Yes, Frosine, I'll not deny it.

FROSINE   But do you know who he is?

MARIANE   No, I don't. Imagine my torment, Frosine, when I compare him with the man they wish to foist upon me.

FROSINE   Good heavens! I admit that those pretty boys have their charm, but they could never provide for you as would a rich, older man. I am aware of the sensual deprivation you would have to endure with an older husband, but that would only be for a short time. Once he dies, you'll be free to choose whomever you like.

MARIANE   What a strange state of affairs! Having to wait until someone dies to be happy...and since when does death always conform to our wishes?

FROSINE   Are you serious? You shall marry him only on the condition that you be widowed within three months... Here he comes in the flesh.

Scene 5: Harpagon, Frosine, Mariane

HARPAGON   Please don't be offended, my beauty, that I appear before you wearing my spectacles, but you are among the most beautiful and brightest stars in the universe. **(Aside)** Frosine, she doesn't seem very pleased to see me.

FROSINE   Girls are always reluctant to express at first hand what they feel in their hearts.

HARPAGON   You're right. **(To Mariane)** There now, my pretty one. Here comes my daughter to greet you.

Scene 6: Elise, Mariane, Harpagon, Frosine

MARIANE	(**Curtsying**) Kindly excuse my delay in visiting you, Madame.
ELISE	(**Curtsying in return**) It is I who should ask pardon for not having visited you first.
HARPAGON	See what a big girl she is; but, then again, weeds always do grow fast.
MARIANE	(**Aside to Frosine**) Oh, how he revolts me!
HARPAGON	What did that beauty say?
FROSINE	That she finds you truly admirable.
HARPAGON	You do me too much honor, my adorable morsel.
MARIANE	(**Aside to Frosine**) I can't stand this any longer.
HARPAGON	Here, too, is my son, who comes to pay his respects.
MARIANE	(**Aside, softly to Frosine**) Ah, Frosine! There he is in the flesh! The man of whom I spoke!
FROSINE	(**Aside to Mariane**) A marvelous turn of events!
HARPAGON	I see that you are astonished that my children should be so grown-up; but don't worry, I'll soon be rid of them both.

Scene 7: Cleante, Mariane, Harpagon, Elise, Frosine

CLEANTE	Madame, this is a most unexpected encounter. I was also surprised when my father advised me of his intentions.
FROSINE	I share in your surprise
CLEANTE	Truly, my father could not have made a better choice, and I am deeply pleased and honored to see you. However, I must admit that I derive little pleasure from the prospect of having you as a stepmother. The fact is, Madame, that the very thought of this marriage repulses me. Indeed, with my father's permission, I would

like to say that, if it were up to me, this marriage would never take place.

HARPAGON Just listen to the impertinence of that compliment!

MARIANE And may I say, in turn, that the thought of having you as a step-son is no less repugnant to me, and that this marriage would never take place were I not so bound to it by absolute power.

HARPAGON She is right. One stupid compliment deserves another. I beg your pardon, my beauty, for my son's impertinence.

MARIANE I found nothing offensive in what he said. On the contrary, I enjoyed hearing his true feelings. Were he not to have done so, my respect for him would have diminished.

HARPAGON It is so good of you to excuse his faults.

CLEANTE Allow me to serve as my father's spokesman and confess that I have never known anyone as charming as you, and that the joy of being your husband would excel that of being the greatest prince on earth.

HARPAGON Gently now, my son, if you please.

CLEANTE I'm only complimenting her on your behalf

HARPAGON I have my own tongue to express myself. Quickly, some chairs.

FROSINE No. It would be preferable to leave now for the fair so that we'll return early enough for the lengthy discussion.

HARPAGON **(Calling offstage to Jacques)** Harness the horses to the carriage. **(To Mariane)** Please excuse me, my beauty, for neglecting to provide you with some refreshment before leaving.

CLEANTE	That's already been arranged, father. I'm having some mandarin oranges, sweet lemons, and preserves sent up on your behalf.
HARPAGON	**(Aside to Valere)** Valere!
VALERE	**(To Harpagon)** He's lost his senses!
CLEANTE	Do you feel that I should have offered more, father?
MARIANE	That really wasn't necessary.
CLEANTE	Just look at that ring my father is wearing on his finger, Madame. Have you ever seen a diamond shine like that?
MARIANE	It certainly does sparkle.
CLEANTE	**(Removing it front his father's finger and giving to Mariane)** You must look at it closely.
MARIANE	Such marvelous reflections! It's truly beautiful.
CLEANTE	**(Standing in front of her as she tries to return it)** No, Madame, your hands form too beautiful a setting. Keep it as a gift from my father.
HARPAGON	From me?!
CLEANTE	Is it not true, father, that you wish to give it to her as a token of your love?
HARPAGON	**(Aside to Cleante)** How's that?
CLEANTE	A fine question, indeed! He's gesturing his approval.
MARIANE	I don't want to
CLEANTE	You jest, Madame. He wouldn't dream of taking it back.
HARPAGON	**(Aside)** This is outrageous!
MARIANE	But this would be...
CLEANTE	**(Still preventing her front returning the ring)** No, I tell you, you would offend him.
MARIANE	Please...
CLEANTE	In no way.

HARPAGON (Aside to Cleante in menacing tones) Conniving brigand that you are.

CLEANTE It's not my fault, father. I'm doing my best to
convince her to keep it, but he's very obstinate.

HARPAGON (Aside to Cleante furiously) Scoundrel!

CLEANTE Resist no more, Madame, I beseech you, lest
you make him ill.

FROSINE Good heavens, why such ceremony? Keep the
ring and make him happy.

MARIANE Very well. Since I have no wish to upset you, I
shall keep the ring, but only temporarily.

Scene 8: Harpagon, Mariane, Frosine, Cleante, Brinda-voine, Elise

BRIND'INE Sir, there's a man out there who'd like to speak
to you.

HARPAGON Tell him I'm busy and to come some other
time.

BRIND'INE He says that he's got some money for you.

HARPAGON Excuse me. I'll be right back.

Scene 9: Harpagon, Mariane, Cleante, Elise, Frosine, La Merluche, Valere

MERLUCHE (Enters running and topples Harpagon) Sir...!

HARPAGON Ah, I'm dying!

CLEANTE What is it, father? Did you hurt yourself?

HARPAGON I'll wager anything that my debtors paid that
traitor to make me break my neck..

VALERE No cause for alarm.

MERLUCHE I'm here to tell you that both your horses have
lost their shoes.

HARPAGON Bring them to the smithy at once.

CLEANTE   While they're being shod, father, I'll do the household honors for you and escort madame to the garden where I'll have the refreshments served.

HARPAGON   Valere, see that he serves as sparingly as possible and send back whatever you can to the food merchant.

VALERE   Understood. (EXITS)

HARPAGON   **(Alone)** Impertinent son that you are! Do you want to bankrupt me?

ACT IV

Scene 1: Cleante, Mariane, Elise, Frosine

CLEANTE   Let us return here where we can speak freely.

ELISE   Yes, Madame, my brother has spoken to me of his love for you, and I understand.

MARIANE   How consoling it is to have the support of a person like you.

FROSINE   It's unfortunate that you did not consult me before this. I could have certainly avoided this unpleasant turn of events.

CLEANTE   To what end? This is my cruel destiny; but in any event, my beautiful Mariane, what have you decided?

MARIANE   Alas! My state of subservience does not allow for any decision on my part. All I can do is wish.

CLEANTE   Is wishing the only solace your heart can offer? No assuaging pity? No helpful kindness? No relieving affection?

MARIANE   What can I say? Were you in my position, you would comprehend the futility of my situation. I place myself in your hands, for I know that you would never suggest anything that would compromise my honor and propriety.

CLEANTE   Alas! Why must I always be constrained by the dictates of honor and propriety?

MARIANE   What would you have me do? Even if I were inclined to ignore the restrictions imposed upon those of my sex, I still have my mother to consider. She raised me with extreme kindness and I could never displease her. You, however, have my permission to do your utmost to win her over. Do and say whatever you must, and should the situation demand that I reveal to her my love for you, I shall do so freely.

CLEANTE Frosine, my poor Frosine, would you help us?

FROSINE With the greatest of pleasure. When it comes to serving love's true cause, I'm really quite sentimental. How may I be of service?

CLEANTE Think of something, I beseech you.

MARIANE Show us a way out of this.

CLEANTE Find a way to undo what you have wrought.

FROSINE This will pose quite a challenge. (**To Mariane**) Since your mother is not a totally unreasonable person, I may be able to persuade her to transfer to the son the gift she planned for the father. (**To Cleante**) However, the problem stems from the fact that the father is none other than your father.

CLEANTE I understand.

FROSINE What I mean is that to reject him is to incur his wrath, and this would hardly incline him to consent to your marriage. (**To Mariane**) Therefore, we must find a way to have you appear less desirable in his eyes so that it will be he, and not you, who does the rejecting.

CLEANTE You are right.

FROSINE Yes, I know, but the problem is how to go about it. Wait! Suppose we found an older woman with a talent equivalent to mine, capable of playing the role of a lady of quality. For the sake of believability, she could engage a quickly improvised retinue and adopt some exotic title, such as Marchioness or Viscountess, and could originate from, let us say, lower Brittany... I could then easily convince your father later that she is a woman of enormous wealth, hopelessly in love with him, and willing to transfer all her possessions to him in a contract of marriage. I am certain that your father would be receptive to such a proposal, for his love of money surpasses his love for you. Subsequently, after he takes the bait and provides you with the consent you seek, it matters little what he does upon learning of the Marchioness' true worth.

CLEANTE   A thoroughly ingenuous plan!

FROSINE   I've just thought of a friend of mine who'll make a perfect Marchioness!

CLEANTE   If your plan succeeds, Frosine, I'll be deeply grateful to you. However, my charming Mariane, preventing this marriage will be no small task, and you must do what you can from your end. You can begin by trying to win your mother over to our side. Make liberal use of the irresistibility that Heaven has placed in your eyes and lips.

MARIANE   I'll do whatever I can.

Scene 2: Harpagon, Cleante, Mariane, Elise, Frosine

HARPAGON (Aside and still unseen) Aha! My son kisses the hand of his future stepmother, and she does little to discourage it! Is there more to this than meets the eye?

ELISE   There's my father.

HARPAGON The carriage is ready. You may leave when you wish.

CLEANTE   Since you're not going, father, I'll take them myself

HARPAGON No. You stay. They can go quite nicely by themselves; besides, I have need of you. **The Ladies EXIT.**

Scene 3: Harpagon, Cleante

HARPAGON   Aside from the fact that she's to be your step-mother, what have you to say about the lady?

CLEANTE   What have I to say?

HARPAGON   Yes, of her manner, her figure, her beauty, her intelligence.

CLEANTE   To speak frankly, she fell far short of my expectations. I find her demeanor blatantly coquettish, her figure ill-proportioned, her facial attributes mediocre, and her wit far from spectacular. However, you must feel that I'm trying to downgrade her in your eyes, for as far as stepmothers go, I suppose I like this one as well as I would any other.

HARPAGON   But you were just saying to her that

CLEANTE   I was speaking gallantly on your behalf merely to please you.

HARPAGON   You are, therefore, not attracted to her?

CLEANTE   I? In no way.

HARPAGON   I'm sorry to hear that. I got to thinking about what people would say about marrying such a youngster. I was about to give up the whole idea and have her marry you instead. But, now with this aversion you have for her, I don't

CLEANTE   You'd give her to me?

HARPAGON   Yes, to you.

CLEANTE   In marriage?

HARPAGON   Yes, in marriage.

CLEANTE   Although I don't find her terribly attractive, I would somehow force myself to marry her, if only to please you, my dear father.

HARPAGON   No, no! Without love, no marriage is happy.

CLEANTE   But that's something that may come in time.

HARPAGON No, no... I'll stick to my original plan and marry her myself

CLEANTE Well, father, I am compelled by the present turn of events to inform you that I have loved Mariane at first sight, and were it not for your feelings toward her and my fear of displeasing you, I would have already asked for your consent to marry her.

HARPAGON Have you visited her?

CLEANTE Yes, father.

HARPAGON Have you declared your love for her and your intention to marry her?

CLEANTE Of course, and I even broached the subject with her mother.

HARPAGON And did she listen to your intentions concerning her daughter?

CLEANTE Yes, very civilly.

HARPAGON And does the daughter love you in return?

CLEANTE Judging from appearances, I am convinced that she cares for me.

HARPAGON (Aside) Aha! Just what I wanted ...to worm that secret out of him. (To Cleante) My son, there are three things you must do: first, purge yourself of this love; second, you must discontinue the courtship of a lady whom I claim for myself, and finally, you must get married soon to a girl chosen for you.

CLEANTE So this was all a little game. I shall tell you flatly that I will never renounce my love for Mariane, that I shall stop at nothing to prevent your having her, despite the mother's consent that you possess.

HARPAGON How's that? You'd dare to intrude on my domain?

CLEANTE It is you who are intruding in mine, for it is I who knew her first.

HARPAGON Am I not your father? And do you not owe me respect?

CLEANTE Love reigns supreme even over a father's authority.

HARPAGON Yes, and I'll rain some supremely fine blows on your head!

CLEANTE All your threats are to no avail.

HARPAGON You shall give up Mariane!

CLEANTE Never!

HARPAGON **(Shouting to Jacques)** Jacques! Fetch me a stick immediately!

Scene 4: Maitre Jacques, Harpagon, Cleante

JACQUES Now, now, gentlemen. What's all the commotion?

HARPAGON Maitre Jacques, to show how right I am in this matter, I'll let you be the judge... I love a girl whom I wish to marry, and this scoundrel has the audacity to love her, too, and to seek her hand in marriage despite my orders.

JACQUES Ah, he is wrong.

HARPAGON Is it not disrespectful of a son to compete with his father in the matter of love?

JACQUES Without a doubt.

CLEANTE I am in love with a young lady who returns my affection most tenderly. My father, however, intends to destroy our affair by claiming for himself the hand of the lady in question.

JACQUES He is most assuredly wrong.

CLEANTE Should he not leave affairs of the heart to the young?

JACQUES   You are right. Let me have a word with him. **(Turns to Harpagon)** Your son is now ready to submit to your demands, provided you treat him better than previously and provide him with a marriage partner to his liking.

HARPAGON   Tell him he can expect to marry whomever he wants with the exception of Mariane.

JACQUES   Let me handle this. **(To Cleante)** You must treat him more civilly and display the respect and submissiveness that a son owes to his father.

CLEANTE   Ah! Maitre Jacques, if he gives me Mariane, I will be the most submissive of men and would never do anything against his will.

JACQUES   **(To Harpagon)** It is done. He agrees to everything you say.

HARPAGON   Excellent!

JACQUES   **(To Cleante)** Everything is settled. He is satisfied with your promises.

CLEANTE   Heaven be praised!

JACQUES   Gentlemen, the way is cleared for amicable discussion.

CLEANTE   Maitre Jacques, all my life I will be indebted to you for this.

JACQUES   Your servant, air.

HARPAGON   Maitre Jacques, you have pleased me greatly, and for that you deserve a reward. **(He reaches into his pocket, giving Jacques the impression that he is about to receive something. All that emerges, however, is a handkerchief which Harpagon uses to blow his nose.)**

HARPAGON   Off with you now, and be assured that I will remember this.

JACQUES   I kiss your hands **(But he doesn't and EXITS)**

Scene 5: Cleante, Harpagon

CLEANTE   I promise you, father, that to my dying day I shall never forget your kindness in this affair. Ali, father, what more can I ask of you after your giving me Mariane?

HARPAGON   What did you say?

CLEANTE   I said that when you granted me Mariane you granted my every wish.

HARPAGON   Who said anything about granting you Mariane?

CLEANTE   Why you, father.

HARPAGON   I?

CLEANTE   Most assuredly.

HARPAGON   How's that? Why, it's you who promised to give her up.

CLEANTE   I? Give her up?

HARPAGON   Yes.

CLEANTE   Never!

HARPAGON   I'll fix you, you traitor!

CLEANTE   Do whatever you like.

HARPAGON   I forbid you to ever see me again.

CLEANTE   How refreshing.

HARPAGON   I'll disinherit you!

CLEANTE   Whatever you wish.

HARPAGON   And I give you my curse!

CLEANTE   I've no need of your gifts!

Scene 6: La Fleche, Cleante

LA FLECHE **(Entering from the garden, money box in hand)** Ah! Sir! Follow me quickly.

CLEANTE   What is it?

LA FLECHE Follow me. I tell you we're in luck.

CLEANTE   How's that?

LA FLECHE This is it.

CLEANTE What?
LA FLECHE I've been guarding it all day.
CLEANTE What is it?
LA FLECHE Your father's treasure I filched it!
CLEANTE How did you do it?
LA FLECHE I'll explain everything, but I can hear him shouting. Let's withdraw.
HARPAGON (Shouting "Stop! Thief! "front the garden and entering hatless) Stop! Thief! Assassin! Murderer! Justice! Just Heaven! I am lost! I am assassinated! They've cut my throat! They've stolen my money! Who can it be? Where is he hiding? How can I find him? Where shall I run? (To the Audience) You all look suspicious to me! Any one of you could pass for a thief! Please, if any of you knows who he is, I implore you to tell me... Quickly now: policemen, archers, provosts, judges, racks, gallows, and hangmen. I'll have everybody hanged, and after that, if I still don't find my money, I'll hang myself!

ACT V

Scene 1: Harpagon, the Officer, Officer's Clerk

OFFICER   Leave it to me. I know my job. Now, then, how much money did you say was in the box?

HARPAGON Ten thousand crowns in cash.

OFFICER   Ten thousand crowns?

HARPAGON Ten thousand crowns.

OFFICER   That's quite a theft.

HARPAGON There's no torture horrible enough to meet the enormity of this crime.

OFFICER   Whom do you suspect of the theft?

HARPAGON Everybody. And I want you to arrest the town and suburbs.

OFFICER   We must instead, pursue a course of quiet diligence leading to the recovery of your money.

Scene 2: Maitre Jacques, Harpagon, Officer, Officer's Clerk

JACQUES   **(Speaking to someone offstage while entering)** I'll be right back. Have his throat cut, his feet grilled, his body immersed in boiling water, and then hang him from the rafters.

HARPAGON Who? The man who stole my money?

JACQUES   No, that suckling pig your steward just sent to me.

HARPAGON Right now there is another matter to discuss with this gentleman.

OFFICER   Don't be alarmed. It is not my intent to promote scandal. All will be gentleness and discretion.

JACQUES   Is the gentleman one of your dinner guests?

OFFICER   My dear friend you must not hide anything from your master.

JACQUES   In faith, sir, I'll show you all I know and will treat you as well as I can.

HARPAGON   That's not the point!

JACQUES   If my dinner is not what I would have it to be, it's the fault of the niggardly steward.

HARPAGON   Traitor! We're not talking about the dinner! You must tell me what you know about the money they took from me!

JACQUES   They took money from you?

HARPAGON   Yes, scoundrel! And if you don't cough it up, I'll have you hanged!

OFFICER   Good heavens! I can tell by his face that he's an honest man. Yes, my friend, if you confess, not only will you be spared of any punishment, but you will also receive an appropriate reward from your master. His money was stolen today, and I'm sure you must know something about it.

JACQUES   **(Aside)** This is the chance I've been waiting for to get back at that steward for the beating he gave me. **(To Officer)** Sir, since it is your wish that I be forthright, I shall tell you that the guilty party in this affair is none other than the steward.

HARPAGON   Valere?

JACQUES   Yes.

HARPAGON   The one who appeared so faithful to me?

JACQUES   The very one. He's your thief, I believe.

HARPAGON   On what do you base this?

JACQUES   On what?

HARPAGON   Yes.

JACQUES   I base it on...er...on what I base it on.

OFFICER   But you must produce evidence.

HARPAGON Did you see him loitering where I kept my money?

JACQUES Indeed, I did. Er...where was your money?

HARPAGON In the garden.

JACQUES Precisely! I saw him loitering in the garden, What was the money put in?

HARPAGON In a money box.

JACQUES That's it! I saw him with a money box!

HARPAGON And this money box...describe it to me. I'll tell you in a second if it's mine.

JACQUES Describe it to you?

HARPAGON Yes.

JACQUES Well, it was ...er...it looked like...er...a money box.

HARPAGON Most of them do. Can you give a more detailed description?

JACQUES It's a large money box

HARPAGON The one stolen from me is small.

JACQUES Oh, yes...it's small if you're talking about size. When I said "large," I was talking about its contents.

OFFICER And what color was it?

JACQUES Color?

OFFICER Yes.

JACQUES It's color was... It had a certain color... Perhaps, you might help me describe it?

HARPAGON Eh?

JACQUES Was it red?

HARPAGON No. Gray.

JACQUES Ah! Yes! Grayish-red! That's exactly what I meant!

HARPAGON That's the one! No doubt about it!

JACQUES Sir, here he comes now. Please don't tell him that I'm the one who revealed his guilt.

Scene 3: Valere, Harpagon, Maitre Jacques, Officer, Officer's Clerk

HARPAGON   Come here! Come and confess the foulest offense ever committed.

VALERE   To what offense do you refer?

HARPAGON   Don't put on that act with me! The truth is out and I know everything. How could you abuse my goodness and gain entry to my household solely to betray me?

VALERE   Sir, since they've told you everything, I shall not deny the matter.

JACQUES   (Aside) Aha! Could I have guessed right without even knowing it?

VALERE   I intended to discuss it with you but was waiting for the proper moment. I implore you to control your temper and to listen to my explanation

HARPAGON   And what possible explanation can you proffer, infamous thief that you are?

VALERE   It is true that I wronged you, but what I did was excusable.

HARPAGON   Excusable? An ambush? A murder like that?

VALERE   When you've heard me out, you'll realize that the wrong is not as great as you're making it.

HARPAGON   Not as bad as I'm making it? It's my very flesh and blood, you scoundrel!

VALERE   Your blood has not fallen into bad hands.

HARPAGON   Who made you do this?

VALERE   A god who excuses everything done in his name... Love.

HARPAGON   Love?

VALERE   Yes.

HARPAGON   There's a fine kind of love, indeed...the love of my gold pieces!

VALERE   You are mistaken, sir. I am neither dazzled nor tempted by your wealth, and I make no claim on any of your possessions if only you leave me with the love I have.

HARPAGON   Never in a million years!

VALERE   Nothing but death can separate us.

HARPAGON   How you lust for my money!

VALERE   I have already told you, sir, my motives were far more noble than you might imagine.

HARPAGON   Next you'll be telling me that taking my money was an act of Christian charity! You'll have the law to answer to and I'll have my satisfaction!

VALERE   You may do as you wish, but I implore you to believe, however, that if any wrong has been done, it is I who is solely responsible. Your daughter shares none of the blame.

HARPAGON   What's my daughter got to do with this?

VALERE   And I say to you, sir, that because of her sense of modesty, it was not without considerable difficulty that she complied with the dictates of my heart.

HARPAGON   Whose modesty?

VALERE   Your daughter has signed a promise of marriage to me.

HARPAGON   By the saints! Another disaster!

JACQUES   **(To the Officer's Clerk)** Start writing, sir. Start writing.

HARPAGON   Misfortune at every turn... Come, sir, do your duty and draw up an indictment of him as a thief and...

VALERE   I am not deserving of those names, and once my identity is known...

Scene 4:   Elise, Mariane, Frosine, Harpagon, Valere, Maitre Jacques, Officer, Officer's Clerk

HARPAGON Ah! Shameless daughter! So, you would pledge your troth without my consent! You're both mistaken if you think you'll get away with this! **(To Elise)** The four walls of a convent will provide the restraint you need. **(To Valere)** And, as for you, the gallows will cure your audacity!

VALERE I shall be heard before being condemned.

HARPAGON Did I say "gallows?" I'll have you alive on the wheel with your bones broken

ELISE **(On her knees)** Open your heart, father. You have a completely false impression of him. It was he who rescued me from a watery grave, and it is to him, therefore, that you owe the life of the very daughter whom ...

HARPAGON So what? Better he let you drown rather than rob me.

ELISE Father! I call upon your love for me as my father to...

HARPAGON No. I'll listen to none of this. Let justice take its course.

JACQUES **(Aside)** He'll pay for that beating he gave me.

FROSINE Now, this is a strange kettle of fish.

Scene 5: Seigneur Anselme, Harpagon, Elise, Mariane, Frosine, Valere, Maitre Jacques, Officer, Officer's Clerk

ANSELME What is it, Lord Harpagon? You seem quite upset.

HARPAGON Ah! Lord Anselme! Observe before you a scoundrel who wormed his way into my household posing as a domestic for the purpose of stealing my money and seducing my daughter.

VALERE Your money is of no concern to me.

HARPAGON Yes, and they are engaged to be married. This is also an affront to you, Lord Anselme, and it therefore behooves you to prosecute to the full extent of the law...at your own expense, of course.

ANSELME I do not intend to marry a woman against her will, nor would I lay claim to a heart already promised to another.

HARPAGON Charge him for the criminal he is!

VALERE What is criminal about loving your daughter? And once my identity is revealed...

HARPAGON Enough of that claptrap! The world today is full of these impostors.

VALERE I'll have you know, sir, that I would consider it unworthy of me to claim anything that was not mine, and that all Naples can bear witness to my station.

ANSELME Hold on, sir. You happen to be speaking to someone who is totally familiar with... Someone who is in a position to challenge what you may say.

VALERE **(Proudly putting on his hat)** I have nothing to fear, and if as you claim, you are thoroughly familiar with Naples, you must be acquainted with the name of Don Thomas d'Alburcy.

ANSELME I most certainly am ... probably better than anyone else.

HARPAGON I don't give a hoot about Don Thomas nor of Don Martin, for that matter.

ANSELME Let's hear what he has to say.

VALERE What I have to say is that Don Thomas d'Alburcy is my father.

ANSELME He is your...

VALERE Yes.

ANSELME Come now, sir, you jest, of course. There's no salvation in playing the impostor.

VALERE May I ask that you weigh your words more carefully, sir? I am not an impostor and can verify whatever I claim.

ANSELME How's that? You dare pretend to be the son of Don Thomas d'Alburcy?

VALERE Yes. And I can prove it!

ANSELME I marvel at your audacity. May I advise you that the gentleman of whom you speak died at sea with his wife and children at least sixteen years ago in an attempt to flee the persecution of the nobility during the Neapolitan Uprising?

VALERE Yes, but I must inform you that his seven year old son, along with a servant, were both rescued by a Spanish ship. And it is that very son who stands before you now. The ship's captain, moved by my plight, raised me as his son. As soon as I was of age, I joined the military. I recently learned that, contrary to my long-held belief, my father was not dead. It was while passing through here in search of him that heaven ordained that I should meet the charming Elise. My love for her was so intense that I decided to have someone else continue my search for my father so that I might be free to enter the service of this household, where I enjoy her proximity and protect her from the severity of her father.

ANSELME But what evidence can you provide other than words?

VALERE The Spanish captain, a ruby signet ring once belonging to my father, an agate bracelet given to me by my mother, and finally old Pedro, the servant who, with me, was spared from the shipwreck.

MARIANE You speak the truth, and what you say convinces me that you are my brother.

VALERE You? My sister?

MARIANE Yes. I have been deeply moved by everything you have said. Our mother has spoken to me at length of our family's misfortune, and how great will be her joy in seeing you! Our lives were spared during that shipwreck, but only at the expense of our liberty. While clinging to some floating debris, our mother and I were picked up by a pirate ship, and after ten years of slavery, by a stroke of luck, we regained our liberty. Upon our return, we found that all our possessions were sold, and we were unable to locate father. We then went to Genoa, where our mother collected the remnants of a depleted inheritance. From there, fleeing the inhumanity of her relatives, she came here to a life of continual languish.

ANSELME Oh, Lord, how wondrous is thy power! Come, my children, let us embrace and share this moment of joy!

VALERE You are our father?

ANSELME Yes, my daughter; yes, my son. I am Don Thomas d'Alburcy. I survived that shipwreck and believed both of you to be dead, along with your mother. After sixteen years, I have been searching for a gentle and wise woman with whom I could experience once again the joys of family life. Naples remained too hazardous for me to ever return so I sold my possessions there and settled here under the name of Anselme.

My other name was too painful a reminder of the past.

HARPAGON   If he is your son, I shall sue you for the ten thousand gold pieces he stole from me.

VALERE   Who told you that?

HARPAGON   Maitre Jacques.

VALERE   You told him that?

JACQUES   You know I would never say anything like that,

VALERE   **(To Harpagon)** Do you really believe me capable of such a foul act?

Scene 6:   Cleante, Valere, Mariane, Elise, Anselme, Jacques, Frosine, Harpagon, Officer, Officer's Clerk

CLEANTE   Stop making such wild accusations, father. If you allow me to marry Mariane, you'll have your money back.

HARPAGON   Where is it?

CLEANTE   You either give me Mariane or lose the money box.

HARPAGON   Nothing has been taken from it?

CLEANTE   Nothing at all. Do you agree to this marriage?

MARIANE   Don't you realize that his consent is no longer sufficient and that you must now address yourself to my father and brother?

ANSELME   God has not reunited us, my children, for me to counter your wishes. Lord Harpagon, surely you must realize that a young girl would prefer the son over the father. Consent with me to this double marriage.

HARPAGON   Before I decide anything, I must first see my money box.

CLEANTE   You will find it in excellent health.

HARPAGON   I don't have the money to spend on marriages for my children

ANSELME   Be not concerned for it would be my pleasure to pay.

HARPAGON   Are you saying that you'll pay all the costs for both marriages?

ANSELME   Yes, I will. Does that satisfy you?

HARPAGON   Yes! Providing you have new clothes made for me for the wedding.

ANSELME   Agreed. Let us rejoice now in the glorious events of the day

OFFICER   Hold on, gentlemen. Who'll pay for my depositions?

HARPAGON   We don't need your depositions.

OFFICER   Yes, but I do not intend to have drawn them up for nothing.

HARPAGON   **(Pointing to Jacques)** As a form of payment, I offer this man to hang.

JACQUES   What is a man to do? If I tell the truth, I get beaten. If I lie, I get hung.

ANSELME   Lord Harpagon, we forgive his deception.

HARPAGON   So then, you'll pay the officer?

ANSELME   So be it. **(To Valere and Mariane)** Let us go quickly to your mother so that she might share our joy.

HARPAGON   And I with haste, to my beloved money box.

THE END

MELODY FOR A SERENADE

JEANNE'S SONG

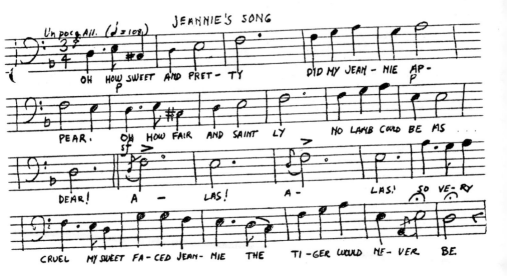

DIALOGUE TO MUSIC

DANCING MASTER'S MINUET

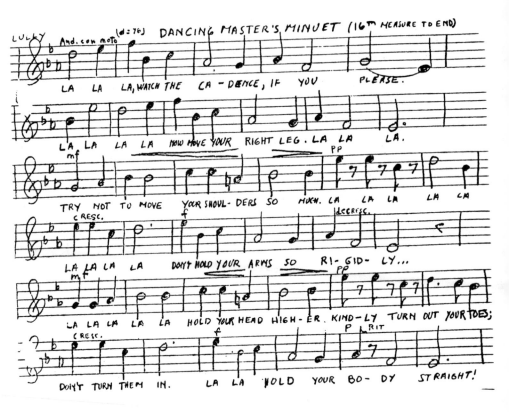

SOPRANO SOLO FOR BANQUET

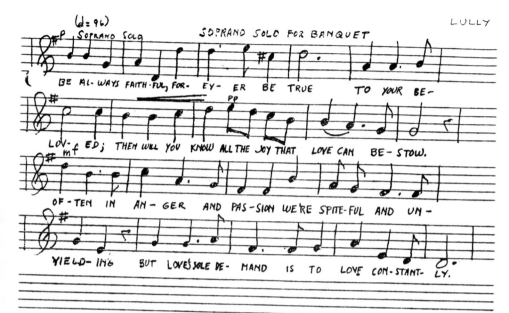

BE AL-WAYS FAITH-FUL, FOR-EY- ER BE TRUE TO YOUR BE-

LOV-ED; THEN WILL YOU KNOW ALL THE JOY THAT LOVE CAN BE-STOW.

OF-TEN IN AN-GER AND PAS-SION WE'RE SPITE-FUL AND UN-

YIELD-ING BUT LOVE'S SOLE DE-MAND IS TO LOVE CON-STANT-LY.

DRINKING SONG

MINUET FOR THE OBOES OF POITIERS

HSTEW   842
        M721

MOLIERE
    MOLIERE : FOUR PLAYS

09/04

                    HSTEW   842
                            M721

HOUSTON PUBLIC LIBRARY
STELLA LINK